# Theological Reflection

Elaine Graham is Samuel Ferguson Professor of Social and Pastoral Theology at The University of Manchester. She is the author of *Making the Difference: Gender, Personhood and Theology* (Mowbray, 1995), *Transforming Practice* (Mowbray, 1996, 2nd edition, 2002) and *Representations of the Post/Human* (Manchester, 2002).

Heather Walton is Lecturer in Practical Theology at the University of Glasgow and co-director of the Centre for Literature, Theology and the Arts. She researches in the field of literature and theology and is co-editor, with Elizabeth Stuart, of the journal *Theology and Sexuality* (Sage).

Frances Ward is an Anglican parish priest and Honorary Canon of Manchester Cathedral in the Diocese of Manchester, UK. She is author of *Lifelong Learning: Theological Education and Supervision* (SCM Press, 2005), co-editor of *Studying Local Churches: A Handbook* (SCM Press, 2005) and Editor of the journal *Contact: Practical Theology and Pastoral Care*.

# Theological Reflection:

## Methods

Elaine Graham, Heather Walton
and Frances Ward

## scm press

British Library Cataloguing in Publication data

A catalogue record for this book is available
from the British Library

0 334 02976 7/9780 334 02975 5

First published in 2005 by SCM Press
9–17 St Albans Place, London N1 0NX

www.scm-canterburypress.co.uk

Second impression

SCM Press is a division of
SCM-Canterbury Press Ltd

Printed and bound in Great Britain by
William Clowes Ltd, Beccles, Suffolk

# Contents

# Introduction

## Method or Mystique?

Students and teachers in adult theological education, ministerial formation and the twin disciplines of pastoral studies and practical theology have become familiar over the past two decades with the frequently used phrase 'theological reflection'. A sizeable literature has developed in this area of work, reflecting a growing body of research material (Ballard and Pritchard, 1996; Elford, 1999; Pattison, Thompson and Green, 2003; Walton, R., 2003; Warren, Murray and Best, 2002). Prevailing understandings and expectations have consolidated to the stage that practitioners in various contexts – seminaries, universities and local churches – now have a range of pedagogical techniques and resources to use as they reflect theologically.

So why another book on the subject? Our argument – and correspondingly, our intention in writing – is to point out that often the reality does not fit the rhetoric. 'Theological reflection' is still easier said than done. Received understandings of theological reflection are largely under-theorized and narrow, and too often fail to connect adequately with biblical, historical and systematic scholarship. So we hope that this book will enable participants to engage in patterns of theological reflection that are richer in the sources they draw on, more diverse in their knowledge-base, more rigorous and more imaginative, so that those undertaking theological reflection today may gain confidence and insight from a realization that what they do is a perennial and indispensable part of the history of Christian doctrine. It is our contention that 'theological reflection' is not a novel or exceptional activity. Rather, it has constituted Christian 'talk about God' since the very beginning.

## From 'Applied Theology' to 'Theological Reflection'

Over the past twenty years the history and identity of pastoral and practical theology has been subject to intense revision. Broadly, this period has seen an epistemological shift from a discipline that regarded itself as supplying practical training for the ordained ministry, often within a clinical or therapeutic context, to one that understood theology as critical reflection on faithful practice in a variety of settings. Yet this shift occurs at the end of a long history of different conceptions of the relationship between the practice of Christian ministry and theological discourse. The practice of pastoral care and the exercise of ministry are activities both ancient and modern, linking the earliest gathered Christian communities to the present-day context. Yet they continue to be vigorously debated. Perhaps we can usefully divide the history of pastoral/practical theology into six broad historical periods.

1  The earliest development, during a period extending over the first two centuries of Christianity, of caring within Christian communities where members were inspired by a concern to build up one another in the faith.
2  A process of increasing institutionalization of apostolic ministries and the regulation of individual and community care by clergy under the aegis of Church authority. This period saw the emergence of 'moral theology' in which the practice of pastoral care was linked to sacramental ministries, a tradition that endures in much Roman Catholic pastoral theology to this day.
3  The post-Enlightenment systematization of theological enquiry into the discipline of 'applied' theology, represented by the work of Friedrich Schleiermacher in establishing a particular area known as 'practical theology' in the German academies of the eighteenth century.
4  The rise of professionalism and secularism at the beginning of the twentieth century, resulting in the further 'professionalization' of the clergy.
5  A turn to secular sources of therapeutic knowledge, especially modern psychologies and their corresponding clinical applications. This emphasis came to predominate in the training for ordained ministry in the West during the second half of the twentieth century.
6  The questioning of the 'psychological' and 'clerical' paradigms and new directions in the theory and practice of Christian caring. This entailed a transition from a *therapeutic* to a *hermeneutic* model of

pastoral engagement in which the activity of *theological reflection* assumes centre stage. The focus shifted to 'the way in which the faith of the Church works out in practice in the world and raises questions about what it sees, addressing them back to theology' (Tidball, 1995, p. 42).

The transition to phase six reflects a number of developments – in academic theology, the life of the churches and wider society – that have transformed the theological curriculum. Since the systematization of Christian theology in Germany (phase 3 above), academic theology was divided into sub-disciplines. Schleiermacher advanced a threefold structure, of 'philosophical', 'historical' and 'practical' theologies. This gave rise to a hierarchy of knowledge in which a clear distinction was made between 'systematic' and 'applied' or pastoral theologies, with the latter as the 'hints and helps' of pastoralia in the service of the Church. In this way of thinking, pastoral care and Christian ministry were not regarded as generative of theological insight, but were merely applications of truth found within systematic theology.

This model of 'applied theology' developed into an altogether more integrated and dialogical relationship between the practice of ministry and the resources of theological understanding. First, the second half of the twentieth century saw a reappraisal of the status and role of the laity in many of the major Christian traditions. For Protestants and Roman Catholics alike, a recovery of the Lutheran maxim of the 'priesthood of all believers', and the reclamation of Christian vocation as the task of the whole Church, signalled a realignment of the nature of ministry. Baptism, not ordination, came to be seen as the most important sacrament of ministry. Ministry was no longer solely equated with the activities of the clergy, but rather became something exercised by the whole people of God, in Church and world. Theological education responded by realigning itself away from what Edward Farley (1983, p. 127) has termed a 'clerical paradigm' (something orientated towards ordained ministry) towards patterns of learning and teaching that sought to foster theological literacy among the whole people of God.

Theologies of liberation introduced the Western discipline of practical theology to the notions of the 'theology of experience' and of 'theologies from below'. Although the chief impact of liberation theologies is often thought to be the way they *politicized the churches* there is also a sense in which they have served to *'democratize' theology* as the 'work of the people', in an effort to return it to those on the 'underside of history' whose voices and perspectives were formerly neglected. The history of the basic ecclesial communities, informed by the pedagogy of Paulo Freire, provided an educational model to facilitate this process (see Chapter 6). As a result, a more integrated, inductive approach to theology has developed that refuses any separation between 'theory' (or systematic theology) and 'practice' (or pastoral studies). It also poses questions concerned with the agents and authors of theological discourse, and the purpose of theology as a body of knowledge (Chopp, 1995). Such theologies of experience ask: Who 'does' theology? What are the ends of theological reflection? What use is theology?

Similarly, within ministerial training there has been a turn away from teaching pastoralia towards educational methods intended to form 'reflective practitioners'. The influential work of Donald Schön on professional identity has resonated with anxiety within the churches concerning appropriate roles for ordained leaders within the contemporary context. Schön identified what he termed 'the crisis of the professions', by which he meant an erosion of public trust in the authority of experts, a suspicion of abuse of professional power, and a questioning of technocratic expertise:

> The crisis of confidence in the professions, and perhaps also the decline in professional self-image, seems to be rooted in a growing skepticism about professional effectiveness in the larger sense . . . But it also hinges centrally on the question of professional knowledge. Is professional knowledge adequate to fulfil the espoused purposes of the professions?
>
> Schön, 1983, p. 13

Schön also points to 'the redundancy of technical rationality'. Instead of displaying theoretical knowledge, professionals must now demonstrate an ability to respond with flexibility to situations of change and flux. They need to be proactive learners and risk-takers. Practitioners must 'move into the center of the learning situation, into the center of their own doubts' (p. 83). Professional learning and knowledge-gathering needs to become 'reflection-in-action'.

Schön argues for a distinctive epistemology of practice that will best facilitate professional practice and development. The reflective practitioner's expertise is different from technical rationality and scientific precision. It is reflexive, problem-based, intuitive and synthetic. Knowledge and expertise are generated from the inside-out and not the outside-in; they require the practitioner to 'act in order to see what the action leads to' (p. 145). In this frame expertise is only ever articulated in relation to the field of practice and is therefore always contextual and contingent to a particular situation. Action and reflection are intertwined, and theory cannot be distilled from practice. Once more, therefore, we see resistance to 'applied' models of understanding in favour of epistemologies that are contextual, implicit and problem-based.

Other educational thinking in the West has stimulated interest in the way adult learners use 'experience' as the root of critical understanding leading to action. For example, David Kolb's model of experiential learning emphasizes the importance of starting from experience and reflecting on practical contexts of engagement, rather than beginning with abstract theory. He characterizes education as a process with four stages: experience, reflection, conceptualization and experimentation. Kolb describes a cyclical movement in which a concrete situation or experience generates observation and reflection, which is then tested out in the context of revised practice (Kolb, 1984).

As a result of these various trends, Christian ministry comes to be understood as being less about the application of expertise and more about facilitating the vocation of all Christians through processes of understanding, analysing and reflecting. The purpose of theological education, therefore, is to equip people with skills and strategies to enable them to reflect theologically. There is a renewed emphasis on *experiential* learning and on the agenda for learning coming *from the learner* – from the dilemmas and questions generated by the practice of ministry. Theology emerges as a practical problem-solving and inductive discipline, which connects with practical issues in a way that illuminates and empowers. It also emerges as a way of reflection that draws on other disciplines in its analysis of experience in order to do justice to the complexity of any given situation.

## Theological Reflection Outlined

All of these movements have had an impact on the theological curriculum. Theological discourse is now seen as *process* rather than *product*. Rather than the discipline of church management, or training in the therapeutic skills of pastoral care, the field of practical theology is now understood as centred upon 'the life of the whole people of God in the variety of its witness and service, as it lives in, and for the world. It asks questions concerning Christian understanding, insight and obedience in the concrete reality of our existence' (Ballard and Pritchard, 1996, p. 27). In other words, theological reflection is an activity that enables people of faith to give an account of the values and traditions that underpin their choices and convictions and deepens their understanding. Theological reflection enables the connections between human dilemmas and divine horizons to be explored, drawing on a wide range of academic disciplines including social sciences, psychotherapeutic and medical disciplines and the arts.

At the heart of theological reflection, therefore, are questions about the relationship of theory to practice, and how to connect theological discourse about the nature of God to the exercise of faith. This is an endeavour shared by laity and clergy: Christian practice is not simply about the duties of congregational ministry but the entire life and witness of the Church. It is predominantly a critical, interrogative enquiry into the process of relating the resources of faith to the issues of life. The exercise of theological reflection is thus one 'in which pastoral experience serves as a context for critical development of basic theological understanding' (Burck and Hunter, 1990, p. 867).

## The Limitations of Theological Reflection

The growth in popularity of theological reflection is evident from its widespread adoption within the theological curricula of seminaries and universities. Yet in other ways its currency seems less useful, if recent research is to be believed. A survey of ordinands in the UK about their experience of theological reflection on their courses recorded that many experience the process as 'mystifying, alienating and non-specific rather than relevant or accessible' (Pattison, Thompson and Green, 2003).

In fact, the exercise of theological reflection seems to have provoked as much bafflement as illumination for at least two decades. In the mid-1980s, Lewis Mudge and James Poling from the United States suggested that programmes that purported to enable Christians to engage in theological reflection were often ill-resourced and poorly designed. In reality, they argued, few congregations were given the resources to think intelligently about their faith. Despite references to theology as 'the work of the people of God',

> any pastor knows that if a typical congregation of Christian people is simply told to go and 'do theology', what will come out will be a mishmash of favorite [sic] scripture verses quoted out of context, superstitions, fragments of civil religion, vague memories of poorly taught Sunday-school lessons of long ago, and the like. Not an inspiring picture.
>
> Mudge and Poling, 1987, p. xiv

Mudge and Poling's argument is prescient and important. The cultivation of reflective discipleship in which rigorous use of theological tradition and analysis of experience is guaranteed requires more than pious hopes. Stephen Pattison, a leading practical theologian and one of the researchers in the Cardiff study, had also expressed similar sentiments concerning the under-resourcing of theological reflection. In a memorable image, he argued that theological students exhorted to 'theologically reflect' are, essentially, being required to manufacture *bricks without straw* (Exodus 5.16), in that few substantial resources or guidelines are ever given to facilitate the process (Pattison, 2000). Once again, it was assumed that theological reflection comes naturally, with little preparation or grounding in possible sources, procedures and norms.

This is not intended to deny or undervalue those who have worked over the years to provide stimulating resources for those engaged in the endeavours of theological reflection. In fact, much of that expertise 'on the ground' still remains to be brought to wider scrutiny, something that we hope this book will stimulate. Yet the problems remain, and may be summarized as follows.

1 Theological reflection is often weak in its use of traditional Christian sources. Practical theology often has an uneasy relationship with the study of the Bible, as a recent study has argued (Walton, R., 2003). Roger Walton surveyed the use of the Bible in theological reflection among selected institutions and commented on the 'paucity' or complete absence of guidelines on how the Bible and Christian tradition are to be used in theological reflection' (p. 135).

2 The analysis of local contexts and socio-economic factors, which theological reflection frequently requires, is often more accomplished than engagement with Church history, doctrine and Bible. This is because patterns of theological reflection are often divorced from the study of systematic/historical/biblical disciplines on the curriculum in theological colleges, courses and seminaries. Pastoral studies is left, then, to deal with practical ministry and contextual analysis, with the imperative to reflect theologically in the context of a field-based placement in a congregation or local neighbourhood while the academic theological curriculum continues uninterrupted back at college.

3 The activity of theological reflection, as well as being seen as something that happens in practice and on the more experiential frontier of ministerial formation, is also often viewed as a contemporary novelty; a new-fangled concession to fashionable theories of

student-centred learning, but essentially unrelated to the processes of theological formulation in the classic Christian tradition.

We ask what would happen if this were to change. What if, for example, theologians and educators started to teach their biblical criticism, their historical and systematic theology *contextually*? If all theology were seen as *practical* theology? What if we could reclaim the project of 'theological reflection' as something that has been fundamental to the evolution of Christian thought and tradition from the very beginning? It might mean, for example, that:

- theological enquiry would be seen as something generated by problematics, dilemmas, contexts, practical tasks;
- the process of theological formulation would become one of making creative use of available thought-forms and concepts – contemporary and inherited;
- 'talk about God' would be recognized as a human activity intending to bring practical perspectives faithfully into critical and creative interplay with divine horizons;
- theology would be a kind of 'practical wisdom'; a way of living wisely, shaped by reflection and faithful obedience;
- the practice of theology would be a disciplined reflection, providing indicative models of understanding how talk about God emerges from human experience and questions.

## Recontextualizing the History of Doctrine

So far, we have argued that practical theology should have the status of a primary theological discipline because of its roots in concrete human dilemmas and the way it requires practical responses from people of faith. Interestingly, voices from systematic and historical theology now also make a similar case. For Ellen Charry, for example, the history of Christian doctrine has found its origins in practical purposes from its very beginnings. For her, Christian doctrine emerges from an ethics of character-formation designed to shape lives that were centred on understanding and knowing God:

> The theologians who shaped the tradition believed that God was working with us to teach us something, to get our attention through the Christian story, including those elements of the story that make the least sense to us. They were interested in forming us as excellent persons. Christian doctrines aim to be good for us by forming or reforming our character; they aim to be salutary. They seek to

form excellent persons with God as the model, and this in a quite literal sense, not as metaphors pointing to universal truths of human experience that lie beyond events themselves. In other words, I came to see that the great theologians of the past were also moralists in the best sense of the term. They were striving not only to articulate the meaning of the doctrines but also their pastoral value or salutarity – how they are good for us.

Charry, 1997, p. vii

Charry presents theology as a body of knowledge designed to articulate the nature of God in order that people might lead godly lives. It is a discourse of character-formation with a practical bearing, rather than abstract or disengaged truths. It is always orientated towards the practice of discipleship. Charry argues that such an understanding of a practical or 'sapiential' wisdom was eclipsed by modernity, in which the practice (and the practices) of faith became divorced from intellectual articulation. To restore theology to its proper role is to remember (re-member) it as essentially a practical discipline, emerging from concrete human situations, informing patterns of faithful living. The purpose of Christian doctrine is to inculcate habits of life by which God may be apprehended and followed, and by which the divine will may be enacted.

Charry's account of historic Christian teachings asks how they would have functioned to make a pastoral or practical impact on the recipient and what dispositions would have been fostered and what norms commended. She uses the term 'aretegenic', which means 'conducive to virtue', to describe 'the virtue-shaping function of the divine pedagogy of theological treatises' (p. 19). This invites us, then, to consider theology as a body of knowledge with function and purpose, directed towards the cultivation of Christian virtue.

> The classic theologians based their understanding of human excellence on knowing and loving God, the imitation of or assimilation to whom brings proper human dignity and flourishing . . .
>
> Christian doctrines function pastorally when a theologian unearths the divine pedagogy in order to engage the reader or listener in considering that life with the triune God facilitates dignity and excellence.

p. 18

This is an important statement. It introduces the idea that theology, and talking, or thinking, about God has practical ends. Yet Charry's notion of divine pedagogy in pursuit of Christian excellence needs further elaboration. Is the educational task of theology simply shaping individual lives, or about framing the collective life of communities of faith? And is the concept of Christian excellence sufficient to describe the desired outcomes of theology; or are there other issues such as justice, social transformation and the celebration of the glory of God which also constitute practical tasks of Christian life, and call forth implicit understandings of who and what God is and how God is best apprehended and manifested in the world?

Together with Charry, we would wish to argue that theology has always been contextual and is best understood as possessing a practical function: to nurture, to inform identity, to communicate. The earliest developments of Christian writing and talking about God, the beginnings of coherent and public communications about the meaning of faith and the nature of Christian truth-claims arose in response to very specific practical circumstances. To take Charry's work further, we would suggest that, historically, theology emerged as a result of three key tasks in relation to practical circumstances.

First, theology informs the processes that enable the *formation of character* (Charry's chief emphasis). Second, theology assists in building and maintaining the *community of faith* (including determining where the normative boundary of faithful practice might lie, and thus the distinctiveness of the collective identity of Christians). Third, theology enables the relating of the faith-community's own communal identity to the surrounding culture, and the *communication of the faith* to the wider world. Is the task of the Church, for example, to withdraw from the world around it; or to proclaim the gospel against many competing world-views? In what ways is the Church called to a duty of care and compassion or the establishment of justice amidst oppression, in the world around it? These three core tasks – of adult formation and nurture, of corporate identity, and of gospel and culture – are fundamental to the conduct of theological reflection that seeks to engender 'talk about God' in ways that are capable of informing the practice of faith in all these dimensions.

## The tasks of theological reflection

1 *The induction and nurture of members.* What does it mean to be a Christian? Who am I as a Christian believer?
2 *Building and sustaining the community of faith.* What does it mean to be the 'body of Christ' in this place and time? How are we to live faithfully and authentically?

3 *Communicating the faith to a wider culture.* How is God to be apprehended and proclaimed? What does it mean to preach 'Good News'? In what ways are Christians called to be signs of God's activity in the world? How are the demands of 'Christ' and 'culture' (see Niebuhr, 1951) to be reconciled in the way that faith is proclaimed and lived?

## Methods of Theological Reflection

In taking the idea of methods of theological reflection, we are deliberately placing ourselves in an important tradition in sociology of knowledge and Christian social thought, which has adopted a typological approach to the diversity of expressions of theological discourse and Christian witness.

The German political scientist and sociologist Max Weber (1864–1920) developed an analytical construct known as the *Ideal Type*. Given the complexity of social reality, and the richly textured nature of human interaction, Weber argued for the distinctiveness of an interpretative social scientific method. He deployed the notion of ideal types, which he described as 'analytical constructs that enable us to simplify a set of social relationships, to detail what is relevant and exclude misleading complexities' (Weber, 1949, p. 78) – as a means of delineating the general contours of a more complicated phenomenon. Ideal types were necessarily more abstract than the realities to which they pointed; but they served as essentially heuristic devices to aid description and explanation.

Later sociological and theological writers adapted Weber's thinking. In *The Social Teaching of the Christian Churches* (1911) Ernst Troeltsch constructed a pair of types he called 'church' and 'sect' to delineate the contrasting world-affirming and world-denying tendencies within early Christian communities. This was a distinction later supplemented by H. R. Niebuhr in his book *The Social Sources of Denominationalism* (1929) by a third type, 'denomination'. Niebuhr's later book, *Christ and Culture*, published in 1951, is perhaps one of the best-known works of this genre and an example of an attempt to categorize the various ways in which the relationship of, and the interaction between, Christianity and culture – as 'total process of human activity' – has been understood. He proposed a fivefold typology to describe a variety of ways in which their relationship has been understood: opposition, agreement, synthesis, duality and conversion; and while his work continues to stimulate critical debate, it also continues to be widely emulated. Perhaps Niebuhr's most enduring legacy is an insistence on the inherent pluralism of the Christian tradition and an acknowledgement that diversity has characterized Christian theology from its very beginnings. He also maintained an emphasis on the historical continuities that can be discerned within, as well as between, specific traditions. This remains one of the chief strengths of a typological analysis.

For example, the Roman Catholic theologian Avery Dulles (1974) elaborates five different 'ideal types' or 'models' of the Church, characterized by a series of different patterns of leadership, engagement with a wider community and understandings of ecclesiology. Subsequently he has developed a similar approach to models of revelation (1992). Stephen Bevans (2002) and Robert Kinast (2000) have also used typologies to identify different models of 'contextual' theology, although their discussions carry little in the way of an historical perspective, drawing on examples from contemporary scholarship.

Our approach to theological reflection stands in this tradition of constructive analysis. We advance seven indicative *methods*, which are genuine, if stylized, representations of authentic theological traditions. We do not intend them to be transhistorical, a criticism often levelled at ideal typical forms; instead, we have chosen to take a number of historical 'snapshots' that we think are indicative and exemplary of the development of each method, and suggest processes of creative theological thinking. Each method enables contemporary practices of reflection and action to locate themselves in relation to received traditions.

Our aims in writing this book can therefore be summarized as follows.

- *To provide basic introductions to a variety of models of theological reflection, and to identify their strengths and weaknesses.* We will examine how the elements often regarded as the conventional well-springs of Christian theology – namely sacred text (scripture), history (Church teaching and tradition), experience (cultural information and human experience) and philosophical systems (reason) – are deployed within each method, and why.
- *To identify the process of 'theological reflection' as the common methodology of theological thinking.* We will ask what identifies each method as 'theological' and trace how each distinctive genre of reflection has taken shape over successive generations and centuries of Christian discourse. We are not seeking to provide a systematic or exhaustive genealogy, but to point towards family resemblances and continuities across a variety of examples.

- *To point to historical and contemporary examples of these methods and to provide extracts from primary texts.* We will illustrate the most significant and indicative ways in which each method finds expression in different contexts with reference to the writings of key figures in their own words.
- *To reflect the diversity of Church and global traditions and approaches to theological reflection.* While our examples are drawn primarily from Western Roman Catholic and Protestant traditions, we are concerned to honour the catholicity of Christian tradition as embodied in the different methods of theological reflection. We will also attempt to highlight the multifaceted nature of theological reflection, asking in whose hands the activity of theological reflection actually rests; where it takes place and in what modes of expression (for example, literary, liturgical, philosophical, artistic) it has been articulated.
- *To enable readers to apply models of theological reflection appropriate to their own context and practice.* While this is not a theological workbook, we hope that it will be a resource for contemporary practitioners of theology. For this reason, we have included questions for discussion, which we hope will stimulate further creative and analytical work.

## How to read this book

The seven main chapters set out our types, or methods, of theological reflection. These are as follows.

1. **Theology by Heart** God is experienced as immanent, personal and intimate, speaking through the interiority of human experience. Records of such experience – journaling, autobiography, psychotherapeutic accounts of self – are vehicles of theological reflection and construction.
2. **Speaking in Parables** The authoritative narrative of Scripture is augmented and challenged by the voices of alternative experiences. Often, theological insights are gained from unexpected sources and woven into the canonical accounts to produce a richer tapestry of perspectives.
3. **Telling God's Story** Here the emphasis is on Scripture as 'canonical'. Christian identity, both individual and corporate, is shaped around 'God's story' as found in biblical narrative. The world stands in judgement under the power of that revelation.

4 **Writing the Body of Christ** The corporate identity and self-understanding of the 'body of Christ' forms the raw material of theological reflection. The community of faith generates theological language in its life together, whether that be in its rules of pastoral discipline or corporate liturgies or in the metaphors it uses to describe its distinctive self-understanding.

5 **Speaking of God in Public** Theological reflection occurs via a process of conversation or correlation between Christian revelation and surrounding culture. The fruits of human reason – scientific, artistic, socio-economic – offer raw material for divine disclosure.

6 **Theology-in-Action** Faithful discipleship rests in being able to realize the power of 'love-in-action'. God is understood as active in history, which is ushering creation towards an ultimate vision of redemption. The task of personal and corporate discipleship is to make common cause in solidarity with the suffering of the world in order to work for justice.

7 **Theology in the Vernacular** The emphasis of this method is on how the gospel finds expression across cultural differences of historical or geographical context. To what extent do the metaphors, values and aspirations of a 'host' culture provide legitimate raw material in the task of theological reflection on the Christian life?

Readers will also discover a common structure to each chapter.

*The Method in Outline* gives a brief anatomy of a particular method and its key characteristics. Basic terminology will be introduced.

The *Introduction* offers an overview of the method, and in particular how certain themes may provide continuity across different historical and cultural contexts. We introduce some of the most distinctive qualities of each method, emphasizing in particular how its own particular process of theological reflection informs the threefold task of articulating Christian identity, forming and sustaining the body of Christ and engaging with culture and society in the name of the gospel.

*Reflections from History* is a substantial section that introduces selected biblical and historical illustrations, drawn from the Western tradition. This section builds up a distinctive paradigm for the method in question and indicates significant exemplars.

*The Method Realized* identifies particular circumstances from the recent past in which the historical antecedents are crystallized in a more sustained fashion, and sketches how each method continues to inform contemporary theological reflection.

The *Critical Evaluation* section scrutinizes the chief critical perspectives on each method, followed by a series of *Questions* that return us to the core themes of theological reflection in relation to Christian formation, corporate identity and attitudes to culture.

An *Annotated Bibliography* identifies a selection of the most significant illustrations of each method, and offers suggestions for further reading.

While the chapters are intended to be read as a critical anatomy of each method in turn, we also hope that readers will engage in comparative analysis across the chapters. Within each chapter, the themes of the *threefold task* of theology (see pages 10–11) remain a constant, and therefore form a thread for readers to follow throughout. A second issue addressed by each chapter is the question of how each method understands and uses the *sources and norms* of theology: how it draws upon the enduring resources of Scripture, tradition, reason and experience to inform its endeavours and how the criteria by which theological communities evaluate the authenticity and adequacy of the truth-claims they make also vary. Readers are invited to consider how and why such diversity has come about.

## Conclusion

This book works with an understanding of theology as *process* as well as *product.* We attempt to lay bare the processes and methods that fuel theological formulation and expression. We have argued that theological reflection has developed out of specific circumstances and historically came to birth in order to resolve particular demands experienced by the earliest Christian communities. The challenges of Christian formation and nurture, of articulating collective identity and the encounter between Church and world form a threefold problematic that has always provided the impetus to generate theology. It exists to enable faithful people to articulate the values and visions that motivate their responses to those three questions of practical living.

Actual human speech about God, thus, is not abstract logical talk about an 'ultimate limit' but rather talk about life and the world, about our deepest problems, about catastrophe and triumph, about human misery and human glory. It is about what is really important in life, how we are to live, how to comport ourselves, which styles of life are genuinely human and which dehumanizing. But it is and can be talk about these matters only because it claims to be about that ultimate point of orientation to which all else must be referred.

Kaufman, 1995, p. 17

The emphasis we have placed on 'theological reflection' as lying at the heart of the formulation of theological discourse enables us to forge new connections with the history of Christian doctrine. We are effectively recontextualizing that history by returning to the particular problems and challenges that prompted previous generations into their own 'talk about God', and showing how particular genres, each with their own distinctive approaches, emerged and developed over the centuries. This is not an exhaustive account, but one by which we hope the divisions between 'systematic' and 'practical' theology might begin to be closed.

Finally, our overarching objective in writing this book has been to return people to the primary sources; to the writers and movements, both historical and contemporary, that continue to inspire and stimulate theological reflection. If we succeed in rekindling interest in some of the great theologians of the past, and of awakening new interest in what impelled them to write, speak and act as they did, then we will be content. To these ends, the companion volume to this work, *Theological Reflections: A Reader* (SCM Press, 2006), will provide more extensive primary material for study and debate.

## Annotated Bibliography

Bevans, Stephen B. (2002), *Models of Contextual Theology*, New York: Orbis, 2nd edn. Emerging out of contemporary interest in the 'inculturation' of theology (see Chapter 7), which constructs five models based on different responses to the tensions between tradition and experience.

Kinast, R. (2000), *What Are They Saying About Theological Reflection?*, New York: Paulist Press. This book also seeks to construct a number of ideal-typical approaches to theological reflection, in which God-talk is understood as emerging from human experience. Its focus is chiefly upon contemporary theological writers rather than an attempt to place theological reflection in any kind of historical perspective.

Mudge, L. and Poling, J. eds (1987), *Formation and Reflection: The Promise of Practical Theology*, Nashville: Abingdon. An early example of the re-evaluation of the identity of practical theology as an academic and vocational discipline, reflecting the beginnings of the shift away from 'applied theology'.

Pattison, S. and Woodward, J. W. eds (2000), *The Blackwell Reader in Pastoral and Practical Theology*, Oxford: Blackwell. An excellent digest of the state of practical theology by the beginning of the twenty-first century, demonstrating its multidisciplinary nature and reflecting how the discipline has effected a more hermeneutical and interpretative turn.

Niebuhr, H. R. (1951), *Christ and Culture*, San Francisco: Harper & Row. A classic of Christian theology, incorporating the exercise of 'ideal types' to demonstrate the enduring diversity of expressions of faithful negotiation between the claims of 'Christ' and 'culture'.

# I

# 'Theology by Heart':
# The Living Human Document

## The Method in Outline

This method of theological reflection looks to the self and the interior life as the primary space in which theological awareness is generated and nurtured. To transform heart-felt inner experience into a theological resource the method employs journal-writing, personal letters, verbatim accounts of pastoral encounters, spiritual autobiography, and other contemporary forms of creative writing, as the means to 'turn-life-into-text'. Such texts can be described as 'living human documents' in the sense that they are authentic accounts of lived experience presented in a form that can be read and analysed. These documents are always dialogical. They do not only contain the perspective of their authors but also witness to their conversational encounters with other people, other world-views and with God. This method of theological reflection, therefore, presents the self as formed through intimate relations with God and others. Looking within, the method seeks to discern how attention to deep personal feelings can become a source of theological sensitivity that results in faithful, and often adventurous, living.

## Introduction

We begin to explore 'theology by heart' through examining reflections of this method found in history. These are sources that can be used to locate the current practice of this method in the traditions of faith. The first example, from Psalm 139, indicates that reflection upon the relationship of the self to God is present in some of the most profound writing in the Judaeo-Christian tradition. A passage from Augustine of Hippo's *Confessions* describes how an encounter with a friend, Ponticianus, stirred Augustine to further examination of his own response to God. The letters of Abelard and Heloise show how letter-writing provides the opportunity for intense exploration of self among the strenuous demands of life in a convent and monastery. John Wesley's journals, written for a public audience, capture a Pietistic turn within the Christian tradition, where the renewed inward life becomes the foundation for a new vision of the Church and engagement with the world.

Although present throughout Christian history this method of theological reflection came to full realization as psychology developed as a discipline that focused critical attention on the significance of the inner self. The works of scholars such as Sigmund Freud and William James were quickly recognized as immensely important for theology. The conflicts, turmoil and pleasures experienced within the self had long been regarded as having theological significance. It now became necessary to offer more rigorous means to explore the psychological processes that were seen as fundamental to the formation of human identity.

Marion Milner, a psychoanalyst and therapist whose life spanned the twentieth century, used journaling techniques to explore her relationship with God, and we examine what she achieved through this process. Anton Boisen, the founding father of the Clinical Pastoral Education (CPE) movement, influenced the way in which psychological insights could be used within pastoral care. His work is still widely used within theological education. The Clinical Pastoral Education (CPE) movement has developed Boisen's use of verbatim accounts of pastoral encounters in order to analyse pastoral practice. The verbatim report is taken here as a way of 'turning-life-into-text' and Frances Ward's recent work on life-long learning demonstrates the continuing creative potential of this method.

Within the wider sphere of professional development, the process of turning-life-into-text has entailed the use of creative writing. The work of the Quaker poet and educator Gillie Bolton illustrates the exciting use of this process in developing reflective practice among those whose work demands a high degree of personal self-awareness. Finally we examine the claims of Riet Bons-Storm that those who have been denied a public voice often find the strength to challenge their exclusion through the written expression of their experiences. Bons-Storm's work demonstrates that 'theology by heart' can become a vital resource to those seeking social justice and transformation.

With its stress on the importance of the interiority of the self as it finds expression through texts, the notion of *reflexivity* becomes a key word in this method of theological reflection. Reflexivity can be defined as an acknowledgement of the significance of the self in forming an understanding of the world. The word can be differentiated from *reflection* where the focus is more upon what can be seen by looking outwards to what lies beyond the limits of the personal. This method can seem overly individual in its application, and it needs to be remembered that self and identity are always formed through interaction with others.

To summarize, this method enables reflection upon the self by examining documents that turn-life-into-text. The context of religious life or church community is often important in the development of understanding of self and identity, and the methods outlined here can be used in professional practice and prophetic engagement with the world. Within the three categories that are used in this book – *Christian induction and nurture, corporate identity* and *gospel and culture* – this method is obviously highly useful in the nurturing of a deep sense of Christian identity within the individual. However, this process of identity-formation is dialogical and the relation to the faith community is also of crucial importance. The Church can be experienced as the space in which personal growth takes place but also, on occasions, where the witness of the heart may be denied, resulting in struggle with and resistance to authority for the sake of truth. Finally, theology by heart is important not only to achieve personal growth but also in order to relate creatively with others in every sphere of life.

## Reflections from History

For it was you who formed my inward parts;
You knit me together in my mother's womb.
I praise you, for I am fearfully and wonderfully made.
Wonderful are your works;
That I know very well.
My frame was not hidden from you,
When I was being made in secret,
Intricately woven in the depths of the earth.
Your eyes beheld my unformed substance.
In your book were written all the days that were formed for me,
When none of them as yet existed.
How weighty to me are your thoughts, O God!
How vast is the sum of them!
I try to count them – they are more than the sand;
I come to the end – I am still with you.

Psalm 139.13–18 (NRSV)

A profound sense of intimacy with God permeates this passage from Psalm 139. The psalmist praises God for the intricacy of creation in the hidden place of the womb; an initial formation that becomes the frame for a subsequent 'fearful and wonderful' development that continues to be sustained right to the end of the 'vast sum' of God's thoughts. This passage captures a sense of God's knowledge of each individual part of creation, from the bones and sinews that are knit together in the womb through to the all-encompassing knowledge that God has of all the days of a person's life. The psalmist expresses praise to God for the immensity of God's thoughts that embrace the beginning and the ending of life, and all that is between – and beyond. The self, in this passage, is placed in the context of God's creation, and yet, despite the awful wonder and the cosmological scale of God's works, it is given a sense of individual worth and dignity.

The passage links knowledge of the God of the heavens with the inward working of the interior life, and to reflection upon the 'secret' self, intricately woven in the depths of the earth. This inward movement illustrates what we will later explore as reflexivity: the concern to understand more deeply the ways of the self, positioned within the networks of society. Here, created by God, the reflexive self seeks to understand more profoundly the nature of its own creation and life-long relationship with God as a being whose days are formed as a book.

The metaphor of the book – a text – to explore the closeness of God to the self as it grows and changes through life is particularly important. 'In your book were written all the days that were formed for me, when none of them as yet existed.' The psalmist gives the sense that the book is God's, but it is unclear whether all the days that are written are to unfold in a predetermined way, as if God knows and plans out the course of a life, or whether the days do not yet exist and are open to the future. In either case the metaphor of a book introduces the sense that the self can be read as a text, open to interpretation leading to enhanced self-awareness and thereby deeper theological understanding. The writer uses the creative form of a psalm, traditionally sung in worship, to encourage reflection upon life as a text to be read, on the nature of the self in relation to God. The metaphor of life as a text in God's hands is a distinctive feature of the method of theological reflection in this chapter.

## The Spiritual Autobiography: Augustine of Hippo's Confessions

St Augustine (AD 354–430) was 43 when he wrote the *Confessions* in 397. He had been consecrated bishop of Hippo the year before. The former civilization of the Roman world was crumbling and Christianity was forging itself into a dominant faith by engaging in fierce debate with classical philosophy, other religions, and different interpretations of the Christian faith itself. Augustine's own life and thinking reflected many of these debates and his writing portrays a personal life that displays in microcosm the conflicts of his time. For whom was he writing? Certainly himself, it seems, as he sought to review his life. But also, undoubtedly, he wrote to be read by a public audience. Astutely, he addressed his text to God, making the whole work a prayer of praise and confession, and leaving it open as to how others might engage with it. His 'living human document' was both an account of his life, and a text to inspire theological reflection in others.

The genius of *Confessions* lies, among other things, in its intensity. Addressed to God, it reveals a man fiercely driven to honest reflection upon his own motivations and passions. The book shows a man who yearns fervently for God and who desires more than anything to be known by God and to know himself. He writes:

> Who is to carry the research beyond this point? Who can understand the truth of the matter? O Lord, I am working hard in this field, and the field of my labours is my own self. I have become a problem to myself, like land which a farmer works only with difficulty and at the cost of much sweat. For I am not now investigating the tracts of the heavens, or measuring the distance of the stars, or trying to discover how the earth hangs in space. I am investigating myself, my memory, my mind. This is nothing strange in the fact that whatever is not myself is far from me. But what could be nearer to me than myself?
>
> *Confessions*, Bk X, Chapter 16

This yearning to know himself led Augustine relentlessly to analyse his feelings and passions. His conversion to Christianity had been a profound experience due in part to the long, persuasive influence of his mother Monica upon him. Augustine's dialogues with friends were also central: he talked at length and in depth with them on all manner of topics and concerns. Friendship provided for him the opportunity for exploration of self. It was through others he experienced the mediation of the love of God as the following passage about his mother illustrates:

Surely the words which rang in my ears, spoken by your faithful servant, my mother, could have come from none but you? . . . Yet the words were yours, though I did not know it. I thought that you were silent and that she was speaking, but all the while you were speaking to me through her, and when I disregarded her, your hand-maid, I was disregarding you, though I was both her son and your servant.

*Confessions*, Bk II, Ch. 3

Augustine here is at the point of conversion, relinquishing as false the philosophy of the classical world and the dualist religion of his youth, Manichaeism, which had captured his intellect but which he knew could not provide the satisfaction he sought. He struggled with the need for a change of heart and described it in terms of a profound tension between his conscience and the forces of habit that controlled his soul. One of the only things that could move the will from its enslavement to past habits of life was delight. He wrote:

And sometimes You fill me with a feeling quite unlike my normal state, an inward sense of delight, which, if it were to reach fulfilment in men, would be something entirely different from my present life. But my heavy burden of distress drags me back: I am sucked back to my habits, and find myself held fast; I weep greatly, but I am firmly held. The load of habit is a force to be reckoned with!

*Confessions*, Bk X, Ch. 40

The struggle is apparent in his famous account of a conversation with Ponticianus. It is as if the words of his friend speak directly to his condition and prompt deep and painful introspection, a sense of nakedness and shame, and a realization of the necessity for a change of heart, yet the awareness of a silent and fearful soul that could not relinquish its habits of old.

But now, the more my heart warmed to those two men as I heard how they had made the choice that was to save them by giving themselves up entirely to your care, the more bitterly I hated myself in compassion with them. . . . As a youth I had been woefully at fault, particularly in early adolescence. I had prayed to you for chastity and said 'Give me chastity and continence, but not yet'. For I was afraid that you would answer my prayer at once and cure me too soon of the disease of lust, which I wanted satisfied, not quelled. I had wandered on along the road of vice in the sacrilegious superstition of the Manichees, not because I thought that it was right, but because I preferred it to the Christian belief, which I did not explore as I ought but opposed out of malice.

I had pretended to myself that the reason why, day after day, I staved off the decision to renounce worldly ambition and follow you alone was that I could see no certain goal towards which I might steer my course. But the time had now come when I stood naked before my own eyes, while my conscience upbraided me. 'Am I to be silent? Did you not always say that you would not discard your load of vanity for the sake of a truth that was not proved? Now you know that the truth is proved, but the load is still on your shoulders. Yet here are others who have exchanged their load for wings, although they did not wear themselves out in the search for truth or spend ten years or more in making up their minds.'

All the time that Ponticianus was speaking my consciences gnawed away at me like this. I was overcome by burning shame, and when he had finished his tale and completed the business for which he had come, he went away and I was left to my own thoughts. I made all sorts of accusations against myself, I cudgelled my soul and belaboured it with reasons why it should follow me now that I was trying hard to follow you. But it fought back. It would not obey and yet could offer no excuse. All its old arguments were exhausted and had been shown to be false. It remained silent and afraid, for as much as the loss of life itself it feared the staunching of the flow of habit, by which it was wasting away to death.

*Confessions*, Bk VIII, Ch. 7; see Augustine, 1961, pp. 169–70

Augustine's *Confessions* remains a classic piece of spiritual writing that speaks to each generation. It reveals an intense relationship with God who was present to Augustine through his friends and other people, and it encourages readers to view their own lives with the same degree of introspection and desire for understanding.

## The Letter: Abelard's and Heloise's Correspondence

The next example of theology by heart that we consider is a dialogue between two lovers, married secretly yet separated by brutal circumstances. Abelard (1079–1142) and Heloise (c.1100–1163/4) married without the permission of Heloise's guardian, who responded by ensuring that Abelard was castrated. Both then took the vows of the religious life and rose to positions of leadership within their respective orders. As we shall see, initially for Heloise this was not a straightforward transference of affection from human lover to Christ, and it was only through correspondence with Abelard that she became reconciled to her new life and was able to integrate her internal passions and frustrations with the external work of running a religious community. We shall read here a letter from Heloise and then Abelard's response, showing how he offers spiritual direction that gives Heloise no real choice but to redirect her love. Thereafter their correspondence is firmly based on service of community and God. The philosophical and political climate of the age is evident in the writing of these two eminently well-educated people and Heloise's own erudition, unusual in a woman of the twelfth century, shines through her closely argued and well-constructed prose.

### Heloise to Abelard, letter 1

I beg you then to listen to what I ask – you will see that it is a small favour which you can easily grant. While I am denied your presence, give me at least through your words – of which you have enough and to spare – some sweet semblance of yourself. It is no use my hoping for generosity in deeds if you are grudging in words. Up to now I had thought I deserved much of you, seeing that I carried out everything for your sake and continue up to the present moment in complete obedience to you. It was not any sense of vocation which brought me as a young girl to accept the austerities of the cloister, but your bidding alone, and if I deserve no gratitude from you, you may judge for yourself how my labours are in vain. I can expect no reward for this from God, for it is certain that I have done nothing as yet for love of him. When you hurried towards God I followed you, indeed, I went first to take the veil – perhaps you were thinking how Lot's wife turned back when you made me put on the religious habit and take my vows before you gave yourself to God. Your lack of trust in me over this one thing, I confess, overwhelmed me with grief and shame. I would have had no hesitation, God knows, in following you or going ahead at your bidding to the flames of Hell. My heart was not in me but with you, and now, even more, if it is not with you it is nowhere; truly, without you it cannot exist. See that it fares well with you, I beg, as it will if it finds you kind, if you give grace in return for grace, small for great, words for deeds. If only your love had less confidence in me, my dear, so that you would be more concerned on my behalf! But as it is, the more I have made you feel secure in me, the more I have to bear with your neglect.

Radice, 1974, pp. 116–17

Abelard to Heloise, letter 4

It was he who truly loved you, not I. My love, which brought us both to sin, should be called lust, not love. I took my fill of my wretched pleasures in you, and this was the sum total of my love. You say I suffered for you, and perhaps that is true, but it was really through you, and even this, unwillingly; not for love of you but under compulsion, and to bring you not salvation but sorrow. But he suffered truly for your salvation, on your behalf of his own free will, and by his suffering he cures all sickness and removes all suffering. To him, I beseech you, not to me, should be directed all your devotion, all your compassion, all your remorse. Weep for the injustice of the great cruelty inflicted on him, not for the just and righteous payment demanded of me, or rather, as I said, the supreme grace granted us both. For you are unrighteous if you do not love righteousness, and most unrighteous if you consciously oppose the will, or more truly, the boundless grace of God. Mourn for your Saviour and Redeemer, not for the seducer who defiled you, for the Master who died for you, not for the servant who lives and, indeed, for the first time is truly freed from death.

p. 153

The poignancy and passion of these passages speak of the power of the discipline that shaped their lives, led under vows of obedience, where devotion is sublimated into the practice of faith. Abelard's plea that Heloise's devotion to him should be redirected shows his firm spiritual direction that she should understand her own feelings and the cruelty that he suffered in a different way by seeing them as borne by Christ. It could be argued that they had no option but to accept the mores of the Church and society in which they lived, and at least by basing their relationship on Christ they could continue to correspond within the framework of communal life where they were accountable to others besides themselves. On the other hand, the way in which Heloise was disciplined by Abelard and instructed to understand her feelings differently shows the way in which sublimation as a religious devotion and practice could be deeply manipulative, even abusive. The letter as a form remains open to interpretation as it captures here an intimacy of relation in the experience of Abelard and Heloise as they attempt to shape their lives in accordance with their theological understanding of Christ's love.

Heloise writes: 'While I am denied your presence, give me at least through your words – of which you have enough and to spare – some sweet semblance of yourself.' In terms of the way in which life becomes text in this method of theological reflection, we have here a sense of substitution: the words will have to stand for the presence of the person himself. She pleads with Abelard to continue to write to her so that she may live, if not with him, with a sweet semblance of him. Abelard counters this plea with Christ: it might almost be said that instead of his own words of love and comfort, she is to focus upon the Word of God, bringing her will into line with that Word, rather than rely upon Abelard's letters. From a renewed devotion to 'the Master who died for you', rather than Abelard, 'for the first time truly freed from death' she would receive boundless grace of God, the supreme grace 'granted us both'. These letters convey the tension of love and emotion, of denial and separation. They show two people who struggle to survive and understand themselves in a relationship that, for whatever reason, could not continue as it had done. Their words to each other poignantly demonstrate how letter writing offered the means to reflect theologically in intimate correspondence. With Augustine, his *Confessions* was an extended prayer, addressed to God. Letters exchanged, as with Abelard's and Heloise's correspondence, allow an interchange of feeling, appeal, opinion and guidance. Their passion and sexual drive are negotiated and managed as both found ways to continue their love in directions other than sexual and personal, giving a powerful example of theological and spiritual direction conveyed through the written text.

The epistolary form has a long history. It belongs in this method of theological reflection because of the way in which letters can capture the concerns of the correspondents and enable reflections and ideas to be exchanged. Letters, as living human documents, enable theological reflection, as we see here how Heloise and Abelard came to understand their passion for each other within a greater context of their love and discipleship of Christ.

## The Journal: John Wesley's Writing

We turn now to the eighteenth century and to the life and work of a preacher who emphasized the inward life and personal relationship with God, to counter the sterility and distant forms of the expression of established religion of his day. John Wesley (1703–91) kept one set of personal diaries intended as private documents, and another journal, recording his extensive travels as he preached and travelled throughout the British Isles. This journal was a record of his life of faith, and was written for public consumption as well as in order to encourage his followers and, at times, justify his actions to a world that seemingly found his forthright style and confident judgement sometimes hard to take.

Wesley came increasingly to be influenced by Pietism. This was a movement that looked to Luther's doctrine of 'justification by faith alone' and the response of the believer to the knowledge that Christ was Saviour, rather than to external trappings, printed prayer books or more formal expressions of religion that characterized the Church of England of the day. Wesley came into contact with Moravians on his visit to the colony of Georgia in 1736, and was particularly impressed by their strong faith in the storms encountered on the sea voyage. Challenged by questions, on that visit to the Americas, from the Moravian leader A. G. Spangenburg, Wesley was increasingly inclined to acknowledge the importance of an internal acceptance of the reality of Christ in his life. A few years later, back in England, he had long conversations with another Moravian, Böhler, and came to see that such acceptance of Christ was a conversion or 'new birth'. In 1738 Wesley experienced an internal event that led him to a different understanding of faith. The Methodist scholar Henry Rack explains it like this:

> Given their Lutheran background (and despite their stress on practical piety and the religion of the heart rather than mere theological correctness as regards the doctrines of grace and faith), it is not surprising that the Moravians should have stressed that salvation cannot come by 'works' but only by faith. And the transition from works to faith was seen by them as producing a 'new birth', typically experienced as an instantaneous conversion. This was what Böhler and his friends taught Wesley. Before the end of April 1738 Wesley had accepted intellectually that salvation was by faith alone, through an instantaneous experience, on the testimony both of Scripture and living witnesses. But he had not actually experienced this happening to himself. The event on 24 May appears to represent this truth becoming a part of his experience. It also appears to have been combined with an explicit 'assurance' of the change having happened – if anything, this is perhaps the dominant aspect of the experience.

> Rack, 2002, pp. 148–9

When Wesley describes in his journal what happened, it is as if the experience itself becomes real in the telling of it, and certainly it was important to Wesley to be able to describe the sense he had of external assurance of this intensely interior conversion. More and more distanced from the Anglican churches of his upbringing because of their distrust of his emphasis upon that interior response to Christ, Wesley's physical sensation of his heart being strangely warmed gave important credibility to his experience. To write publicly of this event in his journal transformed an essentially private, pietistic moment into a religious moment of widespread consequence as a new movement took shape on the eighteenth century landscape.

Sunday 21 May (Whitsunday) 1738
I preached at St John's Wapping, at three, and at St Benet's, Paul's Wharf, in the evening. At these churches likewise I am to preach no more.

Monday, Tuesday, Wednesday, I had 'continual sorrow and heaviness' in my 'heart'. What occurred on Wednesday the 24th, I think best to relate at large.

I think it was about five this morning, that I opened my Testament on those words, 'There are given us exceeding great and precious promises, even that ye should be partakers of the divine nature' (2 Peter 1:4). Just as I went out, I opened it again on 'Thou art not far from the kingdom of God.' In the afternoon I was asked to go to St Paul's. The anthem was, 'Out of the deep have I called unto thee, O Lord: Lord, hear my voice.'

In the evening I went very unwillingly to a society in Aldersgate Street, where one was reading Luther's preface to the *Epistle to the Romans*. About a quarter before nine, when he was describing the change which God works in the heart through faith in Christ, I felt my heart strangely warmed. I felt I did trust in Christ, Christ alone for salvation; and an assurance was given me that he had taken away *my* sins, even *mine*, and saved *me* from the law of sin and death.

I began to pray with all my might for those who had in a more especial manner despitefully used me and persecuted me. I then testified openly to all there what I now first felt in my heart. But it was not long before the enemy suggested, 'This cannot be faith; for where is the joy?' Then was I taught that peace and victory over sin are essential to faith in the Captain of our salvation; but that, as to the transports of joy that usually attend the beginning of it, especially in those who have mourned deeply, God sometimes giveth, sometimes withholdeth them.

Wesley, [1986] 2003, pp. 48–9

John Wesley's journal was written for a public readership. He wrote to encourage his colleagues and followers in a world that could be hostile to his new interpretation of and enthusiasm for the gospel of Christ. The strategy of writing a personal document for publication is a good one if, as Wesley intended, he wanted to appeal to new followers by showing his own devotion and dedication in the face of hardship and rejection. It was also an effective way to incorporate the different theological emphasis he was propounding. As a living human document, Wesley's journal engaged with his readers in a direct and immediate way as it relayed his life, thoughts and his own theological reflection upon the relationship between God and person.

In these passages from history we have seen how the turn to the interior life in the poetry of the psalms, journals, letters, and spiritual autobiography can generate theological reflection. As the often intense experience of a relationship with God is framed into words, a process is begun that enables reflection, both by the initial writers, but then also by other readers. We have seen how this method of theological reflection is essentially dialogical. The conversations can be internal, such as those Augustine records with his mother, his friends or with God. They can also be accounts of real conversations and correspondence. Heloise and Abelard communicated directly with each other and each person was enabled to gain understanding and insight of their faith and practice. In the writings we have examined, biblical sources, or other philosophical or theological resources, can be incorporated as a way of enriching the dialogue. The written text is crucial to this method as the experience of life is described and interpreted. As it provokes further reflection, the text becomes a living human document that generates further theological enquiry.

## The Method Realized

From our consideration of these historical examples of theology by heart we turn now to examine this method of theological reflection as it is practised in contemporary times. With the work of Sigmund Freud (1856–1939), and others such as William James (1842–1910), the birth of psychology as a formal discipline emerged, offering a new discourse through which to analyse the inner life. James's classic *The Varieties of Religious Experience: A Study in Human Nature* (2002), first published in 1902, interrogated religious experience from a psychologist's point of view. He analysed records of religious experience as phenomena, defining religion as 'the feelings, acts, and experiences of individual men [sic] in their solitude, so far as they apprehend themselves to stand in relation to whatever they may consider the divine' (p. 50). He excluded what he called institutional forms of religion, choosing to focus upon the individuals' relationship with the divine, and included examples from many different traditions, arguing for a universality of religious experience. He drew parallels between the 'mind-cure' of psychology and the 'Lutheran and Wesleyan movements' (p. 119), indicating a continuation between the discipline of psychology as it developed in the early years of the twentieth century and the strands of interior religious expression from past centuries that we have been examining in this chapter. The development of self-awareness and reflection upon the self took a decisive step with the work of James as he considered the primary impulse of religion and reflection upon it, which he believed was an activity of a secondary order: 'I do believe', he wrote, 'that feeling is the deeper source of religion, and that philosophic and theological formulas are secondary products, like translations of a text into another tongue' (pp. 414–15).

With William James's work of bringing together the insights of psychology and philosophy with religion we have a sense in which this method of theological reflection develops a language: 'a translation of a text into another tongue'. We look now at the work of a psychoanalyst and therapist, Marion Milner (1900–98), whose life spanned the twentieth century, and who kept journals in which she focused attention on herself and her own reactions and responses to the events of life, integrating her psychological analysis by her quest to understand her religious sensibilities.

## The Journaling of Marion Milner

Throughout her life Marion Milner was fascinated, from a psychological point of view, by herself. She kept journals in which she explores her own actions, reactions and motivations with an analytical honesty. She published *A Life of One's Own* ([1934] 1986) and a companion volume, *An Experiment in Leisure*, ([1937] 1986), and then completed the trilogy in 1987 with *Eternity's Sunrise: A Way of Keeping a Diary*. Her work is particularly interesting because of the methodological approach she adopts, and the way she critiques her own value system and her unconscious motivations. At the beginning of *Eternity's Sunrise* she outlines what she hopes to achieve in her work.

This book, which I began in 1958, is an extension of one I wrote in 1936, called *An Experiment in Leisure*, which was blitzed out of print in the 1940 raids on London, and was itself an extension of my first one, *A Life of One's Own*. That had been partly stimulated by reading Montaigne's essays and his insistence that what he calls the soul is totally different from all that one expects it to be, often being the very opposite. It was this that gave me the idea of keeping a diary to see if I could find out at all what this soul of mine was really like. There was, however, something else that led directly to the diary-keeping. I had been trying, in 1926, to do a mental training course (called Pelman) in order to improve my erratic powers of concentration, and the course insisted that the first thing one must do was find out what one's aim in life was. As I had no idea at all what mine was, I decided that in the diary I would try to put down what seemed to be the most important thing that happened each day and see if I could find out from that what it might be that I really wanted. It was the surprise that what turned up as most important was not at all what I had expected that led me to write that first book. In addition, there was the surprise at what appeared when I tried writing down whatever came into my head about certain words with strong emotional overtones, such as, for instance, the word 'God'.

Milner, 1987, p. ix

The disciplined and creative way in which Milner carries forward this exploration into what 'this soul of mine was really like' reflects her keen psychoanalytic awareness. She draws upon anything and everything that seemed 'momentous', significant and 'of the moment' and deliberately focuses on the business of writing, thus making explicit a key feature of this method of theological reflection: the reflexive self using writing to bring to light the experience of life in order to deepen self-awareness and generate understanding of God. And so she writes of her first volume that it 'is a contemporary journal of an exploration which involved doubts, delays, and expeditions on false trails, and the writing of it was an essential part of the search' ([1934] 1986, p. 13). Later she stated how struck she was by the effect of writing things down:

It was as if I were trying to catch something and the written word provided a net which for a moment entangled a shadowy form which was other than the meaning of the words. Sometimes it seemed that the act of writing was fuel on glowing embers, making flames leap up and throw light on the surrounding gloom, giving me fitful gleams of what was before unguessed at.

1986, p. 69

In the search for her purpose in life, Milner tried to free herself of the burden of assumed aims and attend to what delighted her senses. Her efforts led her to experiments in 'free writing'. At the end of *A Life*, Milner reviewed her writing over the previous seven years. She recognized what she called 'blind thinking' – thinking that was the unconscious monologue that went on in her mind, and wrote: 'I had discovered that different things made me happy when I looked at my experience from when I did not' ([1934] 1986, p. 198). As she worked at the method and then reviewed what she had gained from the experience of keeping a journal, she came to the conclusion that:

> I could say that my failure to reflect, my inability to know what I liked or what I wanted, or to draw any conclusions from the welter of my experience, was due to letting my musings remain in the form of an unconscious monologue . . . I had undoubtedly been quite at sea about how to live my life until I had learnt to make that active gesture of separation and detachment by which one stands aside and looks at one's experience.
>
> p. 217

Writing brings a sense of separation between the interior life and an external text and this is an important step in this method of theological reflection. Writing about one's inner life becomes a conscious self-reflexive activity.

## Anton Boisen and the Living Human Document

We next look at the influential work of the founder of the Clinical Pastoral Education (CPE) movement, the pastoral theologian and Congregational minister, Anton Boisen (1876–1965). On 9 October 1920 Boisen suffered an acute psychotic disturbance and was taken to Boston Psychopathic Hospital, Massachusetts. He reflected upon his own illness and determined that out of the horrors of the experience, good might come. He went through a process of reflection and self-evaluation and was able to gain critical distance to reflect on his illness.

In his letter to Worcester, Boisen is claiming the right (for which he had to fight) of interpreting his own experience for himself. He tried to talk with the doctors about his illness but '. . . they did not believe in talking with patients about their symptoms, taking the common somatic point of view that symptoms are rooted in some as-yet-undiscovered organic difficulty' (p. 40). Boisen began to read Freud, and his experience and reflection led him to see that psychoanalysis had much to offer in pastoral practice, not least in understanding that

*Westboro State Hospital*
*20 November 1921*
*Dr Elwood Worcester*
*Emmanuel Church*
*Boston, Mass.*

Dear Dr. Worcester

In the interview of last Monday the following ground was covered, if I remember correctly:

The precise nature of the original trouble.

The character of the first abnormal condition.

Some facts regarding the love affair around which the whole thing centers.

Your advice that I take up some outdoor work.

I hope that the following facts have been established:

The original trouble was primarily a mental one. There was no habit of masturbation and no perversions, as I understand those terms. There was difficulty in controlling the wayward sex interests.

The first abnormal condition, while containing many morbid elements, was a clear-cut conversion experience with effects which were wholly beneficial.

The love affair was not rooted in friendly association but rather in inner struggle and in what might be called quite accurately the need of salvation. The motive power has been the deep feeling that this was for me the right course, the only one I could follow and be true to my best self.

The danger that I may underestimate the gravity of these abnormal conditions and the necessity of avoiding future recurrences. This danger I recognise. The horror of the recent catastrophe is with me still. It has been terrible beyond the power of words to express. And yet I do not regard these experiences as 'breakdowns'. If I am right in believing that through them difficult problems have been solved for me and solved right, and if through them help and strength have come to me, am I not justified in such a view?

Quoted in Stokes, 1985, p. 58

the troubles experienced by someone in mental anguish required sensitive listening skills and respect as both client and pastoral practitioner worked together to interpret feelings and behaviour. Boisen had a distinctive part to play in ensuring that the insights of Freud became accepted in clinical and pastoral practice in the following decades.

As he first suggested that pastors should include in their preparation 'the study of living human documents', Boisen is generally considered as one of the principal progenitors of the twentieth-century pastoral counselling movement that brought together theological training and the insights of psychotherapy. Only the careful and systematic study of persons struggling with the issues of the spiritual life in the concreteness of their relationships could, in Boisen's view, restore that connection. Boisen's pioneering efforts have ensured that CPE remains today an important location for the development of reflective skills among pastoral practitioners (see Graham, [1996] 2002a, pp. 65–6; Stokes, 1985).

## *The Use of Verbatim Reports in Life-Long Learning*

As CPE has developed, verbatim reports have assumed a central place as a method to bring the experience of pastoral practice to supervised reflection. On the basis of a verbatim report, which captures the conversation *verbatim* between a pastoral practitioner and client or patient, the practitioner is enabled through dialogue with a supervisor (or a supervisory group) to reflect upon what was said and done, and to experiment with alternative interventions and listening skills. The verbatim report need not be long. Often it will capture a brief part of a longer conversation which left the practitioner uncertain that what they said or did was the best response, or puzzled by behaviour patterns stirred in themselves or in the client that seemed to suggest other, unspoken things were going on. The practitioner will be encouraged to write down as much as she or he can remember of the conversation, including silences and body language. If they fail to remember, then the omissions also need to be recorded, as what is forgotten can be as telling as what is remembered. The practitioner will be asked to present the verbatim report by numbering the different interventions of each person in the conversation for easier reference, and to leave a wide margin down one side so that comments and notes can be made during the supervision process.

The text box offers an example of a verbatim report, taken from a phone conversation, brought for supervision by Helen (H). She was concerned about whether she had listened carefully to what was being asked of her, and was also interested in the way her response was shaped in part by her own recent experience of establishing a relationship of spiritual direction with someone else. She began the verbatim report with a brief note that set the conversation in context.

---

Verbatim
*Conversation between myself (Helen) and Jane over the phone. Jane is a curate, a female priest in training. I'd seen her earlier in the day at a meeting. I knew that her sister was very ill and dying, but hadn't talked of it with her at the meeting.*
*(My own reactions and thoughts in italics and bracketed.)*

H1   Hallo . . .

J1   Hallo, Helen, It's Jane.

H2   Hallo. Did you phone earlier? Ray said someone, had phoned
     . . . I was wondering who it was *(then suddenly thinking that
     I was going too fast in the conversation)* how are you? how's
     your sister?

J2   She died a couple of weeks ago. It's all right.

H3   I didn't know. I'm sorry. I'm really sorry. I've been thinking of
     you. *(Do I sound hollow?)* How can I help?

J3   I'm wondering if you do spiritual direction? Does anyone
     come to you? The bishop thought you might be a good person
     to ask.

H4   *(Taken aback, and instinctively not wanting to admit that no
     one does see me strictly for spiritual direction though one or
     two do come for supervision – do I go into this now? And
     then also worried about whether I've got time. And suddenly
     remember that I have only just started seeing a new spiritual
     director which has been large in my mind and at very early
     stage, this seems important.)*
     Well, one or two. Why?

J4   I've been thinking of asking you. I need to get my head sorted.
     And you know where I'm coming from. *(Do I?)*

H5   Jane, why don't we meet to discuss it? It would help to know
     what you're wanting in a bit more detail. And I might not be
     the right person. But we could certainly meet. Have you got
     your diary with you? *(Feeling a bit more tuned in now perhaps
     because using the same response I got when I first approached
     my new director . . .)*

J5   Uh huh.

H6   I'm looking on into June, now. Week beginning the 23rd? How about Thursday that week? (*Am I stalling – quite a way off?*)

J6   No, I can't do that, I'm afraid.

H7   Oh. Hold on. Perhaps there's something earlier. What about Thursday 12th? (*Why didn't I start here? Wanting to be careful not to be too enthusiastic?*)

J7   Yes, that's OK.

H8   11?

J8   Fine.

H9   Do you want to come to me?

J9   Yes. Then I won't need to get rid of Andy. (*Husband. Is there an issue here? 'Rid of' sounded strong. Stored in back of mind.*)

H10  It helps, too, I think, to come somewhere else. To get out of our own patch. (*Similar point discussed with my new director.*)

J10  Yes.

H11  It would really help me if you could put down some thoughts about what you're wanting and email them to me beforehand. Would that be OK?

J11  Yes, fine.

H12  OK then. I'll see you. Take care, Jane.

J12  Bye.

H13  Bye.

In supervision, which could be either one-to-one or in a group, Helen could be encouraged to explore why she had brought this particular conversation and what she said in conversation with Jane in some detail. The different perspectives of each interlocutor, and even those of others not directly present (Andy, the husband and Helen's new spiritual director) could also be incorporated into the discussion as Helen made use of the time and space to understand more clearly her developing role and potential as someone who offered spiritual guidance to others.

The work of supervision is often set within a putative framework that enables different aspects of the work to be considered. Frances Ward's book *Lifelong Learning: Theological Education and Supervision* (2005) takes the work of supervision away from the predominantly therapeutic milieu in which it began and into a theological and educational context. She sets the work of supervision within the wider context of theological education and ministry in a changing society, so that a pastoral encounter is understood within wider social and political issues, with the accountabilities and power relations taken into account. For example in the verbatim that we have presented here the issue of gender emerges as the two women begin to explore the possibilities of meeting for spiritual direction within Church structures where the suggestion has come from a bishop, setting their relationship within the social and political context of a Church where bishops are currently male and women have not long been ordained priests. The shadowy presence behind this conversation of the bishop and the spiritual director, and the two husbands who are mentioned, hints at potential areas for subsequent exploration of the ways in which this ordained woman understands and practises her ministry in a largely male-dominated Church, and as various different expectations upon her at home as roles change within society. A verbatim report such as this could offer rich exploration in supervision of issues of gender and expectations in the practice of ministry.

In *Lifelong Learning* Ward develops the idea of supervision as a place that can provide the opportunity for a playful encounter with otherness, with difference. The supervisor does not look on in a disinterested or superior way, but does have oversight for establishing the boundaries and the creation of a good-enough facilitating environment for learning. Much of the learning that is formative of self and identity will be as a result of the engagement with 'alterity' or difference, an engagement that is at the heart of ministry. To dialogue well with difference is perhaps one of the most important skills for a minister in today's world. In supervision such skills can be learned and developed as the reflective practitioner brings the other spaces and times of their work in communities, in different contexts and different practices. The interplay of supervision becomes a constant interaction between different others, a dynamic interplay of standpoint, of dialogue, of power, of difference (Ward, 2005).

Ward also draws on previous work in this field by Foskett and Lyall (1988) and Hawkins and Shohet (2002), where frameworks are offered that enable both supervisor and reflective practitioner to set their work in a social context, and explore the complexities of interrelationships and dialogues that are explicit or implicit within the verbatim as a living human document. The verbatim then becomes a way of turning-life-into-text for further reflection, which can enable pastoral practitioners to explore the situations in which they find themselves, alternative interventions and other possible outcomes. The experience of supervision, using verbatim reports or case studies, can greatly enhance self-awareness. It can also generate theological reflection as different resources from the Christian tradition are brought into vital conversation with the questions that emerge in pastoral encounters.

## Reflective Practice and Creative Writing in the work of Gillie Bolton

The use of writing to generate further reflection is at the heart of Gillie Bolton's book *Reflective Practice* (2001). Here she describes how creative writing in its many different forms can be used to enable different professional groups to reflect upon their work and wider life. She encourages her clients to make sense of their professional experience by writing creatively. An exercise she frequently uses is to ask those she works with to write for six minutes, without stopping, reflecting upon or censoring the words as they come, a technique very similar to Milner's free writing. At the initial stage of writing it is important that the person does not think about what they are writing in a critical way, or worry about punctuation, spelling or grammar. Bolton states it does not matter if what is produced appears disconnected or even if it seems rubbish afterwards! The point of the exercise is to give busy people permission to stop and to begin to reflect, and to do so by creating the first form of a living human document that might offer material for further exploration (see Bolton, 2001, ch. 8).

Another exercise she uses is to ask her clients to write, again for six minutes, on a generative theme such as 'A time when I learned something vital'. This work is then shared in a safe and supportive environment in which writers can respond to the writing of others and engage with their own narrative in a deeper way. A contribution that is offered to the group is received in silence, before the corporate work of reflection begins to amplify the meaning of the contribution further. The use of silence in Bolton's work is similar in many respects to the place of silence in Quaker worship that Bolton has found helpful in her own spiritual journey. Surprising things can happen as a result of this process. Understandings that have been taken for granted begin to emerge as problematic and people find they have within themselves unexpected resources to solve longstanding problems. Bolton is at pains to stress that although highly creative writing is often produced by groups of practitioners, the purpose is always to foster the development of increased awareness rather than the production of a perfect end product.

This is an approach in which the learner is encouraged to be as reflexively aware as possible of their own social, political and psychological position, and to question it, as well as their environment. In this dynamic state things will appear to be strange, back to front, and to operate in unusual ways: they should do so. One of my students called it 'making the ordinary extraordinary'. It is this very strange-seemingness or extraordinariness which will enable students to formulate their own questions about the situation in which they find themselves (reflective), and the self they find there (reflexive). These questions are almost bound to be different from the ones they thought they might ask before they undertook the reflective and reflexive processes. The questioning will be undertaken in a spirit of enquiry which will lead to a process of more specific, usefully appropriate and meaningful questioning. Interim answers will appear, but will still be markers along the way rather than finishing posts.

Bolton, 2001, pp. 31–2

Bolton offers a very helpful distinction between 'reflexive' and 'reflective', and an illustration of how reflexive activity (attention to oneself in a particular situation) will be often closely linked with reflective processes (attention to the situation or context in which one finds oneself). Bolton's work of encouraging practitioners to write enables them to reflect upon their work and life in a complex world. She sees close links between the written word and the sense of identity that someone develops as they begin to write. A reflective practitioner, Jenny, made the comment: 'I even enjoy the physical holding of the pen, the shaping of the words, and I like the way it unfolds before you, like thought unravelling. The rest of the book is blank; I wonder what the next chapter will be?' (p. 154).

## Riet Bons-Storm and the Incredible Woman

We have seen in this chapter how the interior life can generate theological reflection through the practice of writing. We have explored the ways in which journals and diaries, letters and spiritual autobiography can capture intensely private reflection upon the self and its relationship with God and then, by turning-life-into-text, those living human documents become public so others can gain from the method and from the content. A text written down also enables the writer to return after a period of time to review and develop self-awareness by interaction with what has been written previously.

In many ways this method of reflection has been particularly important for women who have frequently not had access to public arenas of
expression, and so have made use of letters, journals and diaries as an
opportunity for reflection upon their lives and in order to affirm their
own identity. We look now at the work of a contemporary theologian
who has examined the ways in which women can be silenced within
the church life and the discourses of pastoral care. In her important
book *The Incredible Woman* (1996) Riet Bons-Storm writes as a
practical theologian who is well acquainted with the work of leading
male scholars, such as Charles Gerkin, who have used the methods of
CPE.

Her argument is that, despite their very public commitments to
active listening and personal awareness, these male theologians have
been blind to their own gendered assumptions that have structured
their pastoral encounters with women. Because the problems that
many women encounter in daily life (such as deep anger against those
who they spend their lives caring for or the wounds of sexual abuse)
are rarely given voice in church, women often find it hard to express
a sense of pain. They have problems finding language with which
to address these issues for themselves and this problem is further
exacerbated when speaking to a man who may, for them, represent
the authority of a male-centred religious tradition. This often results
in women remaining silent and Bons-Storm argues that pastoral carers
must become more aware of the nature of the silences that permeate
dialogue, as these silences are often the result of a 'lack of voice'.
Marion Milner, in her journals, explored at length the difficulty of
expression – a point we find reiterated in Bons-Storm's work. Milner
wrote in *A Life of One's Own*:

> My determination to write an account of this search had begun
> from the conviction that unless I wrote about it I would lose my way
> . . . I was tempted to write my experience as the story of what
> happened to a friend, an imaginary character, for the tradition of
> reticence in which I was born and bred was hard to fight against.
> What helped me most was the gradually growing conviction that
> silence might be the privilege of the strong but it was certain a danger
> to the weak. For the things I was prompted to keep silent about were
> nearly always the things I was ashamed of, which would have been
> far better aired and exposed to the cleansing winds of confession. I
> knew then that though my decision to write in direct personal terms
> would lead me on to dangerous ground yet it was the very core of
> my enterprise.

Milner, [1934] 1986, p. 32

In this passage we see how words are written out of silence, and the self is heard into speech. Bons-Storm's work focuses not only upon the difficulty women have in breaking silence but also upon the 'incredibility' of women; that they often go unbelieved in situations where the terms of discourse are set by dominant belief systems that traditionally have excluded them. In her book she demonstrates how male counsellors, shaped in their practice by dominant (gendered) discourses, have been unable to hear what is expressed by women. She critiques, for example, Gerkin's horizon of interpretation in pastoral encounters, arguing that it concurs too uncritically with the 'dominant sociocultural narrative' in society. He consequently fails to hear the silences of those who are non-dominant in the nexus of power, knowledge and interpretation. She writes:

> Most men don't think of themselves as 'gendered'; they just think of themselves as 'human'. As such they are the norm of humanity, just like Whites and heterosexuals think of themselves as the norm . . . These hidden privileges of the 'superior people' concentrate on the fact that they are considered 'normal' and that any faltering, fault, or misfortune will not be attributed to their sex, sexual preference, or race.

1996, p. 138

In her work Bons-Storm uses the letters and autobiographical writings of women who have been prepared to turn their silences into text. These are moving documents in which women speak, often for the first time, of issues that are at once deeply personal and which also affect the lives of many other women. These texts are the testimonies of women who have been silenced by their experience of living as non-dominant people in a culture where professional carers are unable to hear and believe the stories that they tell.

Does the sociocultural narrative with its proper roles also govern pastoral communication? As an example, I show how the North American pastoral theologian Charles V. Gerkin, also widely read in other parts of the world, writes about women in his books.

In the span of three of his books he gives seventeen cases of women needing pastoral counselling, alongside eight cases of men. This is typical for books about pastoral care: the cases are mostly about women. Obviously women either have more problems, or need more help than men do, or they are more ready to go to a pastor with their problems. Writing about the women, in ten of the seventeen cases Gerkin mentions something about their outer appearance:

- 'dressed in frilly pink bed jacket, her nails freshly polished, . . . her hair set and colored . . . blue-white' (Gerkin, 1979, p. 84)
- 'attractive wife of an upwardly mobile, hard-driving man' (p. 151);
- 'her hair was bleached and silvered very becomingly and her face looked immature, yet careworn' (p. 173);
- 'she wore an ill-fitting black dress;' Gerkin describes her with her underclothes showing, her hair dishevelled 'as if it had received no care for several weeks' (p. 189). Later, however, this woman has improved: 'her hair was quite becomingly arranged and tinted' (p. 189);
- 'a rather attractive woman of forty-two, the daughter of . . .' (p. 250);
- 'a slight, wispy sort of girl of 19' (p. 278);
- 'a talented and beautiful woman' (p. 280);
- 'a short, stocky woman' (p. 297);
- 'fortyish, slightly plump but attractive' (1984, p. 125)
- 'an attractive, 39 year old housewife' (1986, p. 111)

We find the adjective 'attractive' four times. He mentions favourably the women who take care of themselves in a traditional way: slender, slightly plump but attractive, nails colored, and hair tinted (twice mentioned). Two women are described in relationship to a man – 'wife of' and 'daughter of' – while none of the men is described in relationship to a woman.

None of the eight cases of males describes the man's outer appearance. Instead Gerkin defines them by emphasizing their jobs, definitely in a positive sense: 'a surgeon and a good one,' 'a hard-working man . . . worked for G.M.,' 'a business man,' 'a salesman for a large national corporation,' 'a highly successful corporation executive . . . a leader in community affairs,' 'a professional architect in a large metropolitan firm,' 'he came to seminary'.

This short survey gives the impression that Gerkin – although perhaps unaware – perceives women counselees in the context of the dominant sociocultural narrative of our society and culture. What he looks upon as positive in a woman and in a man concurs with what the sociocultural narrative says about their proper roles. By common consensus, a woman is 'proper' if she is dominant neither as wife to husband nor as mother to father.

Bons-Storm, 1996, pp. 66–8

In order for these women to receive proper pastoral care Bons-Storm argues that there must be a change of culture and a recognition of the pervasive misogyny that exists within the Christian Church. Pastors need to develop a 'transgender empathy' through which the gap between carer and client of different genders can be crossed. Bons-Storm argues that this takes time, likening it to 'a journey into the desert' (p. 143). 'Transgender empathy has to go through this strug-gle with images of the Divine, images of Woman/women, and ulti-mately with the deepest longings for truth and security. Only through this struggle is it possible for a pastor or counsellor to be open to the woman who comes seeking an attentive ear' (p. 143).

To develop such empathy requires that self-awareness is valued and sought. As a method, this way of doing theology from the heart takes us into the depths of self, and the ways in which we grow in knowledge of ourselves as we reflect and seek to understand ourselves 'before the face of God'. For each person engaged upon learning through life about God and about their own response to God, to use writing as a creative and reflexive activity can be a highly significant means to generate theological insight.

## Critical Evaluation

In this method of theological reflection, writing is a crucial element. Whether it be in journal form, or as correspondence by letter, or as spiritual autobiography, or in the form of a verbatim report, or as creative writing, turning-life-into-text offers the opportunity to reflect upon identity. Each of the forms can set that exploration of self within the context of a relationship with God.

One of the most obvious strengths of this method is its immediacy and availability to individuals in the business of life. Letters, a journal, e-mail correspondence, creative writing, can be done with ease in any time or place. The insights gained allow us to consider options before us, to redirect passions and to seek guidance from others. As the con-trol of who reads the material lies in the hands of the practitioner, the writing can be for the person alone, or for a public audience – to explain, to encourage, to stir a response. The method is not solely self-centred, for reflexivity requires that the writer is in dialogue with inter-nal interlocutors, with a supervisor when using a verbatim account, with a correspondent by letter or e-mail. The writing process can also enable the writer to see her or himself 'as another' (see Ricoeur, 1994) and as a creature before their creator.

It could be argued that a weakness of this method of theological reflection is that it does not necessarily lead to action and change in the world. The method strongly emphasizes the inner life and this could be at the expense of the practice of ministry or social action. In its favour, however, is the argument that reflexivity enables the recognition of social, institutional and political contexts in which the practitioner operates. Reflective writing can offer 'time out' to decide upon the best course of action, taking into account a whole range of considerations: value systems, the place of faith, a sense of vision and justice, a sense of what is possible in a given situation. Writing can aid an analysis and engagement with social and political realities.

As a method that relies upon writing and the production of text it also lends itself to entry within the world of publication. Just as Wesley, and Milner, and many others have written journals for a wider audience, so the ways in which life can be turned into text can also, with further revision and redrafting, produce texts that reach a wider readership and influence them. The way in which journal writing and creative writing have been particularly used by women indicate that these forms of writing, which ostensibly belong in the 'private sphere', offer those who are silenced within a dominant socio-cultural milieu a way of reaching a public readership.

## Questions

- How can reflection 'by heart' take into account both critically and constructively the embeddedness of practitioners in the webs of the social, institutional and political power?
- Does this method rely too heavily upon the *written* text? How might it be used by people who are challenged by a heavy reliance upon literary forms, for example, those with dyslexia? What other cultural 'texts' and media might be used to enable a living human document to be performed or produced?
- Throughout the chapter there have been suggestions as to how the presence of God may be discerned within this method of reflection. Do you think the method lends itself adequately to *theological* as opposed to *personal* reflection?

## Annotated Bibliography

Bolton, G. (2001), *Reflective Practice: Writing and Professional Development* London; California; New Delhi: Paul Chapman Publishing Ltd. This book offers an accessible and creative introduction to the practice of creative writing within professional contexts. The author draws on her experience of working with different individuals and groups and offers a useful exploration of the practice of journaling.

Hawkins, P. and Shohet, R. (2002), *Supervision in the Helping Professions: An Individual, Group and Organizational Approach*, Buckingham, UK; Philadelphia, USA: Open University Press. This book is a comprehensive introduction to the processes and practice of supervision written for secular professional contexts.

James, William [1901–2], 2002 *The Varieties of Religious Experience: Centenary Edition* with a Foreword by Micky James and new introductions by Eugene Taylor and Jeremy Carette, London: Routledge. A 'classic' of modern religious writing, which did much to establish the psychological study of religion as an academic and clinical discipline. James's account of 'religious experience' through the ages is methodologically flawed but remains a fascinating introduction to the concept and its significance for contemporary psychology of religion and pastoral care.

Ward, Frances (2005), *Lifelong Learning: Theological Education and Supervision* London: SCM Press. This book is written for any involved in theological and continuing ministerial education who are interested in how they can sustain habits of life-long learning. It draws on the literature on supervision and journaling to enable reflective practice for individuals, one-to-one supervision and groups.

# 2

# 'Speaking in Parables': Constructive Narrative Theology

## The Method in Outline

This method of theological reflection employs the creative potential people have to construct meaningful stories out of the varied circumstances of their lives. Such stories may have coherent form, understandable plots, establish the identity of the author and make clear the meaning of apparently puzzling events. And yet the meaning of a story always exceeds these functions, and so narratives also serve to emphasize the mysterious and indefinable aspects of human experience. Contemporary biblical scholarship reminds us that the stories Jesus told, and the actions he performed, were often shocking and difficult to interpret. There is a *parabolic* quality to his ministry that is always surprising and is often reflected in the stories that believers tell of their own encounters with God. The stories recounted in Scripture are important within this method of theological reflection but these do not determine the pattern of the believer's own narratives. It is rather that threads from these foundational traditions are woven with many other strands into new stories which are vivid and original. They testify through diversity and particularity to a God who is known through the stories we tell, as individuals or communities, about experiences that have become revelatory for us.

## Introduction

Our exploration of this method of theological reflection begins with a consideration of the parabolic nature of Jesus' ministry. We see how the stories that Jesus told about the kingdom of God were integrally related to his ministry of healing and liberation. Furthermore, we witness how the writer of the Gospel of Luke constructed his Gospel in such a way as to enable those who heard and read the story of Jesus to understand his life as a parable in itself.

It is an important fact that some of the earliest forms of Christian theology are life stories. If early Christians were well able to discern how the stories told about the events of Jesus' life contained the keys to understanding God's startling presence among them, the question quickly arose as to whether the stories believers began to tell about the very different circumstances of their own lives had a similar power. *The Passion of the Holy Martyrs Felicity and Perpetua* inspired deep popular devotion but quickly became a problem to the Church because of the radical reversal of social roles it celebrates. *The Story of Margery Kempe* is another extraordinary document that has similarly troubled the institution but for different reasons. It is the prosaic and antiheroic qualities of this work that cause the greatest controversy. Kempe, an uneducated housewife and certainly no pious virgin, insists that her life is like a book through which the work of God can be read.

Because John Bunyan's *Pilgrim's Progress* is widely regarded as a Christian classic it is difficult for contemporary readers to understand the daring step Bunyan took in using the devices of fiction and imagination to describe the life of faith. What is also frequently overlooked is that this is a story of adventure and uncertainty entailing much more than a long climb up a steep hill. It is the wager Christian makes with God concerning the fate of his soul that has given this work of narrative theology its enduring power.

These reflections from history allow us to glimpse the creativity with which Christians throughout the centuries have told stories to convey their passionate sense of God's presence in the events of life. Such work creates a threshold of meeting between the sacred and the mundane that enables the Christian story to leave the pages of history and be reinscribed amidst contemporary circumstances. This is a perennial task.

A new impetus to reflect upon storytelling emerged, however, in the second half of the twentieth century. What has come to be called the 'crisis in narrative' was the subject of much debate after 1945 in the wake of the destruction of World War Two and the horrors of the Holocaust and amidst a period of rapid scientific, technical and social change.

In this context a number of influential thinkers began to argue that social health required a renewal of narrative forms. For some theologians, this entailed a return to the Christian story, which is seen as reliable when other stories fail (see Chapter 3). For other philosophers, psychologists and religious thinkers the stories that emerge from the deep resources of a culture enable people to navigate change and have regenerating potential. These stories are *sacred*, whether or not they are conventionally religious, and they have a deep resilience that ensures their endurance through time. Both societies and individuals need such stories in order to construct their world creatively. In the second part of this chapter we see how constructive narrative theology is realized in the work of a number of key thinkers who are concerned not only with the renewal of Christian storytelling but also with the regeneration of society.

The pastoral importance of people telling their own stories is further emphasized by Herbert Anderson and Edward Foley who argue that the divine and human stories must be woven together in pastoral care and also in ritual practice if the Church is to forge an authentic witness in contemporary culture. The chapter concludes with Heather Walton's critical work upon storytelling in theological reflection. Walton argues that it is important to recover a sense of the disturbing parabolic nature of stories if we are to offer an adequate response to the tragic nature of experience.

This chapter begins with life stories and it will be evident that the process of telling a story that enables a person to discern God within the circumstances of their lives is a powerful means of personal formation and deeply affirms individual faith. By the close of the chapter it will also be evident that a church in which people are enabled to tell their stories will need to face the challenges of inclusivity and be open to change.

## Reflections from History

### The Parable of God

Now he was teaching in one of the synagogues on the sabbath. And just then there appeared a woman with a spirit that had crippled her for eighteen years. She was bent over and was quite unable to stand up straight. When Jesus saw her he called her over and said, 'Woman, you are set free from your ailment.' When he laid his hands on her, immediately she stood up straight and began praising God. But the leader of the synagogue, indignant because Jesus had cured on the Sabbath, kept saying to the crowd, 'There are six days on which work ought to be done; come on those days and be cured, and not on the sabbath day.' But the Lord answered him and said, 'You hypocrites!

Does not each of you on the sabbath untie his ox or donkey from the manger, and lead it away to give it water? And ought not this woman, a daughter of Abraham, whom Satan bound for eighteen long years, be set free from this bondage on the sabbath day?' When he said this, all his opponents were put to shame; and the entire crowd was rejoicing at all the wonderful things he was doing.

He said therefore, 'What is the kingdom of God like? And to what should I compare it? It is like a mustard seed that someone took and sowed in the garden; it grew and became a tree, and all the birds of the air made nests in its branches.'

And again he said, 'To what should I compare the kingdom of God? It is like yeast that a woman took and mixed in with three measures of flour until all of it was leavened.'

Jesus went through one town and village after another teaching as he made his way to Jerusalem.

Luke 13.10–22 (NRSV)

Within the space of these twelve verses we gain a remarkable insight into how the author of Luke's Gospel perceives the mission of Jesus. The early verses are concerned with a healing miracle: one of the many in the Gospel that point towards something very special taking place in the actions Jesus performed. There are a number of things of interest about this particular narrative. First, the healing takes place in the context of Jesus' teaching; there being a close association between what is said and what is done. Second, the woman being healed who has been 'bent double' or bowed down is referred to as a 'daughter of Abraham'. In other contexts such a term might be expected to affirm her piety or status, but the term here is applied to someone who has been brought low and regarded as less valuable than an animal. Third, the healing of this woman has wider significance than the miracle that is performed. It is part of the work of Jesus in overthrowing the rule of Satan and inaugurating the kingdom of God. Lastly, the action provokes a mixed response. There are those who welcome what is happening and others who fail to grasp the significance of the miracle. The author of the Gospel explores this ambivalence further by following the miracle with two short and vivid parables.

Familiarity may blind contemporary readers to the fact that these are both strange stories. In the first the mustard seed planted in the garden becomes a great tree and in the second leaven hidden in the dough leavens the whole mixture. But mustard seeds, although they may make sizeable shrubs, do not become great trees in which birds shelter. In rabbinic writing the birds of the air refer allegorically to the Gentiles and a tree providing shelter for wild birds was an image that was used in Jesus' day to refer to an empire in which many nations were incorporated. This parable assimilates these associations to present an improbable image in which a garden seed attains an unnatural stature. In the second parable a familiar scene also becomes strange. The image of leaven was commonly used within Jesus' culture to refer to a polluting or corrupting agent. It carried associations of impurity. Furthermore the amount of flour used by the woman is enough to make more than 50lb of bread, more than is possible for one person to prepare in one batch. So the kingdom of God is portrayed as spreading like a hidden contaminating force. It is also producing something much larger than common sense tells us is possible.

The stories told by Jesus are often odd, surprising and hard to interpret unequivocably. In recent years the question of why Jesus taught in parables has occupied many scholars. The romantic view that these are stories drawn from common life, for common people and are the natural form of expression for a man of the people has been contested. Eduard Schweizer points out that Jesus does not make a straightforward point and then use a story to illustrate it. Rather a story appears to be required in order to communicate something about the nature of the kingdom that cannot be conveyed 'without the language of parables or the performance of parabolic action' such as a miracle (1984, p. 23). Where in the everyday world is Satan overthrown as a woman stands up straight, or where does a mustard seed grow into a tree and where is a banquet for beggars being prepared by a disreputable baker? A story is needed to encourage those who have eyes to see and ears to hear to welcome the impossible thing that is happening among them.

The miracle and the parables thus belong together and are followed by another very significant statement. We are reminded that Jesus' words and actions take place on his journey towards Jerusalem. The whole episode of teaching/healing/storytelling itself forms part of a wider story: one that Luke continually reminds his readers is to culminate in the passion of God's prophet but also in his mysterious exaltation (Luke 13.32–35). What is happening in the miracle and in the parable is also happening in the events of Jesus' life. There is a mystery taking place. He will perform mighty acts but these will not be understood. He will be placed in the earth. He will be hidden but he will also rise again. In this sense Jesus himself can be seen as the parable of God.

## The Passion of Perpetua

We have seen how the Gospel of Luke presents Jesus to us as a teller of stories but also as someone whose life can be read as an extended parable through which God is made manifest. It is easy to concede that this can be allowed in the exceptional case of Christ, but more radical to think that throughout the history of the Church Christians have claimed that in the circumstances of their own lives a continuing *revelation* is taking place. The author of the preface to *The Passion of the Holy Martyrs Perpetua and Felicitas* is clear about the difficulties some might experience in crediting contemporary events with such significance but argues that this is to display a lack of faith and understanding:

> The deeds recounted about the faith in ancient times were a proof of God's favour and achieved the spiritual strengthening of men [sic] as well; and they were set forth in writing precisely that honour might be rendered to God and comfort to men through the written word. Should not then more recent examples be set down that contribute equally to both ends? For indeed these will one day become ancient and needful for the ages to come, even though in our day they enjoy less prestige because of the prior claims of antiquity.
>
> Perpetua in Kraemer, ed., 2004, pp. 357–68

The story that unfolds after this introduction is one of the most stirring to reach us from Christian history. It is all the more important because the main body of the text is narrated by a woman in her own words. The historian Judith Perkins reminds us that we possess hardly any written records of women's lives prior to the Middle Ages and that Perpetua's testimony is 'the clearest woman's voice . . . to speak from the ancient world' (Perkins 1995, p. 38).

Perpetua (d. 203) was an educated young woman aged about 22 whose family had long-standing connections with the imperial government. She had recently given birth to a son and was breastfeeding at the time of her arrest with other Christian catechumens, including the slave Felicitas who was herself pregnant. Perpetua's account of her arrest, imprisonment and trial is divided into three parts. Each of these contain a narrative of events and an account of their religious significance that confirms Perpetua in the status of prophet and martyr.

In the first part of her testimony Perpetua describes her arrest and her father's attempts to persuade her to deny her faith. She refuses in simple and irrevocable terms: '[Can] I call myself anything else than what I am, a Christian?' Her avowal provokes her father to angrily throw himself upon her as if 'he would tear my eyes out'. Shortly after this confrontation those arrested are taken to prison where Perpetua states, 'I was very much afraid because I had never felt such darkness.' Fellow Christians secure the removal of the prisoners to a better area within the jail where Perpetua is relieved to be able to suckle her child, 'now enfeebled by hunger'. In restored spirits Perpetua resumes her prophetic vocation, 'I was privileged to converse with the Lord whose kindness I had found to be so great', and requests a vision concerning the fate of the prisoners. Her request is granted and she sees herself mounting a ladder, guarded by a mighty dragon; as she ascends further, she encounters an aged shepherd, milking a sheep.

### Perpetua's Vision of Heaven

At the foot of the ladder lay a dragon of enormous size, and it would attack those who tried to climb the ladder . . .
'He will not harm me,' I said, 'in the name of Christ Jesus.'
Slowly, as though he was afraid of me, the dragon stuck out its head from underneath the ladder. I went up using its head as my first step, I trod on the head and went up.

Then I saw an immense garden, and in it a grey haired man sat in shepherd's garb; tall as he was, and milking sheep. And standing around him were many thousands of people clad in white garments. He raised his head and looked at me and said, 'I am glad you have come my child'.

He called me over to him, and gave me, as it were, a mouthful of the milk he was drawing; and I took it into my cupped hands and consumed it. And all who stood around said: 'Amen'. At the sound of this word I came to, with the taste of something sweet still in my mouth.

Kraemer, 2004, p. 360

In the second part of the narrative Perpetua recounts the details of her trial and condemnation to death in the arena. Once again her father implores her to recant, saying 'have pity on your babe', but she refuses. In retaliation her father takes charge of the infant but she is comforted as 'the child no longer desired the breast nor did my breast cause me uneasiness, lest I should be tormented by care from my babe and the pain of my breasts at once'. The vision Perpetua receives after this experience is of her little brother, who died from cancer as a child, thirsting dreadfully in the place of the dead. With great earnestness Perpetua prays for his healing and release and later sees him again drinking freely and playing 'joyously after the manner of a child'. Perpetua recognizes that she has secured his relief from the place of punishment.

In the final part of Perpetua's story the day upon which the Christians are to be thrown to wild beasts draws near. Her martyr's resolve is strengthened by a final vision in which she is summoned to the arena where she is confronted by a huge Egyptian. She is stripped down for the fight and becomes a man. A fierce battle ensues in which Perpetua once again stands upon the head of her foe. She is presented with her prize by another man of amazing height who calls her daughter and kisses her. She awakes from this vision confident in the victory that awaits her.

As a testimony to her Christian faith and hope Perpetua's story is powerfully compelling. However, when read as a carefully crafted work of theological reflection it becomes apparent why it has had such an impact upon the Christian imagination throughout the centuries. The work is constructed so as to unify Perpetua's experiences with their theological interpretations. God is present in every aspect of the story and is manifested as powerfully in Perpetua's simple testimony to her father as in the fantastic revelations. One of the most important factors unifying the whole piece is that Perpetua's passion is presented as an embodied testimony. The revelation occurs through her body. The young woman writes of her physical sensations as she endures fatigue, hunger, and painful yearnings for her child. She struggles in her body to mount the high ladder and conquer the Egyptian. The grace of God is experienced as much in the easing of her swollen breasts as it is through the strength she is given to conquer her monstrous enemies.

Many commentators have marked how the psychological and physical traumas of imprisonment are resolved in the visions. Her father's disapproval is countered by the images of a mighty Father who twice welcomes Perpetua as daughter. The forced weaning of her baby is contradicted by visions in which she is able to bring comfort to a thirsty child. While Perpetua appears to be at the mercy of violent powers she treads them underfoot. While she seems to be imprisoned in darkness she is already mounting above this world into a garden of delight.

Such a reversal of values lies at the heart of the Christian narrative and Perpetua's own story (and friendship with the slave Felicity) demonstrates her identification with this radical tradition. However, our understanding of her story is deepened when we become aware how images and symbols drawn from Roman Carthage are deeply interwoven in the tale. Practices of child sacrifice for the good of the polis continued in Carthage long after they died away elsewhere in the Roman Empire. Furthermore, from the time of Dido, female suicide, self-sacrifice, was marked and celebrated at crucial turning points in the city's history (Salisbury, 1997, p. 53). Perpetua's voluntary martyrdom, and the high significance accorded to martyrdom in the Carthaginian church, must be viewed in the light of this cultural inheritance.

So Perpetua's story is a testimony to a God encountered and revealed in a young woman's bodily passion. It displays her convictions concerning the divine significance behind events that faithless observers cannot grasp. It draws upon major themes within the Christian tradition that celebrate the victory of the powerless. The common cultural symbols of the day are employed to convey its message. The passion narrative is also deeply personal and original. The vision of the huge, white-haired shepherd who welcomes Perpetua cannot be traced back to Christian iconography of the day. Nor can Perpetua's descriptions of her longing for her baby or defiance of her father be filtered into the pious formulaic accounts that are often preserved as martyr's testimonies. These striking narrative features have been an embarrassment to ecclesiastical authorities. Augustine's sermons on the feast day of the martyr's display his discomfort with the narrative of this audacious woman and a fourth-century redactor edited Perpetua's account to make her and Felicity appear more suitable models of female piety. However, the narrative of this outspoken and unruly woman survived, and continued to inspire greater popular devotion than the stories of more illustrious and seemly Christian martyrs.

## The Story of Margery Kempe

The story of Margery Kempe (c. 1373–1439) is also a work of narrative theology, constructed in order to reflect the presence of God in the life of a woman whose waywardness was similarly troubling to the Church. It is a remarkable text, which literary scholars have described as the first autobiography written in English and historians have sifted for details of everyday life in medieval times. Christian scholars have generally been less enthusiastic about the book and many have suggested that Kempe, despite her many visions, is better described as a hysteric rather than a mystic.

There are a number of reasons for this negative response. The first is the earthiness, domesticity and vulgarity of the text. Kempe is no romantic figure whose life can be read as a religious allegory or pattern for Christian devotion. The divine invades Kempe's life in humble, commonplace and inconvenient ways. Elizabeth Armstrong argues that Kempe's first encounter with Christ, after she finds herself on the verge of madness after a difficult childbirth, sets the tone for the whole work:

> Kempe's idea about the divine and the human is implied in that the most memorable story of her childbed illness. Its emotional range from the poignant to the mundane, firmly set in the realm of her ordinary life, makes it an epitome of everything she was to write later. Christ comes to her in her ordinary woman's life . . . simply sits on her bed and utters one sentence . . . 'Daughter why have you forsaken me, and I forsook you never' . . . the immediate effect of the visit is domestic. Kempe becomes 'stabled in her wits' and immediately takes up the keys to her kingdom – the pantry – and so steps sane again into housewifery.
>
> Armstrong, 1992, p. 22

The traditional forms of piety recognized in women of her day entailed withdrawal from the world into the enclosure of a convent or anchorage. Kempe, however, is a wife and becomes the mother of 14 children! While her visionary encounters are as vivid as those of any other mystic, and include a divine marriage with the Godhead, her everyday life continues with its toils and temptations. Kempe frankly recalls her struggles with censorious neighbours and soiled linen. She makes it clear that others find her odd and embarrassing because of her obsession with God. She is frank about the sexual temptations that besiege her despite her intimacy with Christ. She confesses to an infatuation with a neighbour who declares that he would rather be 'chopped up as small meat for the pot' (Kempe, 2003, p. 57) than sleep with her.

In every area of her life Kempe is confronted by the contradictions between her experience and the models of female piety that assail her. She describes her struggle to believe that what was being revealed to her, a mere woman, would be of any value in the eyes of the authorities:

> It was twenty years and more from that time when this creature first had feelings and revelations before she began to undertake any writing. Afterwards, when it pleased our Lord, he commanded and ordered her that she should undertake the writing of her feelings

and revelations and the way of her life so that his goodness might be known to all the world . . .

When this book was first being written, the said creature was more at home in her chamber with the priest doing the writing and said fewer beads than she had done for years before in order to hasten the writing. And when she came to church to hear mass, intending to say her Matins and other such devotions as she had been accustomed to before, her heart was drawn away from them and very much set upon meditation. Since she was afraid of displeasing our Lord he said to her soul 'Do not be afraid daughter . . . the dedication with which you have striven to get written the grace that I have shown you please me much, as does he who is doing the writing too. For even if you were in church and both of you wept as bitterly as ever you have done, yet you would not please me more than you do with your writing. For daughter, by this book many people will be converted and believe in me.

Kempe, 2003, p. 103

Dhira Mahoney argues that although Kempe rejects the role of anchorite in order to wander abroad, offering uncomfortable reminders of God's presence, she is granted, or obtains the symbolic means of demonstrating, her status as a holy woman to others (Mahoney, 1992). One of the most significant of these is the ecclesial recognition of her 'celibate' marriage. She achieves this after many years of struggle with her own desires and despite her husband's considerable reluctance. She also takes to wearing white, which causes much consternation. 'Are you a virgin?' asks the archbishop of York. 'Do you intend to lead our wives astray?' ask others who are well aware of the challenge presented by a matron who proclaims sexual independence and refuses to stay at home carding and spinning as other women do.

Kempe's many pilgrimages are also signs of her calling. These were undertaken according to divine promptings and Kempe travelled when she felt compelled to do so even when her journeys were unsanctioned by her confessor. With her characteristic lack of sentimentality Kempe describes the physical discomfort of lice and fleas, the advances of lecherous men, the attempts of embarrassed fellow pilgrims to escape her presence and the generosity of others who sustained her travels with hospitality and blessings. Despite the many discomforts of medieval travel, the pilgrimages are clearly presented as simultaneously physical and spiritual journeys. Through them Kempe achieves deeper visionary communion with her beloved Christ and discerns his iconic presence in the various people she meets along the way. Her ability to discern Christ's form in the holy women, outcast lepers, handsome men and babes in arms she encounters is one of the most endearing features of her idiosyncratic spirituality.

Perhaps the most enduring witness to Kempe's significance is her story itself. In reflecting upon the construction of her narrative Kempe acknowledges that it is not an ordered chronological account that celebrates in conventional terms the recognizable features of a holy life. It is presented, however, as the authentic record of a woman whose life has been disordered by God. The book is intended to fulfil the same role that Kempe herself was called to perform: to serve as a mirror to others seeking glimpses of God in their own pilgrimages. It is thus a work of narrative theology that proudly affirms the link between the creature (as Kempe calls herself) and the creator; a bond imaginatively made manifest in the story of a particular and peculiar life.

## *John Bunyan and* The Pilgrim's Progress

For a lay person to compose and publish an account of their spiritual life was unusual and even dangerous in Kempe's time. However, in the turbulent decades following the English Civil War (1642–45) religious enthusiasm was encountered at every level of society and the mechanisms for regulating piety were in disarray. In this climate many narratives of religious experience began to find their way into print. Christopher Hill argues that there was a gradual democratization in the production of spiritual writings that had not been possible before:

> Anticipation of spiritual autobiographies can be found in diaries (spiritual balance sheets), prefaces to the collected writing of preachers or biographical appendices to funeral sermons. The revolutionary decades saw the publication of this new genre. Spiritual autobiographies of ordinary people could not have got into print before the breakdown of censorship and the establishment of effective religious toleration.
>
> Hill, 1988, p. 64

It was not only a period of social instability that provided greater possibilities for the sharing of literary testimonies. The theology that inspired the Puritans to revolution, and sustained the activities of dissenting groups after the restoration of the monarchy in 1660, emphasized that God predetermined those destined for salvation. The doctrine of predestination raised a difficult challenge for believers. If salvation could not be achieved by an act of faith or will how was it possible for a person to be confident that they were among the chosen? One answer seemed to lie in the painstaking examination of the experiences of the faithful. Roger Sharrock (1976) describes how in the late seventeenth century the word 'experience' came to mean a state of mind or feeling relating to the inner religious life. 'Experience meetings' were held in which believers shared together personal narratives of God's dealings with their lives. The belief that God's elective providence was at work in every area of a person's life made even commonplace occurrences a topic for intense theological reflection.

John Bunyan was born in 1628 in the village of Elstow just outside Bedford. He grew up in this period of religious fervour and in an area where support for the Parliamentary cause was strong. Although his family was not wealthy he was given elementary schooling and learned to read and write. As a young man he served for four years in the parliamentary army. He became increasingly convinced that his way of life was displeasing to God. Morbid fantasies overcame him as he took part in his usual pastimes.

In a state of deep insecurity Bunyan was also overcome by terror when reading the Bible. Many texts seemed to offer promises of hope and comfort but these were accompanied by others that spoke of disobedience, death and damnation. In this terrified condition he encountered members of the Bedford Baptist Congregation; four poor women sitting in their doorways in the sun, 'talking about the things of God . . . they talked about how God had visited their souls with his love in the Lord Jesus, and with what words and promises they had been refreshed' (Bunyan, 1907, p. 16). He began to cultivate the acquaintance of these people. Very gradually through the healing influence of the Bedford church and his own meditations upon Scripture he began to perceive himself to be among the elect and to testify to others through dramatic preaching.

Although persuaded in his faith Bunyan continued to experience many conflicts and temptations that led him to zealous attempts to demonstrate his Christian devotion. His decision to defy the authorities by holding a preaching meeting led to his arrest in 1660. The long years in prison afforded him the opportunity to reflect upon the dramatic journey which had brought him to that place. Out of these reflections he produced his two most famous works: *Grace Abounding to the Chief of Sinners* (1666) and *The Pilgrim's Progress* (1678).

*Grace Abounding* is a work of autobiography that offers some insights into Bunyan's life history but more into the conflicts of his spiritual life. The reader is caught up in the drama of negotiations with a God who in turn comforts and withdraws. This sense of drama is heightened by the vivid language with which Bunyan describes his plight: already drawing upon the vivid allegories of light and darkness, mountain and valley, tranquility and torment that are more fully expressed in *The Pilgrim's Progress*. To its last pages the dialectic of assurance and desperation continues: 'I will leap off the ladder even blindfold in eternity, sink or swim, come Heaven, come Hell; Lord Jesus if thou wilt catch me do; if not I will venture for thy Name' (1907, p. 100).

For a dissenting preacher to employ a writing style that reflects the influence of fairy tale, legend, 'popish' hagiography and 'chapbook' fiction was certainly controversial. Some scholars suggest that Bunyan was a storyteller before he was an evangelist and though he outwardly abhorred romance he could not shake off the love of sensational writings that he had acquired in his youth. Yet this judgement minimizes the singular achievement of *The Pilgrim's Progress*, which breaks new ground in making the narrative of the Christian life not only Bunyan's own story but accessible to all readers. More than this it draws upon the medieval image of life as a pilgrimage (a significant feature of Kempe's writing) and brings this into the modern era. As a work of theological reflection it affirms that God's story can be told in human terms employing all the devices of myth, metaphor, allegory, parable, fantasy, vision and imagination. No better defence of the work of the constructive narrative theologian can be made than that offered by Bunyan in *The Author's Apology for His Fable*:

### From *The Author's Apology for His Fable*

This book will make a Traveller of thee;
If by its Counsel thou wilt ruled be;
It will direct thee to the Holy-Land,
If thou wilt its directions understand:
Yea, it will make the slothful active be
The blind also delightful things to see.
Art thou for something rare, and profitable?
Wouldest thou see a Truth within a Fable? . . .
Wouldst thou be in a Dream, and yet not sleep?
Or wouldst thou in a moment laugh and weep?
Wouldst thou lose thyself, and catch no harm?
And find thyself again without a charm?
Wouldst thou read thyself and knowest not what,
And yet know whether thou art blest or not,
By reading the same Lines? O then come hither,
And lay my book, the Head, and Heart together.

Bunyan, 1907, p. 141

## The Method Realized

### Stephen Crites and the Narrative Quality of Experience

In 1971 an American philosopher (and keen musician), Stephen Crites, published a short essay that was to provoke a massive reaction within the theological world. We can view 'The Narrative Quality of Experience' ([1971] 1989) as emerging out of the experience of the 1960s. American social values had been deeply challenged by the civil rights movement, antiwar campaigns, the rise of feminism and the 'sexual revolution'. Within this context many believed that significant social change was occurring all around them and questions were being raised as to why change happens and how human beings maintain their sense of meaning and identity in revolutionary times.

This context provides the background to Crites's reflections upon the significance of narrative in cultural life. The essay is deeply evocative containing many resonant images drawn from Crites's love of music. It is also, at times, maddeningly imprecise. Crites admits that he has a 'grandiose thesis' concerning the way cultures assume certain forms and change through history but that he has no means of proving this other than by allusion and illustration (1989, p. 65). The lasting impact his article has made is probably due to the breadth of his vision and the musicality of his writing, which resonated deeply with the questions being asked by a generation of radical young theologians.

Crites's paper begins by affirming that human identity is always formed within a specific cultural context. Each society differs from its neighbours and is dynamically developing along its own particular trajectory. He goes on to argue that this cultural identity is established *through narrative*, which is the way in which human beings are both shaped by and give shape to their world. After ascribing this central place to narrative, Crites develops his thesis further by identifying three important forms of narrative that together structure human life. First he describes sacred narratives. These are the subterranean stories that lie 'deep in the consciousness of a people' (p. 69). Sacred narratives are anonymous and communal. They are not the product of individual imagination or creativity and they cannot be easily adapted. Because sacred narratives are foundational to culture they are seldom specifically told as stories in everyday life. Rather they can be traced in the way a culture's other stories are told.

People do not sit down on a cool afternoon and think themselves up a sacred story. They awaken to a sacred story, and their most significant mundane stories are told in the effort, never fully successful, to articulate it. For the sacred story does not transpire within a conscious world. It forms the very consciousness that projects a total world horizon and therefore informs the intentions by which actions are projected into that world. The style of these actions dances to its music. One may attempt to name a sacred story . . . But such naming misleads as much as it illuminates, since its meaning is contained and concealed in the unutterable cadences and revelations of the story itself. Yet every sacred story is a creation story: not merely that one may name creation of the world and self as its 'theme' but also that the story itself creates a world of consciousness and the self that is orientated to it.

Between sacred and mundane stories there is distinction without separation. From the sublime to the ridiculous, all a people's mundane stories are implicit in its sacred story, and every mundane story takes soundings in the sacred story. But some mundane stories sound out greater depths than others . . . in these, as well as in some works of literary art, and perhaps even in some merry little tales that seem quite content to play on the surface, the sacred stories resonate.

Crites, 1989, p. 71

The final narrative form Crites reflects upon is that of consciousness itself. Here Crites makes his most important claim, supported by his reading of Augustine of Hippo, that human consciousness takes narrative form: 'I want to further propose that the form of active consciousness, i.e., the form of experiencing, is in at least some rudimentary form narrative' (p. 82). Crites sees human experience as shaped by memories, which are themselves incipient stories; existing as 'episodes in an image-stream, cinematic'. Human beings never merely draw upon the past, however, they are also able to anticipate the future and again this faculty has a narrative character: 'we anticipate by framing little stories about how things may turn out' (p. 77). It is because human consciousness has a narrative propensity that a resolution can be made between memory and anticipation without eradicating the creative tension between them.

As well as forming cultural identity, narrative sustains, nourishes and protects it. Narrative, as a means of structuring experience, preserves us from both immediacy and abstraction – present in our times in the political threat of totalitarianism (in either fascistic or global-capitalist forms). In times of danger, or rapid cultural change, the permeability of narrative forms enables people to perceive new configurations between their experience and the sacred stories of their culture. These together may generate new symbols, 'causing a burst of light like a comet entering our atmosphere' (p. 81), which enable human beings to reorientate their cultural identity to meet the challenge of new times. As part of this process human beings continually discover new ways of addressing their sacred roots and thus retaining their connection to the divine. Literature and the arts have a crucial role to play in this process of spiritual and social renewal.

The power of Crites's essay lies in the link he proposes between personal biography, sacred traditions and contemporary cultural narratives. All of these mediate in distinct but not separate ways the sense of personal and corporate identity, and provide the resources necessary to negotiate social and political change. His work has been hugely influential in the development of constructive narrative theology in a number of ways (see Goldberg, 1982, pp. 12–16). First he emphasizes the distinctiveness of cultural narratives. Each people has its own particular 'language' and narrative voice. This insight was affirmed by early Black theologians who stressed the importance of turning to the cultural practices that constitute the everyday life of a people in order to tell their distinctive story of God. Second, the importance Crites accords to linking contemporary experience to sacred story resonated with feminist theologians who were becoming aware just how little of the distinctive experiences of women were reflected within the dominant theological tradition. Encouraging women to voice their own experiences came to be seen as important theological work. Third, Crites's work encouraged theologians from all marginalized contexts to look to their literary and artistic heritage as a sacred resource. The sacred story might not be directly told within these forms but its echo and its image could certainly be traced within them.

## Paul Ricoeur: Imagining New Worlds

Paul Ricoeur (1913–2005) was a French philosopher as well as an innovative religious thinker. However, he always preserved a distinction between these two activities, believing that religious conviction and philosophical critique should mutually inform each other but that neither mode of engagement should compromise the other. 'It seems to me that as far back as I go in the past, I have always walked upon two legs. It is not only for methodological reasons that I do not mix genres, it is because I insist on affirming a twofold reference that is absolutely primary for me' (1998, p. 139). Despite this avowal of the importance of preserving the integrity of philosophical thinking, Ricoeur's life-long interrogation of *the ways in which human beings create meaning* provides very important resources for theological reflection.

Ricoeur was brought up within a devout Protestant household and therefore had an early awareness of belonging to a minority community within French society that cherished its own distinctive view of the world. Orphaned when only two years old, his early career was disrupted by the Second World War, most of which he spent in prison camps in Germany. Upon returning to France he had to wrestle with the impact of Nazi occupation and collaboration upon French national identity. An awareness of the human devastation caused by the conflict, and particularly the tragedy of the Holocaust, caused Ricoeur to reflect throughout his life on whether it is possible fully to come to terms with the past and yet to envision a transformed future. With this background it is easy to understand Ricoeur's enduring fascination with the ways in which human beings create, sustain and transform the worlds of meaning they inhabit. We shall now therefore examine first his generative work on the significance of metaphor and then consider some of his later thinking on the narrative construction of identity.

In relation to metaphor, Ricoeur's reflections were provoked by what he regarded as a failure by linguists, critics and philosophers adequately to account for the processes at work in the construction of metaphors. Human language is rich in metaphoric utterances but these are frequently overlooked in the analysis of discourse where it is assumed that metaphors are acting as a straightforward way to enhance rhetorical performance. This, however, is to miss the surprising significance of the human capability to refer to one thing in terms of another. Metaphors bring together what were previously distinct terms into a new conjunction. They represent a disruption of thought and speech: 'metaphor shatters not only the previous structure of our language, but also the previous structures of what we call reality' (Ricoeur in Valdes, 1991, p. 85). The function of metaphor is thus not so much to adorn everyday language but rather to push it to its limits and beyond. And thus through metaphor we receive 'a new way of *being* in the world' (p. 85, our emphasis).

We can see through the momentous language Ricoeur uses here to describe the operation of metaphors that he clearly believes that something extremely important is happening when human beings make a leap of vision that allows them to perceive the world in new ways. From it 'a new vision of reality springs forth, which ordinary vision rejects because it is attached to the ordinary use of words. The eclipse of the objective, manipulable world thus makes way for the revelation of a new dimension of reality and truth' (p. 10).

> The more imagination deviates from that which is called reality in ordinary language, the more it approaches the heart of that reality which is no longer the world of manipulable objects, but the world into which we have been thrown by birth and within which we try to orient ourselves by projecting our innermost possibilities upon it, in order that we *dwell* there, in the strongest sense of that word. But this paradox is only sustainable if we happen to concede that we have to amend not only our ideas as to what the image is but also our prejudices as to what reality is. Under the shock of fiction reality becomes problematic. We attempt to elude this painful situation by putting beyond criticism a concept of reality according to which the 'real' is what our everyday interests project onto the horizon of the world. This prejudice is not displaced but reinforced by our scientific culture in that for science, reality is what science declares it to be.
>
> Ricoeur, in Valdes, 1991, p. 133

In an insightful essay on Ricoeur's understanding of literature, Rowan Williams argues that the literary text here is accorded a revelatory function. It is not concerned to verify a truth but rather to *embody*, or *manifest*, or to *testify* to an alternative vision. 'It displays a possible world, a reality in which my human reality can find itself, and in inviting me into its world the text breaks open and extends my possibilities' (Williams, 1986, p. 199). Williams reflects that in this context a dynamic understanding of revelation is operative that is not so much about the will being required to submit to prescribed truth as the imagination being called upon to open itself to new possibilities. This perpective sheds new light upon the way in which Jesus proclaimed the kingdom through parabolic fictions and miraculous actions. This can be interpreted, after Ricoeur, as bringing into tension two worlds and enabling those who identified with Jesus' words and actions to enter into a different relation with the everyday world. Its conventional power is challenged and a different way of life becomes appropriate.

Ricoeur's work on metaphor thus has important implications for theological thinking. It challenges Christians to think creatively about the metaphors they use to describe God: as devices that are not merely descriptive but directly shape the way in which Christians live out their faith in practice. In recent times many constructive theologians have argued that Christians need to employ new metaphors if they are to proclaim their faith in today's world (see Kaufman, 1993; and McFague, 1987). Ricoeur also helps us to see poetic writing, literature and other forms of imaginative construction as having sacred significance. Within parables, stories and fictions (whether canonical or otherwise) a power is at work that can become revelatory for us.

Ricoeur's thinking on the narrative propensity that human beings employ to shape their lives was developed in conversational relationship to the work of Crites, and there are many similarities between the views of the two men on this issue. However, perhaps prompted by his own experience, Ricoeur was more concerned about the disparate and discordant elements that constitute a human life. A life story, like a metaphor, must bring together seemingly irreconcilable elements into a unity that becomes both meaningful and illuminating. This process can be observed in fiction when an author uses a plot to generate a creative synthesis so that a story can be told. 'By means of the plot, goals, causes and chance are brought together within the temporal unity of a whole and complete action. It is the synthesis of the heterogeneous that brings narrative close to metaphor' (Ricoeur in Valdes, 1991, p. 18). The same process can be seen in the narrative work of constructing life stories.

> It seems that our life, enveloped in one single glance, appears to us as the field of a constructive activity, deriving from the narrative intelligence through which we attempt to recover . . . *the narrative identity which constitutes us.* I emphasise the expression 'narrative identity', because that which we call subjectivity is neither an incoherent succession of occurances nor an immutable substance incapable of becoming. It is exactly the kind of identity which the narrative composition alone, by means of its dynamism, can create.
>
> Ricoeur in Valdes, 1991, p. 437

Just as individual human beings undertake this task we can also imagine how through hearing and telling stories (particularly the stories of victims and survivors) human cultures can form narrative identities that enable them to move forward through time in healthy and creative ways without forgetting the past.

Ricoeur's work on narrative has taken rather longer to enter the mainstream of theological thinking than that of Crites but it is now increasingly stimulating theological interest. This may be because, in what are avowedly unconfessional philosophical reflections, an implicit model can be traced of God as the narrator of history who brings meaning out of chaos, who continually creates new worlds and in whose image humanity is formed. Furthermore, the concept of narrative identity offers an attractive view of the significance of human agency. It implies that it is possible to redeem unfortunate, or even tragic, circumstances through storytelling. Within practical theology we find that this notion has been enthusiastically received, and facilitating the telling of life stories is now often portrayed as *the* most significant pastoral task, as in the discussion of Riet Bons-Storm in Chapter 1.

Within this enthusiastic embrace of storytelling, however, there lies a disturbing tendency to assume that the redemptive power of narrative can always bring healing and release, that discordant elements can always be reconciled within a life story properly told. Clearly this is a dangerous assumption as some experiences, particularly of trauma and abuse, cannot be so easily synthesized into narrative form. This points to a problem within Ricoeur's work. There is a tension between his work on metaphor and his work on narrative. While the latter attempts to retain an integrity with the former, by emphasizing the heterogenous elements within life experience, it appears that the focus upon emplotment (leading to narrative coherence) may lead us to lose sight of the tension and instability that always characterize metaphoric speech *and* human experience.

## Anderson and Foley: Weaving Together the Human and Divine

Herbert Anderson and Edward Foley are two practical theologians from Chicago whose personal friendship and shared professional interests led them to collaborate in writing a book, *Mighty Stories, Dangerous Rituals* (1998) which explores the relationship between story telling and ritual.

Like the other writers whose work has been explored in this section, Anderson and Foley believe that narrative is a primal form of human expression: 'Human experience is structured in time and narrative' (1998, p. 4) and 'Stories are privileged and imaginative acts of self interpretation' (p. 5). Moreover, they assert, there is a fundamental relationship between narrative and ritual. They characterize this affinity with reference to the different dimensions of human life.

To stress the symbiotic relationship between story and ritual is not to suggest that they are identical . . . they are certainly distinct but this distinction does not suggest that they are separate. Rather, ritual and narrative are analogous to our own existence, which is mediated by body and mind, flesh and spirit, touch and imagination. In our patterned behaviour we explore and express our hopes and dreams. Rituals shape our stories, and our instinct to perceive life as a narrative urges us to rehearse that narrative through our bodies. There is no dualism or conflict here.

p. 27

There is thus a narrative quality to all ritualizing, and story-telling is given depth and profundity through its association with ritual practice. Both storytelling and ritual are also sites where the opportunity exists to bring together the divine and human story. The metaphor Anderson and Foley use to describe this process is 'weaving', an image also beloved of many feminist theologians (see Christ and Plaskow, 1989; Chopp, 1995). By taking an everyday image with associations of human craft and fabrication as the root metaphor for theological reflection, Anderson and Foley are suggesting that within the experiences of ordinary human life we can expect to encounter God. 'When we are willing to admit the possibility of God's presence in ordinary human events we will be more likely to fashion our human narratives – composed of many such events – in the light of that presence' (p. 40). Anderson and Foley believe that the ability to discern the connections between our own stories and the stories of God has redemptive qualities. It promotes personal growth and regeneration, it provides pastoral comfort at times of pain or transition. It allows healing and reconciliation to take place and, crucially, when it fails to happen, a crisis occurs for the Christian community. 'The future of faith communities depends on their capacity to foster an environment in which human and divine stories regularly interact' (p. 40). Ritual provides a dramatic affirmation of the significance of human life-experience, and are a means of navigating change in a healthy way that also generates social solidarity. It may also provide an opportunity to affirm that what is taking place is being taken up and inscribed within the life of God.

Sadly, this process is inhibited by the fact that the rituals of faith communities often fail to connect with the life stories of believers themselves, and have nothing at all to offer those from outside the community who wish to celebrate or mourn in the presence of God.

While many of the biblical narratives that can still be encountered in our rituals are vivid accounts of human experience, lack of awareness of the biblical story in its fullness means that these are frequently encountered as meaningless fragments that have little connection with the life issues of those who hear them. Even when preaching is effective, unless the ritual itself can be experienced as rooted in the life of the community, its performance will lack authenticity: 'The ceremony may be proper but the rituals have no soul' (p. x).

Given their analysis of the current difficulties experienced in connecting the human and divine in a 'coauthored' story it is not surprising that Anderson and Foley present the work of constructing new narratives and rituals as an urgent theological task. It is one that they believe will transform not only the worship of the Church but also pastoral care and prophetic witness. The initiative for generating constructive narrative theology may fall to the pastoral practitioner whom the community chooses to lead its worship and embody its care. However, while the pastor might be instrumental in encouraging a renewed emphasis upon storytelling and ritual this is a task that should be owned by the whole Church: 'The people who are part of the worshipping assembly are not the "object" of the stories of salvation but participants and even coauthors in the work of [constructing] a new narrative from human and divine stories' (p. 163). Those who share in this work, Anderson and Foley believe, are 'sacramental agents' who have learned to recognize that 'Jesus is not only present in baptisms, church weddings or the weekly celebration of the Lord's Supper but in the bathing rituals between mother and child, the sexual intimacy of marital partners, and in the ordinary meals that punctuate our existence' (p. 163).

Anderson and Foley's work is persuasive and engaging – particularly as it includes many powerful narratives that support the case that they are making. And yet there will be many questions raised as to whether this constructive theological work can really generate the renewal they wish to see. The authors themselves admit there are some problems that are not easily resolved. It is easy to talk about telling stories in the context of faith but there are stories of violence and abuse within the Christian community that are yet to emerge as coherent narratives. There is even the danger that in telling them their significance is undermined: 'It is still difficult to fashion stories that include the presence of abuse or violence in human life without camouflaging evil or promoting premature reconciliation' (p. 148). This leads us to acknowledge that not all the stories we tell are 'good'. This may be because they are not well told. It may also be that they are deeply problematic.

Here Anderson and Foley raise the distinction between worship and pastoral care. The carer may wish to encourage stories to be told and rituals enacted so that healing takes place but whether or not these stories or actions will affirm the glory of God is another question.

> We acknowledge that enabling people who have experienced miscarriage or divorce to ritualise these situations in all of its complexity and ambiguity is healthy. The challenge for the pastoral minister, however, is to shape such ritualization so that it is not only healthy at the level of the human story but also redounds to the health and vitality of the divine story.
>
> p. 147

The unease that Anderson and Foley express about bringing some human experiences into close conjunction with the divine story leads us to acknowledge a serious problem that faces constructive narrative theologians when they seek to weave together the sacred traditions and contemporary life narratives. In the next chapter we shall explore the work of theologians who consider that the story of God told through the Bible forms the pattern and shape for the human story. They consider that it is normative and defining while our human stories are always partial, contingent and provisional. From this perspective it is not a creative act to join together the threads of experience and revelation into a variety of creative patterns. There are too many aspects of human life that should be judged by the cutting edge of the biblical narrative rather than brought into conjunction with it. It is certainly the case that constructive narrative theologians continue to wrestle with the question 'what stories should be told in church?'

## *Heather Walton: Beyond Storytelling in Practical Theology*

In this chapter so far we have noted a number of problematic issues for constructive narrative theology. These concern the tension between metaphor and emplotment (or the parabolic and the mythic) and the powerful regulatory forces that are preventing certain experiences from becoming part of the Christian narrative tradition. The work of Heather Walton explores these issues further. She makes clear that storytelling is not always a benign and liberating activity and that the Christian desire to achieve narratives of wholeness and healing can be a violent process that not only denies the tragedy in human life but also prevents us from encountering God in the midst of extreme circumstances. Walton argues that it is necessary to move beyond a naive celebration of narrative as a redemptive force towards an appreciation of the power of *poesis* to embody trauma and enable a dark epiphany of the divine.

Although Walton is a practical theologian she draws much of her inspiration for work in this field from reflecting on the relationship between literature and theology and particularly feminist theology and women's writing (Walton, 2003a, 2005). She notes that there have been powerful traditions of interpretation within Western culture that have placed literature and theology in a complementary relationship. Theology is assumed to employ reason to make clear, coherent and authoritative statements concerning the nature and purposes of God. Literature, in contrast, is portrayed as stimulating the imagination and the senses; compelling us to draw closer to divine beauty and mystery. However, the language of complementarity has often disguised the fact that theology is regarded as the dominant partner. For example, in the influential critical writings of T. S. Eliot, literature is portrayed as playing an important role but one that is brought to perfection when it enjoys a harmonious relationship with theology. Indeed without the guiding hand of theology to restrain it literature can be seen as potentially dangerous. It has a tendency to usurp the place of theology and offer itself as a guide to ethics or a source of spiritual wisdom (Eliot, 1933). In the framework established by Eliot, literature has a role to play in drawing us towards God; but its place is standing alongside theology and not assuming its role or privileges.

The work of feminist theologians appears to contradict the position established by Eliot (which is still dominant today). Within feminist theology, literature has played a hugely important part in providing an alternative source of spiritual insight to the canonical texts of Scripture. Because women are frequently marginalized within established religious traditions, literature written by women has come to serve as alternative sacred text in which many feminists have seen reflected their own aspirations, values and religious intuitions. However, herein lies the problem. In making literature a handmaid to theology, albeit in this case feminist theology, feminist theologians have repeated the gesture of male theologians in seeking to harness the energies of literature to service their own theological or political agenda.

The problem Walton identifies in both these approaches is that when literature is called upon to serve the ends of theology we can lose sight of the fact that the creative arts have a vital role to play in challenging all forms of theology and forcing reconsideration of its most fundamental assumptions. For example, the theological response to the holocausts of the twentieth century was desperately inadequate and it has been left to the literature of testimony (as found in the work of Paul Celan, Elie Wiesel, Etty Hillesum and others) to raise radical theological questions and make clear that the Christian story of God cannot continue to be told without taking account of the massive disruption in its narrative coherence that this scale of human suffering represents.

One of the reasons why literature has been able to touch the depths of human pain in a way that theology could not is the special nature of literary writing. Literature has the metaphoric or parabolic qualities we have discussed previously in this chapter. Walton argues that it is not possible adequately to represent in ordinary language the depth of trauma victims of violence or abuse suffer. As Anderson and Foley recognized, to do so runs the risk of normalizing or containing extreme experiences. Walton draws upon the work of Hélène Cixous to suggest that when attempting to communicate out of the depths of pain it is necessary to put the metaphor in the place of suffering (Cixous in MacGillivray, 1994, p. xlix). In other words, it is necessary to transubstantiate experience through what Walton calls *poesis* in order to be faithful to the horrors that people suffer (Walton, 2002).

Walton draws two important conclusions from her analysis of the way literature is currently used in theological reflection. The first of these is that literature has a significant role to play beyond offering helpful insights into the human condition, or even articulating the experiences of those who have been marginalized by the dominant tradition. It should not only serve as a supplement to theology supplying what is lacking or decoratively illuminating theological texts. It must also be allowed to challenge theology, deconstructing its authoritative status and 'unmaking' theological narratives.

The second insight Walton communicates is that it is not only when we achieve a sense of narrative cohesion or identity that we encounter God. Walton argues that God is as much to be known through painful and chaotic experiences, when our world appears to fall apart, as through those moments when we can see a fit between our own lives and the narratives that make up the Christian story. Here Walton draws upon the work of Paul Roemer (1995) who suggests that the function of storytelling, from ancient folk tales and myths to contemporary cinema, has not only been to establish personal identity, social reality or even enable us to experiment with the construction of alternative worlds. In Roemer's opinion stories do not merely help us achieve a fragile mastery over circumstances, they also allow human beings, who seek to live in safety in their self-constructed worlds, to encounter what lies beyond them. Stories force us to acknowledge

the presence in life of something that we cannot control or comprehend: 'This other is the sacred, fate, nature, process, time, the past, the
generic and the unconscious, all those things that from outside govern
our lives' (1995, p. 56).

Walton's work on literature leads her to adopt a critical position in
relation to the current enthusiasm for storytelling within practical theology. She questions the dominant metaphors of weaving employed
by constructive narrative theologians to describe storytelling work.
She recalls the myth of Penelope who both wove and destroyed her
weaving and argues that an authentic response to the world as it is,
and to the sacred other, requires that theologians and pastors must be
prepared to fulfil both roles. There will be many times when helping
people to tell their stories will lead to healing and peace. However,
there will be other moments in which a pastoral response will entail
entering alongside another person into the death of meaning and loss
of coherence. This does not mean that the pastoral agent has nothing
to offer in this situation but that offering might be *poesis* rather than
emplotment. We may use rituals, symbols or music to allow pain to
be communicated rather than constructing stories that promise an
illusory reconciliation of tragic circumstance.

Furthermore, when stories are told in the context of faith communities we must be careful that these are not ones that have been
constructed to conceal the theological challenges inherent within
them. As Roemer has suggested, many of the best and most powerful
stories that draw us closest to the mystery of the sacred in the midst
of life are ambivalent, painful or strange. In self-reflexive works of
narrative theology Walton uses her own experiences of undergoing
medical interventions intended to help her conceive a child to describe
a liminal state of in/fertility in which she has come to a new awareness
of God. Of her stays in hospital she writes: 'Here I have learned faith.
I know that God is God of the fertile spring and the burning rock'
(Walton 2003, p. 202).

My partner and I get up late. We have to get a taxi and we fight all the
way to the hospital. I am checked in for 'implantation' in a ward for
women with women's troubles. The toilets are full of blood . . .

When my turn comes for implantation my fear makes the insertion
of the tube difficult. It hurts a lot. There is a long tube attached and
an invisible life is slipped inside me. The embryologist is very careful
to check that nothing has been left inside the tube . . .

They wheel me into a side room. My head is upturned so that my
head is lower than my feet. It is horrible. I fight with my partner

again. 'Just leave me alone.' He goes. I try to imagine what I would
ever say if some day, someone asked me 'Mummy how are babies
made?'

I am almost drifting off to sleep when a woman half bent double
and as white as death comes into my room. She has the right to be
here. 'I'm one of you', she says. 'I just came to tell you it works. I got
pregnant. I went four months before I lost my baby. They say that's a
good sign. I've got embryos frozen. Next time I'm sure it will work.'
She smiles and leans over and touches me. And it is all ghastly and
horrible. What right has she got to do this to me? I worked so hard
for this and she has spoiled it all. A conception can never happen
now. Not here. Not with all this trouble. Can you conceive when you
are visited by an angel like this one?

But wasn't everything spoiled long before this? I look at her. Why
not look at her? Silly to turn away. Perhaps I have to welcome her?
She is one of us. Maybe some sort of angel is a necessary part of the
process? You don't get to choose your visitation.

Walton, 2003b, p. 209

Finally, Walton's work has implications for the practice of preaching,
and especially the preacher's use of the Bible. Much of contemporary
homiletics is concerned with making biblical stories acceptable and
useful for contemporary living. However, the stories we encounter
in the Bible are themselves often difficult and disturbing. To fail to
recognize this may be to protect ourselves from their challenge. Walton
(1993) argues that the Church must construct new forms of narrative
preaching that not only use storytelling to engage the attention of the
congregation but also to surprise them with the mysterious, dangerous
and morally questionable nature of God's story. This is not a new
technique. When Jesus taught in parables he was doing something
shocking and disturbing that the Church has been trying to come to
terms with ever since.

## Evaluation

People enjoy telling their stories and often achieve insight, strength
and consolation through this process. When their stories are heard
and affirmed by others, then social as well as personal transformation
can take place. Sometimes traumatic historical events require whole
groups of people to construct new narratives to live by. All of these
processes possess corresponding theological significance. In terms of

the categories we have used in this book, storytelling is an extremely important part of Christian formation, corporate and individual, because it allows people to create links between their own lives and the traditions of faith. As Anderson and Foley point out, storytelling then becomes a means of upbuilding as well as challenging and changing the Church. Furthermore, constructive narrative theologians have helped us to recognize how important sacred stories are to the wider processes of social renewal. It is not surprising, therefore, that narrative has been seen by many contemporary theologians as possessing redemptive power.

However, while recognizing the tremendous importance of stories in constructing personal and corporate identity we have, in this chapter, urged some caution concerning the claims of constructive narrative theology. It is not surprising that, in an age where propositional truth claims and appeals to foundational thinking are treated with scepticism, conservative, orthodox, liberal and progressive theologians alike should turn to narrative as an alternative basis upon which to found theological thinking. It must be admitted that this has proved a very creative turn but extravagant claims are frequently made for narrative that are not subject to critical appraisal.

The influential work of Crites provides a good example of this tendency. He has freely admitted that his essay contains many broad assumptions that cannot be easily proved – although they appear to him to be self-evident (1989, p. 65). There is no real way of testing that experience is structured in the way he proposes and particular problems arise in the case of sacred narratives. These are accorded immense significance and are alluded to in highly metaphoric prose. However, what exactly these deep stories consist of remains elusive. They can be known only by the effect they have upon his other two categories of experience, but in themselves they are shadowy and mysterious. Despite this, theologians following Crites have often taken for granted that his work contains a 'true' description of the way narrative structures human experience, rather than offering a more heuristic account that allows him to speculate further on processes of religious and cultural change.

The role of narrative in creating change is a theme that appears frequently in the work of constructive narrative theologians. Some appear very hopeful that when we begin to listen to the stories that have been marginalized within the tradition then the symbols through which we have expressed faith in the past will also begin to change. And yet experience suggests that it is not so easy to rearrange religious symbols into ethically more acceptable and democratic forms as moral understandings develop, as conflicts deeply dividing the Church (for example on homosexuality and inclusive language) clearly indicate. Others would argue that when we begin to listen to the stories that people tell out of their contemporary experiences and bring these into conversation with the divine story then we will be able to create forms of Christian community that are much more appropriate for our own times than those we have inherited. Here an even deeper problem begins to emerge.

There are many Christians who believe that the divine and human stories are such that it is not possible to weave them together in the way constructive narrative theology suggests. They understand the divine economy and everyday human life to be in fundamental contradiction. There is no evidence that those who hold to this perspective are finding that their churches are empty or that their people lack engagement because their life experiences are unnarrated or unmarked by ritual. While it could be argued that these Christians are simply finding less visible ways of interpreting their own stories in the light of God's story, the caution they express concerning the fusing of human and divine horizons should make their more liberal critics pause for thought.

This is probably the point where it is most fruitful to acknowledge the ambivalence of constructive narrative theology. It does indeed offer great potential to affirm Christian identity and generate new understandings of God and new forms of Christian practice. However, there is a great danger in underestimating the irreconcilable aspects of existence by, for example, seeking to resolve pastoral problems through offering narrative closure or by too readily assuming that God can easily be plotted into human narrative scripts. Jesus taught in parables, uncomfortable and unstable stories with equivocal meanings. They emphasized both the closeness *and* the strangeness of God.

## Questions

- Are there some stories that should not be told in church?
- Is it possible to weave together the divine and human stories?
- How would you differentiate between a parable and a story?

## Annotated Bibliography

Ostriker, Alicia (1994), *The Nakedness of the Fathers*, New Jersey: Rutgers University Press. This moving and funny work by a Jewish feminist weaves together her own life story with the foundational narratives of Judaism. It is a subversive but also deeply faithful text: as the stories are loved so must they also be wrestled with.

Chopp, Rebecca (1991), *The Power to Speak: Feminism, Language, God*, New York: Crossroad. This book celebrates the changes that can take place in Christian communities when those whose voices have previously been excluded begin to tell their stories and recover a sense of narrative agency. It is based upon the author's personal research into contemporary practices in theological education.

Anderson, H. and Foley, E. (1998), *Mighty Stories, Dangerous Rituals*, San Francsico: Jossey Bass. This book is valuable not only for the lucid case it makes for the pastoral significance of linking together human and divine stories but also for the many illustrations it offers of how this occurs in practice.

Valdes, Mario (ed.) (1991) *A Ricoeur Reader*, Toronto: Toronto University Press. This is not an easy read but it does contain extracts from some of Ricoeur's most important works. It also has a brilliant, if lengthy, introduction by Valdes.

# 3

# 'Telling God's Story':
# Canonical Narrative Theology

## The Method in Outline

This method of theological thinking regards the Christian faith as God's self-narrated story told through the life and death of Jesus Christ. The Gospel narratives of Jesus' words and actions are taken as the key to interpreting not only the rest of Scripture but also the unfolding events of human history. As the incarnation, passion and resurrection constitute the central reality of existence, the challenge facing Christians is to pattern their own life in conformity with this great drama. The theological task is to discern how contemporary experience can be interpreted through the story that the Church tells about Jesus and to identify forms of practice that are coherent with this narrative. This method does not establish abstract rules or principles to guide the reflective process. Rather it invites the Christian to develop a *habitus*, or way of life, through which the story of Jesus continues to be told in the life of the story-shaped community of the Church. The appeal of this method of theological reflection is particularly evident in the contexts where Christians have felt the need to affirm their distinctiveness in challenging or threatening environments. In situations of social fragmentation and cultural relativism it provides a basis for the reconstruction of *Christian identity*. However, it has been criticized for failing to offer a means of engaging with contemporary culture or other religious traditions. Questions have also been asked about who decides how the story of Jesus is told today.

## Introduction

In this chapter we shall consider how throughout the centuries Christians have not only told the story of Jesus but also attempted to pattern their own lives according to this narrative. The first worshipping communities met to celebrate the Lord's Supper and thus they set the passion of Christ at the centre of their communal life. The weekly celebration of the Eucharist soon developed into rituals marking other events in Jesus' life. The annual cycle of the Christian year was quickly established and provided a means whereby believers could share symbolically in the journey from Bethlehem to Jerusalem.

Participating in worship is one way in which believers enter into the story of Jesus. However, throughout the centuries many have felt the call to model their lives on Christ in very direct ways. St Francis is one of the most loved of all the Christian saints and this is largely because of the dramatic ways in which he sought to follow the example of Christ and present it to others. It was partly through the influence of Franciscan scholars and preachers that popular devotion to the person of Christ, and a desire to imitate his life, became a key part of medieval spirituality. The impact of Francis upon Ignatius Loyola has been widely recognized but the founder of the Jesuit order did not seek to persuade others to undertake the literal emulation of Jesus that Francis had aspired to. Rather, he sought to develop ways in which, through contemplating the life of Christ, believers could discover their own vocations in whatever way of life they found themselves.

Within the Anabaptist movement the medieval practice of the 'imitation of Christ' found a new form. The Anabaptists discerned within Scripture a clear imperative to adopt a form of life that was in radical contradiction to the practices of both state governments and religious authorities. The Anabaptists' witness was based upon a 'Christocentric' approach to reading the Scriptures. This became the key feature of canonical narrative theology as it emerged as an influential method of theological reflection in the twentieth century.

The Swiss theologian Karl Barth is widely regarded as generating the approach to the Christian narrative that has now become a powerful force within contemporary theology. Barth's own engagement with Scripture was prompted by his disappointment that liberal theology and socialist politics seemed to offer no resources for preventing the appalling disaster of the First World War. In his disillusionment he turned to the Bible and found within its pages a narrative that contradicted the political and theological scripts in which he had previously placed his faith. Barth's rediscovery of 'the strange world of the Bible', and his insistence that the accounts it contains of Jesus are the key to interpreting not only the Bible but the whole of human history, were a major source of inspiration for the Yale theologian, Hans Frei.

Frei and his colleague George Lindbeck argued that the scriptural narratives of Jesus contained the key to renewing the Church. They claimed that the effect of Enlightenment scholarship had been to obscure the fact that Scripture is not a fragmented, historical text but a coherent, 'realistic' story with the meaning of the whole made plain by the passion of Christ. Without the sense that they have a particular story, which creates for them a distinct identity, Christians lose a sense of their special role and mission. In our increasingly plural culture it is now appropriate for Christians to rediscover the resources their narrative provides and shape a Church that can effectively witness to this story in a 'post-liberal age'. This theme is taken up in the work of Stanley Hauerwas, a Methodist ethicist from Texas who has been much influenced by the Yale theologians and also by contemporary Anabaptist thought. For Hauerwas, the heart of Christian ethics lies in the story of Jesus as it is performed within the Church. Christians do not approach ethics on the basis of pre-established views of right or wrong. They must always ask whether this view or action is compatible with the story the Church tells about Jesus.

The work of the British Catholic theologian Gerard Loughlin helps us to reflect upon some of the questions that we have identified as important for each of the methods of theological reflection considered in this book. Loughlin's work presents canonical narrative theology, developed by Barth, Frei and others, as coherent with the earliest traditions of Christian worship. He calls upon his readers to consider Christians as being 'baptized' into a story and 'eating' the words of Scripture. In other words each believer is initiated into the faith and continually nourished by the resources of the narrative tradition. The Church achieves its coherence when worship and practice are centred upon the story of Jesus. Furthermore, Loughlin asserts, in our nihilistic and 'death loving' culture the Church has a duty to present and embody an alternative narrative that has the power to nourish and sustain human life by showing the significance our human story achieves when it becomes part of the unfolding story of God.

## Reflections From History

### Sharing the Lord's Supper

> For I received from the Lord what I also handed on to you, that the Lord Jesus on the night when he was betrayed took a loaf of bread, and when he had given thanks, he broke it and said, 'This is my body that is for you. Do this in remembrance of me.' In the same way he took the cup also, after supper saying, 'This cup is the new covenant in my blood.

Do this, as often as you drink it, in remembrance of me.' For as often as you eat this bread and drink the cup, you proclaim the Lord's death until he comes.

Whoever, therefore, eats the bread or drinks the cup of the Lord in an unworthy manner will be answerable for the body and blood of the Lord. Examine yourselves, and only then eat of the bread and drink of the cup. For all who eat and drink without discerning the body, eat and drink judgment against themselves.

1 Corinthians 11.23–29 (NRSV)

These words concerning the institution of the Lord's Supper are found in what is recognized as one of the earliest documents of the Christian Church. Paul's epistles predate the Gospels, and scholars believe the first letter to the Corinthians was written early in Paul's missionary career. Thus these simple verses represent a precious liturgical inheritance that links the Eucharistic practice of contemporary believers with those of the first Christian converts. However, the words have a greater significance than simply validating the celebration of an ancient ritual: Paul is doing more than just setting out the appropriate way in which the Lord's Supper should be shared. He is also setting the passion of Christ at the heart of the Christian community.

Remembering the passion of Christ is what the Christian community does when it comes together for its central act of worship – but Paul's words convey more than this. When the grammatical structure and context of the words are examined it becomes clear that Paul intends the words 'this is my body that is for you' to refer to more than the broken bread. The way Paul has constructed this phrase allows his readers to infer that it is the community which shares this holy food that is the body of Christ. As Raymond Pickett states, 'Paul . . . pushes this tradition to a new conceptualisation so that [the words] can also refer to the body which is the Church. The dual metaphor suggests a connection between the understanding of the death of Jesus and the idea of the community that expresses it' (Pickett, 1997, p. 120).

The idea that the community which here remembers Christ's passion has become his body, sharing his suffering and resurrection, is one that Paul develops further in 2 Corinthians 4.10 where he makes the audacious claim that believers carry in their bodies, 'the dying of Jesus so that the life of Christ might be made manifest in our bodies'. At this very early stage of Christian devotion we are confronted with the profound vision of a people formed by a Eucharistic practice through which they come to participate in Christ's passion. It is in this sense that sharing the Lord's Supper becomes a proclamation and a testimony. It is not that those witnessing the liturgy would necessarily understand its meaning (although they might) it is rather that through sharing in all that this act entails a corporate body is formed, which is Christ's continuing presence in the world. This is the reason for the grave warning Paul issues against those who eat and drink unworthily. The charge against this group – rebuked earlier in the chapter (1 Corinthians 11.17–22) – is not that it has failed to follow the correct ritual procedures, but that it has divided a holy community that is charged with nothing less than assuming the form of Christ in the world.

The weekly celebration of the Lord's Supper was from earliest times understood by Christians as the way in which they staged a 'little Easter' and were thus drawn into the great drama of Christ's passion. From this liturgical action developed the celebration of Easter and then Holy Week and Pentecost. By the end of the third century the diverse practices of widespread Christian communities were consolidated into the liturgical year we observe today. Thus it was that the Church instituted the means through which believers could pattern their own lives around the sacred events of the life of Christ. The story of Jesus was developed into a narrative framework through which they not only recalled the work of Christ, but also shared in this through enacting it in the life of the Church.

From earliest times, therefore, Christians have found the means of 'indwelling' the story of the life of Christ. It could be argued that the momentum to establish a distinctive Christian identity, in the deeply syncretistic cultures of the Roman world, was sustained by the power of this story to generate new forms of worship and costly, sacrificial action. The generative power of this story can be witnessed in many epochs of Christian history as is illustrated in the following three examples.

## St Francis of Assisi and the Poor Christ

Francis (c. 1181–1226) was born in Assisi, a rich and fertile part of Umbria where art and learning had flourished for centuries. But changing feudal relations and a developing mercantile economy had brought conflict to the region. There was intense (and often bloody) rivalry between competing neighbouring territories. Many peasants had been alienated from the land to endure extreme poverty in urban areas. This situation of social unrest was also one of intellectual ferment. Flourishing trade had facilitated the exchange of new ideas and social discontent proliferated dissident opinions. Millenarian religious movements flourished. These were frequently lay-led, and adherents proclaimed God's impending judgment upon prosperous citizens and corrupt ecclesiastical authorities alike. Lacking evangelical vigour, but rich in land and property, the Church was deeply implicated in secular disputes. In this context its moral authority was severely challenged. In the region of Assisi many chapels lay in ruins and there was widespread cynicism concerning the motives of the clergy.

In this situation the radical identification Francis made with the Christ of the Gospels resonated powerfully with the social questions of the day. In contrast to many of his contemporaries Francis saw the stories of Jesus as offering a literal pattern for Christian living that it was possible to emulate in personal devotion and communal life. The saint brought memory of the Gospels into living focus and although his legendary deeds (relinquishing property, caring for lepers, living in poverty) were simply formed directly from narrative tradition they represented an authentic confrontation with the most significant social and theological questions of his day.

It was the genius of Francis that he was able to synthesize a devotion to the crucified Christ with a deep identification with the suffering poor living on the margins of Assisi. He discovered in the Gospels' stories the 'poor Christ' whose life of poverty was an integral part of his redemptive passion. Francis sought to create in his own life, and through the formation of communities of friars, contemplative sisters and lay people, living examples who could embody the way of Jesus in poverty as a charisma for the whole Church.

### From the Major Life of St Francis by Bonaventure

#### The Foundation of the Order

He was at mass one day on the feast of one of the apostles and the passage of the Gospels where our Lord sends out his disciples to preach and teach according to the Gospel was read. When Francis heard that they were not to provide gold or silver or copper to fill their purses, that they were not to have a wallet for the journey or a second coat, no shoes or staff, he was overjoyed. He grasped the meaning immediately in his love for apostolic poverty and committed it to memory. 'This is what I want' he exclaimed. 'This is what I long for with all my heart . . .'

As the force of his teaching and the sincerity of his life became known others were moved by his example to live a life of penance. They renounced everything they had and came to share his life and dress. First among them was Bernard, a worthy man who was called by God . . . Francis was filled with the encouragement of the Holy Spirit when he realised he was being joined by his first follower and he said, 'We shall have to ask God's advice about this'. In the morning they went to the church of St Nicholas where they spent some time in prayer. Then Francis opened the Gospel book three times in honour of the blessed Trinity asking God to approve Bernard's plan with a three-fold testimony. The book opened the first time at the words, 'If you have a mind to be perfect, go home and sell all that belongs to you and give it to the poor' (Matthew 19.21). The second time they found the phrase, 'take nothing with you to use on your journey' (Luke 9:3) and the third time the word of our Lord caught their eyes, 'If any man has a mind to come my way, let him renounce self and take up his cross and follow me' (Matthew 16.24). 'This is our life and rule', said Francis, 'and everyone who comes to join our company must be prepared to do this'.

Bonaventure, 1991, pp. 646–8

From a contemporary perspective Francis' asceticism can appear extreme and even perverse. It is thus important to recall the significance of his determinedly literal application of the gospel's admonitions concerning the dangers of wealth and re-affirmation of the need for self-denial in discipleship. In a climate that favoured complex, allegorical interpretations of Scripture Francis advocated a *realistic*, or perhaps more accurately *simple*, approach to the narratives that resulted in a rediscovery of the significance of Jesus' words and deeds. This should not be misidentified as fundamentalism. There was no question of a rigid adherence to the written text. Indeed the evidence suggests that Francis never owned a Bible: in twelfth-century Umbria, such a valuable item would have cost more than a horse. One of the most appealing early Franciscan legends describes how the friars gave away their only copy of the Scriptures to a poor widow for 'the gift of it will be more pleasing to God than our reading from it' (Bonaventure, 1979, p. 436). It is rather that Francis sought to re-embody the impulse of the gospel through his own words and actions – as if caught up in and absorbed in the power of the drama. A vivid symbol of this imaginative identification was the delight Francis experienced through staging the tableau of the nativity – a practice inaugurated by him in the small town of Greccio.

I wish to do something that will recall the little child who was born in Bethlehem and how he lay in the manger, how with an ox and an ass standing by he lay upon the hay . . . The manger was prepared, the hay had been brought, the ox and the ass were led in. There simplicity was honoured, poverty was exalted, humility was commended and Greccio became, as it were, a new Bethlehem . . . The people came and were filled with joy over the new mystery.

Bonaventure, 1991, p. 70

There can be no doubting the creativity with which Francis participated in telling God's story. The mysterious accounts of the saint receiving the stigmata give material expression to the conviction that Francis himself functioned as an icon of Christ; a living symbol of his passion. An early biographer expressed his belief that looking on Francis he had seen Christ himself.

Indeed it seemed to this brother and all that great multitude that Christ and the blessed Francis were one and the same person. This does not seem to understanding people to be in any way a rash judgement, for he who cleaves to God is made one spirit with him and God will work all things in all.

Celano, 1991, p. 358

While it is difficult not to be moved by the vivid legends of Francis they do raise many questions. Francis struggled throughout his life to be faithful to the gospel of the poor Christ and to the authorities and traditions of the Church. This caused him much personal suffering affecting both his health and spirits. Many today still experience a conflict between the path of radical discipleship and belonging to the institution of the Church. Some would see this as an irresolvable problem that raises the further question as to whether a vocation to embody Christ can be assumed by communities of people as well as exceptional individuals. Francis himself was deeply troubled by the difficulty of maintaining fidelity to the gospel vision within the community he founded. Bitter disputes over this matter erupted during the lifetime of the saint, and while Francis was loved and honoured as the source of spiritual authority it was found necessary to delegate the temporal affairs of the order to others. Conflicts between vision and pragmatism were not resolved by this arrangement and the issue of fidelity to their founder's vision was to divide the order of friars shortly after Francis' death.

## St Ignatius and the Spiritual Exercises

It is fitting to discuss the contribution of Ignatius (1491–1556) along-side the work of Francis because of the significant influence of Fran-ciscan spirituality upon the founder of the Society of Jesus. One of the achievements of the Franciscan movement was a renewed emphasis upon the significance of the earthly life of Jesus for the believer. This was an inheritance that Ignatius was eager to claim but whereas Francis adopted a way of life that he believed was directly patterned on that of Jesus, Ignatius took the narratives as the pattern for a spiritual journey that could be undertaken by the discerning Christian in whatever way of life they were called to pursue.

Ignatius was born some three hundred years after Francis and into a very different context. The Catholic hegemony over most of Europe began to shatter during his lifetime and the works of the Protestant reformers as well as the humanistic writings of Erasmus were the subject of fiery debates in the university cities in which this intellectual disciple chose to make his home. Fear of heresy, and the evident politi-cal consequences of dissident religious thinking, fuelled a high degree of anxiety concerning all forms of religious enthusiasm. Ignatius himself was to fall under the scrutiny of the Inquisition on more than one occasion and was imprisoned while his work was investigated for a short period in 1524. Nevertheless, it would be a mistake to view the work of Ignatius as a reaction against the emergence of Protestantism rather than as an attempt to provide secure grounds for a renewed sense of Christian vocation within the Roman Catholic Church, a passion that would fuel the first Jesuits to undertake some of the most audacious missionary activity in the history of the Church.

The legends of Francis were among the materials Ignatius studied while recovering from severe injuries during 1521. The narrative of Francis' deep commitment to the way of Christ challenged his heroic predisposition and they contributed to his decision to abandon his former lifestyle and take a similar path in life. Further Franciscan contributions to Ignatius's developing vision came through his attachment to Ludolph of Saxony's *Vita Jesu Christi*. This work appears to have been the most significant source drawn upon by Ignatius in the construction of the *Spiritual Exercises*. Ludolph's book is based largely upon an early Franciscan text, *Meditationes Vitae Christi*. The Jesuit historian John O'Malley writes:

> Ludolph was himself so dependent on the *Meditationes Vitae Christi* that it is sometimes difficult to distinguish this text from his

own. The *Meditations,* once attributed to St Bonaventure and surely influenced by him, were composed by an Italian Franciscan in the late thirteenth or early fourteenth century and were the principal vehicle by means of which Franciscan piety first entered the Jesuit tradition.

O'Malley, 1993, p. 46

It was as a direct result of Ignatius's own spiritual awakening to the challenges of a life lived in conformity to the will of God and patterned on the stories of Jesus that the *Spiritual Exercises* came into being. Ignatius sought to systematize his own experience into a form that could be used by others in order to 'seek and find the divine will with regard to the disposition of one's life for the salvation of the soul (Ignatius in Ivens, 1998, p. 1).

---

### Second Week, Second Contemplation: Nativity

[111] The first prelude is the *history*; here how our Lady, nearly nine months' pregnant (as we might devoutly think of her) and seated on a donkey, with Joseph and a servant girl, taking with them an ox, set out from Nazareth for Bethlehem to pay the tribute which Caesar had imposed on all those lands;

[112] The second prelude is the *composition* made by seeing the place. Here will be to see with the eyes of the imagination the road from Nazareth to Bethlehem, considering the length and breadth of it. Whether it is a flat road or goes through valleys or over hills; and similarly to observe the place or grotto of the nativity, to see how big or small it is, how high, and what is in it.

[113] The third prelude will be the same, and in the same form, as in the proceeding contemplation.

[114] The first point is to see the persons, namely Our Lady, and Joseph, and the servant girl, and after his birth, the child Jesus. Making myself into a poor and unworthy little servant, I watch them, and *contemplate them*, and as if I were present, serve them in their needs with all possible respect and reverence; then I will reflect within myself to draw some profit.

[115] The second point. To watch and notice and consider what they are saying, and reflecting within myself, to draw some profit.

[116] The third point. To watch and consider *what they are doing,*

for example, their journeys and their labours, so that Christ comes to be born in extreme poverty and, after much toil, hunger, thirst, heat and cold, insults and affronts, he dies on the cross – and all of this for me. Then I will reflect and draw some spiritual profit.

Scholars agree that the earliest forms of *The Exercises* were taking shape as early as 1523 and Ignatius significantly developed their use during his stay in Paris between 1528 and 1533. The early dynamism of the Jesuit Order owed much to the impact of this ordered method of reflection, chiefly intended to aid the Christian to discover in what form of life they might best serve the purposes of God.

*The Exercises* are divided into four 'weeks', which constitute four essential stages to be passed through in the process of discerning God's will for the searching soul. The first week is spent in the painful examination of conscience and the confession of sin. The following three weeks take the Christian on a journey with Christ through the events of the incarnation, passion and resurrection. During these latter weeks, Gospel passages recounting events in Jesus' life deliver the basic structure for meditation and prayer evoking a sense of love and obligation in the believer and a desire to elect a course of life in conformity with his. The person making *The Exercises* is invited into active imaginative encounter with the narratives they contemplate. As an aid to this exercise Ignatius employed the 'prayer of the senses', a deeply engaging process using all the faculties in active participation with the narrative event. Although written almost 500 years ago these instructions for contemplation still retain their freshness and are surprisingly resonant with contemporary emphases on the need to draw upon the whole range of embodied experience in the practice of theological reflection.

Although Ignatian-inspired retreats have been practised for centuries they have enjoyed something of a revival in recent times. Retreats in everyday life are now widely offered and the basic principles of Ignatian contemplation have been popularized through such accessible texts as Gerald Hughes' influential book *God of Surprises* (1985). In books such as these the practice of contemplation is not presented as a task undertaken during the fixed duration of the retreat but as a custom to be observed in all circumstances, a process of life, a *habitus*.

*The Prayer of the Senses*

[122] The first point is to see the persons with the imaginative sense of sight, meditating and contemplating their circumstances in detail and to draw some profit from the sight.

[123] The second point. To hear with the sense of hearing *what they say or might say*, and to reflect in oneself and draw some profit from this;

[124] The third point. To smell and taste *with the senses of smell and taste* the infinite *gentleness and sweetness of the divinity*, and of the soul and of its virtues, and of everything else. According to who the person contemplated might be; and to reflect within oneself and draw profit from this.

Ivens, 1998, pp. 96–8

## The Anabaptists: A 'Cross-bearing Community'

We have shown how Ignatius drew upon the legacy of Francis to develop a means through which Christians could imaginatively inhabit the stories of Jesus in order to discover God's will and purpose for their own lives. While the *Spiritual Exercises* are undoubtedly a creative resource of immense importance to the Church, it would be wrong to suggest that meditating upon the life of Christ was something unusual in the late Middle Ages. This was a popular practice, and Ignatius was drawing upon the traditions of medieval piety in a highly effective way in order to nurture spiritual renewal among those eager to live their lives according to the will of God.

Many of Ignatius's contemporaries were also returning to the Gospel narratives seeking to find within them the way of authentic Christian discipleship. For some of these the scriptural witness pointed beyond a transformation of personal life to a reformation of the Church. Amongst these the Anabaptists, part of a movement known as the 'radical Reformation', regarded the stories of Jesus as more than inspiring or exemplary. For these believers being a Christian meant living as Christ lived. As the Anabaptist martyr, Jan Wouterss, wrote from prison concerning 'the little flock who follow Christ':

They do evil to no one; they pray for their enemies; they do not resist their enemies; their words are yea that is yea and nay that is nay

. . . they are also these who bear the cross of Christ, for He says: 'If anyone would come after me let him take up his cross and follow me' . . . join these cross-bearers that you may come to Christ, who bore the cross for us; for we must follow His footsteps and be like our Lord.

Snyder, 2004, p. 157

The origins of the Anabaptist movement are diverse. Albrecht Ritschl argued that Anabaptism had its roots in Franciscan lay movements. Other scholars point to the influence of pre-Reformation dissenting or heretical groups (such as the Waldensians or Cathars). There is now widespread agreement that the work of the reformers themselves inspired the Anabaptists to mount their audacious challenge to civil and ecclesiastical authority. But among the many streams that fed into the movement one of the most significant was the sixteenth-century passion for reading the Bible. This was facilitated by the development of the printing press and the publication of new versions of the Scriptures, including Erasmus's Greek New Testament (see Chapter 7).

In Zurich, Ulrich Zwingli, leader of the Reformation in that city, encouraged his enthusiastic young followers to give serious attention to Bible study. However, he found that some of those he had supported in this discipline wished to take the Reformation process further and deeper than he deemed either wise or necessary. Disputes began to surface concerning the way the Eucharist was celebrated within the city. A group, among whose emerging leaders were Conrad Grebel and Felix Manz, came to believe that Zwingli was failing to return to the pure simplicity of the Lord's Supper because he did not wish to alienate the civil powers. He was thus placing worldly authority before the authority of Christ's example. The group discussed this issue further and came to believe that there were other matters upon which Zwingli was compromising and that the New Testament contained a very different vision of the Church to the one that was being established in Zurich.

One of the discrepancies they noted lay in the practice of baptism. They found no warrant for infant baptism in the Bible and came to see this as an important ecclesiological issue. On 21 January 1521, at the home of Manz, Grebel agreed to baptize a fellow dissident George Blaurock, who in turn baptized the other members of the group. This is frequently taken as the founding moment of the Anabaptist movement; however, it is important to realize that what was at stake for those involved was not, primarily, a dispute concerning the sacraments alone but rather a fundamental principle concerning the nature of the Church. As Balhasar Hubmaier, a gifted Anabaptist leader, was to proclaim a few years later, baptism itself does not cleanse the soul, nor is it necessary for salvation. However, where 'baptism in water does not exist there is no Church, no brother, no sister, no fraternal discipline, exclusion or restoration . . . For there must be some out-ward form of testimony by which brothers and sisters can know one another, though faith be in the heart alone' (Hubmaier in Estep, 1996, p. 89).

Believers' baptism secures the Church as the company of commit-ted believers who seek to live according to the example of Christ. For the early Anabaptists this commitment often meant a martyr's death (usually by drowning or burning) as members of the movement were violently persecuted within both Catholic and Protestant territories. This persecution led the movement to disperse and reform in various parts of Europe and prevented the development of ordered theological confessions or established leadership. And yet, despite the heterogene-ity of early Anabaptist communities, a distinctive way of reading the Bible began to emerge among them.

As a movement whose intellectual leaders were, quite literally, short-lived, an emphasis upon the clarity of the biblical text itself and its accessibility to ordinary believers was vital. The majority of Anabaptists were poor and often illiterate, although many learned to read after conversion. Yet they came to trust the Bible's power to speak directly to them without the necessity of theological scholar-ship. Their persecutors were frequently exasperated by the claims of the uneducated peasants to understand the meaning of the Scriptures, as this extract from an interrogation clearly shows:

> Jacob: Therefore Christ thanked his heavenly Father, that He had revealed and made it known to babes, and hid it from the wise of this world, as it is written, Matthew 11.25.
> Fr Cornelius: Exactly; God has revealed it to the weavers at the loom, to the cobblers on their bench, and to the bellows-menders, lantern-tinkers, scissors-grinders, broom makers, thatchers and all sorts of riff-raff, and poor filthy beggars. And to us ecclesiastics who have studied from our youth, night and day, he has concealed it . . . If the devil and his mother have not had a hand in this I do not understand you people.
>
> Snyder, 2004, p. 119

Not only was the Bible viewed as self-interpreting; the Anabaptists also regarded certain parts of the Bible as obviously more significant than the rest. As a text it was not 'flat' and certain features commanded more attention than others. The New Testament had clear priority over the Old Testament and the Gospels more authority than the Epistles. The teachings of Christ were particularly important because these were the words upon which the Church was to be founded. Stuart Murray argues that: 'The Sermon on the Mount seems to have acted as a further canon within an already Christocentric canon' (2000, p. 79).

This emphasis upon the teachings of Jesus distinguished Anabaptists from other Reformation Christians. Luther, for example, preferred the words and doctrines of the Epistles concerning the salvation wrought through Christ to the stories of Jesus' life and work recounted in the Gospels. Murray argues that the Reformers had a Christological approach to reading the Bible whereas the Anabaptists were Christocentric, 'in the sense of focusing on Jesus himself instead of a doctrine describing the effects of his redeeming work' (p. 84). This Christocentrism issued in a hermeneutics of obedience that the Reformers argued came dangerously close to belief in salvation through works. The Anabaptists not only refused infant baptism, they also renounced the possession of riches, oath-swearing, sword-carrying and the authority of civil bodies concerning matters of faith. Martyrdom was accepted as a likely consequence of joining this cross-bearing community.

> But my children, remember what I write and wherever you hear that there is a plain, rejected little flock that is cast out by the world; join them; and wherever you hear of the cross of Christ depart not away. But flee the shadow of this world, go to God; fear Him alone; keep His commandments; remember all His words . . .
>
> Therefore my children, love your neighbour heartily; and this with a liberal heart. Let the light of the Gospel shine in you. Deal your bread to the hungry, clothe the naked and do not suffer anything to remain with you double, since there are enough that lack (Isaiah 58.7). And whatsoever the Lord grants you possess do that with thankfulness, not only for yourselves but also for your neighbour. In short, my children, let your life be conformed to the gospel of Christ.
>
> The testament of Maeyken Van Deventer for her children,
> in van Braght, 1938

What distinguishes this determination to follow in Christ's footsteps from the 'works righteousness' the Reformers condemned, is the lively spiritual awareness of the early Anabaptists that they were not merely following the example of Christ but sharing in his very body upon earth. As we have seen, the primary concern of those disputing the way that the sacraments were celebrated was the formation of a Church that could truly embody the way of Christ to the fullest possible extent. As Arnold Snyder argues:

> The Anabaptists had come to a stunning conclusion that may well have sounded blasphemous to their contemporaries. They were convinced that when the living Spirit of God in believers worked to bring them together by the outward signs and symbols of their unity (as ordained by Christ), the result would be the establishment of the very body of Christ in the world, visibly working through its members.
>
> 2004, p. 109

This sacramental sensibility is beautifully expressed in the words of an early Anabaptist hymn that was sung at the Lord's Supper:

> All members of His body
> Pursue His work here always
> According to His will, unto death
> They are one bread with Christ here.
>
> Hymn in Estep, 2000, p. 100

## The Method Realized

### Karl Barth and the Strange New World of the Bible

We have taken note of various examples of attempts to indwell God's story. From these it becomes apparent the affirmation of a sense of identity rooted in the foundational stories of the faith is a particularly resilient and generative form of theological thinking – particularly in times of difficulty or uncertainty. Theological systems that are established upon cultural norms which are so engrained as to become invisible are difficult to contest on their own terms. When the systems begin to strain or disintegrate due to the pressures of cultural change then narrative theologies can be a potent means of reforming faith. Possibly the most powerful illustration of this dynamic can be observed in the response made by Karl Barth (1886–1968) to the collapse of the legitimacy of liberal Protestantism at the outbreak of the First World War. Barth's work has been decisive in the development of the forms of canonical narrative theology that emerged in the latter half of the twentieth century.

As a young man Barth received his theological training in the great liberal traditions of German Protestantism. He was an enthusiastic student of Adolf Von Harnack who strenuously affirmed the compatibility of Christianity with the aspirations of modern civilization. Barth records, 'At the end of my student days I was second to none among my contemporaries in credulous approval of the "modern" theology of the time' (Busch, 1976). A first pastorate in the depressed industrial township of Safenwil (1914–21) confronted Barth with a harsher knowledge of life than his progressive theologies could easily accommodate. He became involved with trade union disputes and active in Christian socialist movements (his first son was named Karl Marcus). However, as Europe drifted into war Barth was dismayed to see both his theological mentors and his socialist comrades offering their enthusiastic support for a conflict that Barth strongly felt was contrary to the will of God and against the interest of working people. His biographer, Edward Busch, explores Barth's emotional turmoil. He quotes Barth's personal reflections expressed in letters to friends and colleagues:

> Barth did not know what to make of 'the teaching of all my theological masters in Germany. To me they seemed to have been hopelessly compromised by what I regarded as their failure in the face of the ideology of war.' Their ethical failure indicated that 'their exegetical and dogmatic presuppositions could not be in order' . . .
>
> For Barth, the outbreak of the world war was 'a double madness involving not only his theological teachers but also European socialism.' . . . Surely it was not long since 'in the Cathedral in Basle the socialists of all lands had solemnly assured each other and the world that they would be able to offer effective resistance to the outbreak of any new war'. And what happened instead? 'The apostasy of the party'.
>
> Busch, 1976, pp. 81–2

The linkage Barth makes here between ethical impotence and exegetical/doctrinal failure is crucial. In the years leading up to the Great War he had begun to doubt whether the theological tools he had acquired through study were adequate even for the challenges of a preaching ministry in a country parish. In face of the catastrophe of the trenches they appeared morally unsustainable. For a number of years he had been searching for a firmer ground on which to base his faith and his quest returned him with urgency to reading the Bible. He found a freshness and strangeness in the world of the scriptural texts. 'It was often as if I caught a breath from afar, from Asia Minor or Corinth, something primaeval, from the ancient East, indefinably sunny, wild, original, that is somehow hidden behind these sentences' (Barth in Busch 1976). Barth was engaging with what he was to term 'the strange new world' of the Bible. David Ford, who has written extensively on Barth as a narrative theologian, states:

> When Barth was in Safenwil searching for a new foundation for his theology he found it in the 'strange new world of the Bible'. . . Barth's comprehensive alternative world of meaning is an overarching story which is not the traditional one from creation to parousia but is the life-time of Jesus Christ of whom he was to say, 'His history as such is our history. It is our true history (incomparably more direct and intimate than anything we think we know as history).'
>
> Ford, 1981, p. 165

What Ford is at pains to suggest is that Barth had discovered within the biblical stories of the life and death of Jesus a narrative that breaks in upon the natural continuum of history and is the basis upon which the events of history are to be judged and interpreted. The whole of the Christian teaching rests upon the 'unbelievable' story of Jesus. 'Dogmatics is therefore "much less a system than the narrative of an event". The event effects a takeover of our world of meaning' (p. 24).

> Once more we stand before this 'other' new strange world which begins in the Bible. In it the chief consideration is not the doings of man [sic] but the doings of God – not the various ways we may take if we are men of good will but the power out of which good will must first be created – not the unfolding and fruition of love as we may understand it, but the existence and outpouring of eternal love, of love as God understands it – not industry, honesty and helpfulness as we may practice them in our old ordinary world, but the establishment and growth of a new world . . . This is the new world within the Bible. We are offered the magnificent, hopeful life of a grain of seed, a new beginning out of which all things shall be made new. One cannot learn or imitate this life of the divine seed in the new world. One can only let it live, grow and ripen within him.
>
> Barth, 1928

The strength of this position is twofold. The revelatory power of the gospel can be used to construct a basis from which to resist the current events of human history: Barth's later opposition to fascism is based upon his allegiance to an altogether different narrative to the one offered to German Christians by National Socialism. At the same time, these powerful narratives offer ordinary Christians the gracious invitation to participate in God's story through engaging in the festivals, worship and preaching of the Church. This participation is an act of extreme simplicity; an appropriation of the events of Christmas, Palm Sunday, Good Friday as things that might take place 'any day in Basel or its environs like any other important happening. History? Doctrine? Myth? No – but things actually taking place, so that we can see and hear and lay up in our hearts' (Barth in Ford, 1981, p. 16).

Reading Barth as a narrative theologian has done much to rekindle interest in his work in an age that finds traditional forms of dogmatic theology alien and conceptually unattractive. However, this interpretative strategy does not ameliorate the problems that liberal critics have always argued are inherent in his work. Is a theology of *Krisis*, which finds grounds for hope in what lies entirely beyond human culture, really an adequate Christian response to the complex realities of the twenty-first century? Might not the strange world we encounter all around us be equally as revelatory as the 'strange world' of the Bible?

Another issue is equally pressing. To nominate Barth as a narrative theologian provokes us to enquire further into the narrative strategy he employs in interpreting the biblical tradition. Barth does not deny the significance of biblical scholarship but he clearly differs from those of his teachers (such as Harnack) who sought to identify, through the use of historical critical methods, an irreducible historical kernel in gospel traditions upon which to base an appealingly simple and rational retelling of the Christian story. Similarly he eschews a subjectivist approach that finds the meaning of the stories in the ahistorical, emotional and spiritual satisfaction they provide. Such an approach would leave far too much to the response of the reader and militate against the notion of a radical challenge emanating from the revelation carried within Scripture itself. An alternative to these former strategies is to read the Scriptures on their own terms in the same way that one reads literature in a realist genre. Realist fiction creates a convincing world of meaning that the reader is invited to accept in order to enter the story. They must put aside their own presuppositions and become part of the world the literature presents to them. An approach to the text as 'realistic literature' (see Kelsey, 1979) has enabled later narrative theologians to claim a Barthian warrant for moving beyond some of the pressing problems involved in using the Bible in theological reflection.

## Hans Frei, George Lindbeck and the Rediscovery of Biblical Narrative

This understanding of Barth's reading strategy outlined above was favoured by one of the most famous canonical narrative theologians, Hans Frei. Frei drew upon Barth's insistence that the narratives of Jesus must be taken as the key to understanding Christian doctrine and displayed a particular devotion to the passion narratives as a key to understanding the rest of Scripture. The concern of his most famous text, *The Eclipse of Biblical Narrative* (Frei, 1974) is that the Western churches appear to have lost their appreciation of, and confidence in, the 'realistic' stories recounted in the Gospels. Since the rise of historical criticism in the eighteenth century, scholarly interest has atomized the texts and paid attention to technical problems and textual disputes rather than the narrative coherence they display. Prior to this time, Frei believes, it was widely assumed that the Gospels described real events, had a temporal sequence and could easily be combined into a 'common narrative referring to a single history and its patterns' (1974). For Frei, the loss of confidence in the coherence of biblical narrative represents a great danger for the Church because it entails a weakening of the claim of this narrative upon Christian practice.

In his early writing Frei is particularly indebted to the work of the literary critic Erich Auerbach and his influential text *Mimesis: The Representation of Reality in Western Literature* (1953). In this, Auerbach argues that the Bible differs from other ancient texts in that it does not entertain or instruct the reader but rather draws them into its own world. 'The Bible's claim to truth is not only far more urgent than Homer's, it is tyrannical – it excludes all other claims. The world of Scripture stories is not satisfied with claims to be a historically true reality – it insists that it is the only real world' (pp. 14–15).

As well as arguing that the texts of Scripture make direct claim upon the reader, Auerbach implies that the style in which they are written is at odds with classical narrative form. We are presented with a world that is 'entirely real, average, identifiable' (p. 42). The 'realism' of the text is as crucial for Frei's hermeneutical strategy as for Barth's. For Scripture to perform the role of structuring the life of the Christian Church it must be directly communicable, comprehensible and *gripping*. His later work, *Theology and Narrative* (Frei, 1993) consolidates this position with insights taken from the work of George Lindbeck.

Lindbeck, a colleague of Frei at Yale, shares the narrative assumptions of Barth and Frei that 'To become a Christian involves learning the story of Israel and Jesus well enough to interpret oneself and one's world in its terms' (Lindbeck, 1984, p. 34). Although these narratives are the primary materials of the religious tradition, the way the story is interpreted within the Church depends upon the rules the Christian community generates to inform its reading. Lindbeck argues that the doctrinal formulations of Christianity are the 'grammar' that regulate which understandings of the story can be regarded as authoritative for members of the community. Christian doctrine is thus not the purest and highest form of Christian truth but rather a guide to telling the story in conformity with shared communal understandings.

What is the literary genre of the Bible as a whole in its canonical unity? What holds together the diverse materials it contains: poetic, prophetic, legal, liturgical, sapiential, mythical, legendary and historical? These are all embraced, it would seem, in an overarching story that has the specific features of a realistic narrative as exemplified in diverse ways, for example by certain kinds of parables, novels and historical accounts. It is as if the Bible were a 'vast, loosely-structured, non-fictional novel' (to use a phrase David Kelsey applies to Karl Barth's view of Scripture).

Further, it is possible to specify the prime function of the canonical narrative (which is also the function of many of its most important component stories from the Pentateuch to the Gospels). It is 'to render a character . . . offer an identity description of an agent', namely God. It does this not by telling what God is in and of himself, but by accounts of the interaction of his deeds and purposes with those of creatures in their ever-changing circumstances. These accounts reach their climax in what the Gospels say of the risen, ascended and ever-present Jesus Christ whose identity as the divine agent is unsubstitutionably enacted in the stories of Jesus of Nazareth.

Lindbeck, 2002, pp. 180–81

Lindbeck's ideas enabled Frei to see the Christian Church as a cultural community grounded upon a sacred story and generating its own language rules governing the way in which that story is told and acted upon: 'I'm suggesting that the Church is like that – a culture . . . There is a sacred text – a typical element in a religious system – and there are informal rules and conventions governing how the sign system works' (Frei, in Placher, 1993, p. 17)

To summarize this position, the story of Jesus as interpreted (real-istically) according to doctrinal practice, generates the identity (or culture) of the Church. It is on the basis of internal self-understanding that any relation is made to external events and other communities of meaning. This process is *intratextual*. In Frei and Lindbeck's work, 'intratextuality' refers to a process that is defined by what is internal to the life of the interpretative community rather than what lies beyond it. A return to the sources of Christian particularity is regarded by both men as crucial in a situation in which Christian belief no longer functions as a unifying cultural framework. Lindbeck predicts a decline in the number of Christians until, as a small social minority, they are driven to return to the catacombs in order to 'cultivate their native tongue' (1984, p. 133). Frei envisages the Church faced with the challenge to rise from the ashes of its contemporary dissolution with renewed confidence in its vocation:

> [T]he most fateful issue for Christian self-description is that of regaining its autonomous vocation as a religion after its defeat in its secondary vocation of providing ideological coherence, founda-tion and stability to Western culture . . . One never knows what this community might then contribute once again to that culture or its residues including its political life, its quest for justice and freedom and even its literature.
>
> Frei, 1993, p. 149

As might be expected, liberal theologians have found much to criti-cize in the intratextual approach to theological reflection articulated by Frei and Lindbeck, which places the canonical narrative in opposi-tion to the contemporary cultural challenge. In a significant critique of canonical narrative theology, David Tracy concedes that Frei and Lindbeck have contributed to the development of a broad consensus that the 'plain sense' of the passion narrative united to the common confession generates a working basis for a 'fuller theological crite-ria of what might be deemed appropriate Christian theology' (Tracy, 1990, p. 51). However, he also argues that there are many problems inherent in their project. In particular, the assumption that the Bible is best read realistically marginalizes alternative readings that 'however unrealistic in form maintain hermeneutical fidelity' to the passion nar-ratives. Tracy is concerned that prophetic and mystical readings of the text may be devalued by scriptural realism. This is a particularly acute problem because these readings are often favoured by Christians out-side the Western tradition. Might it not be the case, asks Tracy, that the reading practice which is *supposedly* generated 'intratextually' through fidelity to the texts and the grammar of tradition is *actually* generated by the social milieu in which the texts are read. It thus may 'accord too well with a culturally Anglo-Saxon reading of Christianity: clear, reasonable, moral, firm and realistic' (Tracy, 1990, p. 48).

## Stanley Hauerwas and the Ethics of the Story-formed Community

The post-Barthian work of Frei and Lindbeck offers a creative method for engaging in theological reflection within a canonical tradition. However, the attention of both thinkers is mainly focused upon Christian self-understanding in a cultural context that is alien to the traditions of the faith. Less attention is given to exploring how this model generates distinctive forms of Christian action. It is in the parallel writings of another American scholar, Stanley Hauerwas, that the ethical implications of canonical narrative theology are more fully explored and the focus shifts from theology to Christian practice.

In his early writings Hauerwas is mainly concerned to reinstate the bond between the narratives of Jesus and Christian living. In contrast to those liberal theologians, typified by Ernst Troeltsch (1865–1923), who had argued that the concerns of Jesus must be taken as purely religious and therefore unable to generate a social ethic, Hauerwas claimed that the narratives of Jesus do not inspire a social ethic, they *are* a social ethic. 'By recovering the narrative dimension of Christology we will be able to see that Jesus did not have a social ethic but that his story is a social ethic' (Hauerwas, 1978, pp. 303–24). This social ethic is made real as it is manifested in the life of the Church.

Christian ethics would be unintelligible if it did not presume the existence and recognizability of communities and corresponding institutions capable of carrying the story of God. The most general name we give that community is church, but there are other names for it in the history of Christianity. It is 'the way', the body of Christ, people of God, and a plethora of images that denote the social reality of being Christian and what it means to be a distinctive people formed by the narrative of God . . .

The Church is not the kingdom but the foretaste of that kingdom. In the Church the narrative of God is lived in a way that makes the kingdom visible. The Church must be the clear manifestation of a people who have learned to be at peace with themselves, one another, the stranger, and of course, most of all, God. There can be no sanctification of individuals without a sanctified people.

Hauerwas, 2001, p. 372

In these understandings of the nature of Christian ethics Hauerwas is deeply indebted to the radical thinking of the Anabaptist theologian John Howard Yoder. Yoder refused the distinction between what Jesus taught and who he was, and argued that within the biblical narratives of the historical Jesus were to be discerned the nature of God, the reality of the kingdom and the mission of the Church. Yoder understood Jesus as presenting a powerful challenge to the powers of his age and Hauerwas followed Yoder in discerning in Jesus a warrant for Christian pacifism and a rejection of the values of contemporary capitalism.

However, the location for the Christian opposition to the current world order does not lie in participation in secular movements for social justice but through being a member of the Church; 'the kind of community his story should form' (Hauerwas, 2001, p. 304). Just as Jesus himself *is* a social ethic, the 'cruciform' church should manifest his challenge through its shared life. Christians must 'rediscover that their most important social task is nothing less than to be a community capable of hearing the story of God that we find in the scripture and living in a manner that is faithful to their story' (Hauerwas, 1981, p. 1).

Hauerwas's understanding of the function of the Church dominates his later writings. Through a deep engagement (and personal friendship) with the philosopher Alasdair MacIntyre he came to understand the Church as a community formed by a narrative tradition that develops distinctive characteristics among those who live according to its story (for example, non-violence, perseverance, hope, hospitality to strangers). Hauerwas is well known for his pacificism and his rejection of capitilist values. The Church thus becomes a 'school for virtue' understood as authentic practice, 'a virtue is what causes something to perform its function well (1981, p. 111). It is MacIntyre's thesis in his most famous work *After Virtue* (1981), that the contemporary context might be compared to a new Dark Age in which the authoritative traditions undergirding communal life have collapsed. In this situation a new barbarism ensues in which communal traditions that embody narratives of good living are replaced by fragmentary pluralism and rapacious self-interest. The remedy for this situation is the formation of small communities in which traditions are not only preserved but secretly cultivated – tradition is not static but evolves through the process of intercommunal dialogue – in the hope that these precious narrative resources might provide the seed-corn necessary to regenerate the society.

The apocalyptic tenor of *After Virtue* resounds in much of Hauerwas's later writing. Whereas 'the world' in his early texts is 'other' than the Church it remains a dialogue partner and possible source of inspiration (1981, p. 91). In his later writing it takes on a darker and more threatening character. 'When Christians say "world" we are saying more than "universe" or "society" or "culture". We are saying something more like "Pentagon", that place where the principalities and powers are organised against God for the most noblest of reasons' (Hauerwas and Willimon, 1989, p. 78).

Given this understanding the necessity of maintaining order and discipline within the Church becomes a pressing concern. In his more popular texts, such as *Resident Aliens* (1989, co-authored with William Willimon), Hauerwas compares Christians to resident aliens who must submit themselves to a rigorous alternative regime of life in order to mark out their distinction from the corrupt social order that they reluctantly inhabit. This idea was intended to gain the sympathy of many concerned to respond with integrity to the challenges of the Gospel narratives. However, Hauerwas presses this issue beyond what many would find acceptable. The hyper-authoritarian life at the Parrs Island Marine boot camp is used by Hauerwas and Willimon as an image of the life of the dedicated Christian believer. 'Recruits' are separated from 'civilian society' and subjected to rituals of humiliation, which function to obliterate their former identity and enable them to speak with a new language (1989, pp. 72–7).

So important does the issue of authority become for Hauerwas that he begins to be preoccupied with the means through which the Gospel narratives are to be interpreted within the Church. Hauerwas argues that it is 'spiritual masters' who must mediate the understanding of the tradition to the faithful. He quotes with approval from Vatican II, 'the task of authentically interpreting the word of God, whether written or handed on, has been entrusted exclusively to the living teaching office of the Church' (Albrecht, 1995, p. 49).

Such sentiments as these have drawn forth many criticisms of Hauerwas in recent times, not least from those who share his suspicions of the militaristic and exploitative 'world order'. However, there can be no doubt that his contribution, based on a straightforward use of the methods of canonical narrative theology, has resulted in a radical reappraisal of the nature and purpose of Christian ethics.

## Gerard Loughlin: The Church and God's Story

Canonical narrative theology as articulated in the work of Barth, Frei and Hauerwas has been influential in moves by contemporary theologians to affirm 'orthodoxy' in the face of what is perceived to be the nihilism of contemporary culture. Within this movement a renewed confidence in Christian theology is *orthodox* in the sense that it eschews the scepticism of liberal theology and places confidence in the God revealed in Scripture and venerated through tradition. However, it is also *radical* in the sense that it is willing to question whether traditional Christian attitudes and practices (in relation to women and sexuality for example) are in concordance with this sacred narrative. The movement is also radically critical and willing to question the intellectual roots of contemporary theological trends, often seeking to rearticulate Christian understandings that were formed before the modern era. These are presented as being able to speak a challenging word to a Church and culture that has followed a fundamentally misguided path since the Enlightenment placed humanity at the centre of a world formed by human hands and human reason.

In his book *Telling God's Story* (1996) Gerard Loughlin, a British theologian associated with the Radical Orthodoxy school, sets out clearly a vision of how a renewed awareness of the significance of the divine narrative can generate new confidence within the Church. Loughlin presents the fragmentation of contemporary culture as the result of a collapse of faith in the grand narratives of human progress fashioned by the European Enlightenment:

> When the grand narratives of religion began to lose their credibility the modern world invented itself by retelling the old stories in a new way. It didn't tell stories about God, but about history, evolution, the psyche, about stars and scientific progress, about genetic manipulation and a master race: about human emancipation through enlightenment and 'technoscience'. These stories, however, are now also incredible, undesirable, horrible. And it seems that now there are no master stories left, we have to be our own story-tellers, our own little masters.
>
> Loughlin, 1996, p. 9

Postmodern times are evoked as a context in which story-telling flourishes but where there is profound scepticism concerning the truth and authority of the stories we tell. Loughlin allies himself firmly with the narrative theologians discussed in this chapter by affirming that the Christian does not concede the relativism of the story they tell. This is because it is God's own story; self-narrated through Christ, witnessed to in Scripture and doctrine and embodied in the life of the Church.

It is Loughlin's particular contribution to the method of canonical narrative theology that he focuses upon ecclesiology. 'The text is a dead thing until it is taken up and performed in the life of the Church' (p. 113). He offers many vivid images of how the Church as the body of Christ partakes of the word of God and is thus 'enfolded, incorporated in the very life of Christ' (p. 220). The reality of this incorporation can be discerned through the striking examples of Christ-likeness to be found in the lives of the saints. However, it is also attested to in the common, everyday life of the Christian community, particularly as it engages in worship. For Loughlin, the Eucharist is the paradigmatic example of what sharing in God's story entails. The community gathers to hear and remember the narrative of Christ's passion. As they 'consume' this narrative they are themselves 'consumed' by the story. They are transformed into the very body of Christ and thus become themselves the telling of God's story in the world.

> The biblical story is present not only in the readings of the lectionary but in the very language of the liturgy which, through penitence and acclamation, comes to focus on the life, death and resurrection of Jesus Christ. The participants' absorption into the story is made possible through their absorption of the story in and through its ritual enactment. They are not simply witnesses of the story, but characters within it. They are not simply recall the forgiveness of sins but also ask and receive forgiveness; they do not repeat the praise of others but give praise themselves; they do not merely remember the night on which Jesus was betrayed but, mindful of their own daily betrayal gather with the apostles at that night's table, themselves called by the one who in that darkness called his disciples to eat with him. Above all they do not merely remember the giving of the bread and the passing of the cup. But receiving the bread and passing the cup themselves, they too share in that night's food.
>
> Loughlin, 1996, pp. 223–4

The strong emphasis Loughlin places upon the Christian community as the body of Christ gives his theology a more dynamic quality than is found in the work of some other canonical narrative theologians. The Church does not merely re-enact an archaic script; it tells a story that cannot be finished apart from in and through the Church. However, the Church does not tell the story for its own sake. It has in truth *become* the story of God, which is unfolding with just as much significance today as it had in first century. Indeed, Loughlin's analysis of the nihilism of postmodern culture places a particular imperative on the Church effectively to present an alternative narrative to the ones that are eagerly consumed within our culture but which are failing to nourish our communal and spiritual lives.

## Evaluation

Canonical narrative theology offers a straightforward and coherent vision of the task of theological reflection; it is the process through which individuals and communities seek to embody and act out the story of God told in Jesus. It is impossible to deny the importance this practice has had throughout Christian history or the significance it has attained within contemporary theology. It offers an effective means of *Christian nurture*, a clear basis for *ecclesiology* and a means of affirming *Christian identity* in contradiction to culture. Furthermore, many of those who have sought to live as Christ in the world have offered moving examples of Christian resistance to wordly power. From Francis's embrace of the poor Christ, to Barth's rejection of fascism and the contemporary witness of Hauerwas against American imperialism, we can see very tangible examples of the way this process forms lives of radical discipleship.

However, the attractiveness of many aspects of this understanding of theological reflection should not lead us to ignore the many problems that are inherent in the method. Some of these concern understandings of the Christian narrative as simple and realistic; and the claim that the Church has always seen its story in this way. We are aware from historical scholarship that mystical and esoteric readings of the life of Christ circulated among the very first Christian communities. Allegorical interpretations flourished in patristic and medieval periods and are still very significant in many parts of the Christian world today. It might be argued that realistic readings only gradually achieved hegemony as a result of the forces of cultural modernity in the West. Realism in literature goes hand in hand with empiricism in philosophy and a common-sense approach to a disenchanted universe; it is a literary genre that celebrates the coherence of a narratable world. Would it be possible to read the Bible like a realistic novel if this form had not been precisely the literary type that has developed within, and characterizes the modern era? If this is so, it becomes evident that contemporary experience will always determine how we encounter the sacred canon.

Other questions emerge concerning the relation of the Christian narrative to differing cultural traditions. For example, Lindbeck and Frei offer their methods of theological reflection to a post-liberal world of radical plurality. Within this context they are keen to return Christians to their own distinctive identity, not in order to prove superiority over others, but in order to offer a particular witness. These sentiments appear to accord well with some forms of postmodernism in which it is recognized that all knowledge is radically contextual and that claims to meaning are always based upon prior commitments of faith. When considering the implications of this position, however, it is important to take cognizance of the fact that the 'particularity' of the tradition to which we are returned is itself radically plural. Christians share many sacred narratives with Jews and Muslims and there is a continued debt owed to the living traditions of the faith out of which the Church came into being. Furthermore, there is the suspicion that while some canonical narrative theologians seek to engage fully with the postmodern challenge others are nostalgic for a premodern world in which the Christian narrative provided the predominant epistemological framework for society.

Similarly, there are many questions concerning the ethical implications of the Christian story. Clearly it is in the nature of narrative that there can be many interpretations of the meaning of the same story. Can we really be certain what the implications of the gospel traditions are in relation to the many complex issues of today? One of Hauerwas's most perceptive critics, Gloria Albrecht, has asked why it is that Hauerwas believes Christians living in coherence with their narratives will always oppose abortion, condemn premarital sex and define women's lives through giving priority to their traditional 'nurturing' duties. Is this a faithful reflection on the gospel? Or is Hauerwas reading the story of Jesus according to his own assumptions and predispositions? Are we witnessing the forces of a male-controlled tradition and institution returning under a new guise? (Albrecht, 1995).

Finally, canonical narrative theologians have argued that a return to the Christian narrative offers an effective antidote to the evils of postmodernism. But for whom is contemporary pluralism and breakdown of traditional values a problem but for those who have benefited from 'social order' in the past? All of these criticisms centre on one fundamental question: if the Christian Church is a story-formed community, who determines the way in which the story is told? Are the narratives themselves shaped to reflect the interests of particular groups and repeated at the expense of others? Is it not wise to recognize the diversity and richness of the tradition and celebrate the fact that realistic interpretations are only one way of approaching a multilayered story that continues to unfold and interact with culture in numerous different ways?

## Questions

• Why do some Christians see reflecting on the story of Jesus as a 'spiritual exercise' whereas others see it as a political act?
• Is the Christian narrative in conflict with contemporary culture?
• What are the most significant differences between this method and constructive narrative theology (Chapter 2)?

## Annotated Bibliography

Hughes, Gerard (2003), *Oh God Why? A Spiritual Journey Towards Meaning, Wisdom and Strength*, Oxford: Bible Reading Fellowship. This is a popular and highly accessible book based upon the Ignatian spiritual exercises. It offers helpful advice upon the techniques that can be used to enter into the story of Jesus today. The final section contains material for study groups.

Hauerwas, Stanley and Jones, L. Gregory (eds.) (1989), *Why Narrative? Readings in Narrative Theology*, Grand Rapids: Eerdmans. This is a very useful compilation of extracts from key texts on narrative theology. Most, but not all, are from the 'canonical' perspective.

Yoder, John Howard (1972), *The Politics of Jesus*, Carlisle: Paternoster. This classic text, written by a modern Anabaptist theologian, has been inspirational in developing Christian ethics out of the story of Jesus.

Loughlin, Gerard (1996), *Telling God's Story: Bible, Church and Narrative*, Cambridge: Cambridge University Press. This book not only brings canonical narrative theology into conversation with ecclesiology it also offers a helpful overview of the work of the thinkers discussed in this chapter.

Hauerwas, Stanley (ed.) (2001), *The Hauerwas Reader*, Durham, NC: Duke University Press. This weighty volume forms an excellent introduction to the work of Hauerwas and includes extracts from some of his most famous works.

# 4

# 'Writing the Body of Christ': Corporate Theological Reflection

## The Method in Outline

In this chapter we consider theological reflection as a corporate activity, with a shift of emphasis from the individual to the congregation, church or faith community. We examine how the faith community can construct a sense of corporate identity through the use of a central metaphor, or symbolic practices such as prayer, eating and working together, or by creating a narrative that tells the story of its ongoing life. Such metaphors, practices and narratives provide symbolic and theological power to enable a faith community to develop an idea of itself that sustains it through time and enables it to engage with and express its distinction from its culture. A significant motif that emerges in the different examples used in this chapter is that of 'the body of Christ'.

## Introduction

Throughout the chapter we use the terms 'congregation', 'local church', 'community of faith' interchangeably to cover the wide range of different ways in which people meet regularly to worship and witness to God in the world. As will be seen in the reflections from history section, the faith community shapes itself in various ways. Paul's letters to the church in Corinth are addressed to communities that formed themselves around the household or patron's house, including friends, family and slaves. Paul's concern was to encourage a sense of corporate responsibility so that members developed a different lifestyle based upon their understanding of a life of equality in Christ, rather than upon the former class, gender and economic distinctions. This led him to reflect theologically on corporate life as prefiguring 'the body of Christ'. Benedict's Rule, from the sixth century AD, gave a symbolic structure to the time and space that the brothers shared, and by communal practices, such as eating, praying and working together, a regulated way of life emerged. The Beguines of the later Middle Ages gathered in much more informal ways. Many of them described their life as a *Vita Apostolica*, an apostolic life, which provided theological and symbolic significance for adherents, and gave spiritual authority to those who were normally without a voice in the Church structures of the day. The way Dietrich Bonhoeffer (1906–45) described 'life together' in his book of the same name illustrates from the twentieth century how a community can form with a theological witness that is counter-cultural to the values of its society. Although this example is a relatively recent 'reflection from history' it belongs in this section because it predates the contemporary understanding of corporate theological reflection that has developed only in the past 20 years.

For this method of theological reflection only becomes explicit with the recent development of the discipline of congregational studies. The last 30 years have seen increased interest from sociologists and cultural anthropologists in the way communities sustain corporate identity in societies experiencing rapid social change. For example Anthony Cohen's important book *The Symbolic Construction of Community* (1985) explains how communities use certain symbolic practices, rituals or ideas to establish corporate identity. Cohen views this construction as an imaginative process through which the members of a community will establish boundaries by holding a symbol in common, and indeed the idea of 'community' itself has symbolic power. Symbolic practices are required to provide continuity through time and to consolidate the life together. Symbols construct community precisely because they are imprecise and allow various meanings to be invested in them. This enables communities to develop with a diverse membership that nevertheless can present a distinctive corporate identity to the world around.

Clearly congregations can be seen as symbolic communities in the manner suggested by Cohen and other social scientists. The emerging discipline of congregational studies has used the resources of social and cultural theory to investigate the dynamics of congregational life. In the early 1980s the work of researchers such as Carl Dudley and James Hopewell began to show how congregations existed through the symbolic work of those who belonged to them. Hopewell's book *Congregations: Stories and Structures* (1988) has proved to have enduring influence, and we examine here how he developed the idea of the identity of the congregation as a narrative construction. He wrote that 'from its conception to its death the local church exists by the persistent imaginative construction of its members' (in Dudley, 1983, p. 82). We shall return to this theme and see how he worked with local congregations to draw out their distinctive narratives by focusing upon significant events and people in its history. Greater understanding of their own stories can enable congregations to deal with change and think about their constituted identity more creatively.

Another important development in understanding the local church has emerged from liberation theology, and we examine how Leonardo Boff describes 'ecclesiogenesis'; the birth of churches and base communities 'from below'. Browning's work on congregations as moral communities is also considered as he explores how churches develop forms of practical moral reasoning. Mary McClintock Fulkerson's work is included here not so much because she talks about community-forming processes, but about what happens when the community that is formed does not adequately accommodate some of its members. She analyses how women negotiate their presence and develop strategies for reading the biblical texts that enable them to create space and remain within faith communities whose dominant discourses are more inclined to silence them. We conclude the chapter by looking at styles of emergent churches, and particularly the work of Kester Brewin (2004) on 'the complex Christ'. Here we see how contemporary scholars reflect upon what forms of community will develop within the networked societies of a globalized world.

## Reflections from History

For just as the body is one and has many members, and all the members of the body, though many, are one body, so it is with Christ. For in the one Spirit we were all baptized into one body – Jews or Greeks, slaves or free – and we were all made to drink of one Spirit.

Indeed, the body does not consist of one member but of many. If the foot were to say, 'Because I am not a hand, I do not belong to the body,' that would not make it any less a part of the body. And if the ear were to say, 'Because I am not an eye, I do not belong to the body,' that would not make it any less a part of the body. If the whole body were an eye, where would the hearing be? If the whole body were hearing, where would the sense of smell be? But as it is, God arranged the members in the body, each one of them, as he chose. If all were a single member, where would the body be? As it is, there are many members, yet one body. The eye cannot say to the hand, 'I have not need of you,' nor again the head to the feet, 'I have no need of you.' On the contrary, the members of the body that seem to be weaker are indispensable, and those members of the body we think less honourable we clothe with greater honour, and our less respectable members are treated with greater respect; whereas our more respectable members do not need this. But God has so arranged the body, giving the greater honour to the inferior member, that there may be no dissension within the body, but the members may have the same care for one another. If one member suffers, all suffer together with it; if one member is honoured, all rejoice together with it.

Now you are the body of Christ and individually members of it.

1 Corinthians 12.12–27 (NRSV)

Paul offered the Christians in the communities he founded continued oversight through his visits and his letters. Reading between the lines of the letters that were preserved can be a useful way of understanding some of the issues that these young communities faced. What can we know of the local tensions at Corinth? From his letters to the Corinthians it becomes evident that there were internal pressures and discord, and Paul attempted to remind this new group of Christians of their loyalty to one another. Some contemporary scholars (notably Wayne Meeks (1983); Gerd Theissen (1982), Antoinette Wire (1990)) attempt to read Paul's rhetoric to discern the social world of the early churches, and they argue that it was the case that rich people offered meeting places for the newly converted Christians in their homes (see 1 Corinthians 16.15, 19). Elsewhere in the first letter there are hints that there were relatively poor converts present (1 Corinthians 1.28, 11.22), and Paul was faced with the task of addressing the socially advantaged, and reminding them of their 'unity' with the poorer elements. It also appeared that there were other conflicts, for example, concerning gender. Antoinette Wire (1990, p. 157) argues that Paul's rhetoric is often addressed at confident women prophets whose social status was rising, perhaps threatening Paul's own authority and his own relatively low social status as a tentmaker. Paul identified issues of power and exclusion on the basis of class, and offered the Corinthians a symbol that encouraged them to reflect theologically upon their distinctiveness from the world around whilst dealing creatively with their internal differences.

In this passage Paul encouraged the faith community at Corinth to reflect theologically, particularly about issues of power. He uses a metaphor to catalyse them into a sense of community, the metaphor of 'the body of Christ'. In other letters he uses other metaphors with the same function, for example, 'the household of God' or 'the living temple'. By employing such symbols he encouraged his readers to reflect theologically about their life together, and in doing so to construct their corporate identity in ways that enabled internal diversity to become a strength rather than a weakness.

In this particular case, Paul's use of the metaphor 'the body of Christ' enabled him to call rich and respectable members of the church at Corinth to account. It would seem that the rich had assumed that they could treat those of lower class in ways that reflected the norms of the urban society in which the congregation was located. Paul is at pains to remind them that as 'the body of Christ', they are called to a different way of relating, one where those of lower status should not only be treated with equal care but also be seen as indispensable and of honourable worth. As Cohen would suggest, Paul gave them a symbol by which to order their internal life, but which also presented a public face that spoke of unity.

He was the first to apply the notion of 'the body of Christ' to a Christian community, but in doing so he borrowed a metaphor from current Stoic thought (see Dunn, 1998, pp. 550–51), illustrating his ability to utilize the thought forms prevalent and familiar in the society of the time and bring those ideas into critical tension with the new way of life that emerged with Christianity. In that way, Paul attempted to address tensions of unity and diversity and overturn existing social stratifications.

### St Benedict's Rule: Theological Reflection by Regulation

We turn next to the Rule of St Benedict (480– c.547) and examine how regulated practices of prayer, eating together, reading the Rule aloud at meal times and work – all comprising a 'common rule of life' – provided stability for a monastic community in a world of change and flux. These were communities of structure and peaceful living, based upon 'a gentle rule' that laid down corporate practices and organized time and space in distinctive patterns.

The method of corporate theological practice established by Benedict in the sixth century was to have a widespread impact and lasting influence upon the political and social landscape of the early Middle Ages. Against the backdrop of a world 'where the bonds of civil society were everywhere dissolving' (Southern, 1970, p. 29), Benedict successfully harnessed the urge that many felt to live an ascetic life. Instead of an individual heading off into the desert (where the earliest monasteries were founded) Benedict's Rule enabled the colonization of the waste places of his society, creating the template of ordered community in a world of change. Until the twelfth century the rule provided a communal life that filled a political, social and religious vacuum that Benedict could not have foreseen. Southern writes that 'kings and magnates saw the monks as spiritual soldiers fighting for the safety of the land. Monastic establishments were formed in every main centre of political power' (pp. 224–5). He quotes these words from a title deed for land given in Worcester to the Benedictines:

> Amid this fleeting and transitory world, all visible things hasten to their end more quickly than the wind, but the things which are not seen remain fixed and immutable forever. Seeking therefore to use our transitory and temporal riches to procure eternal rewards and lasting joys . . . I give to the bishop and monastery of Worcester this piece of land to remain free from all human service till the end of time.
>
> p. 29

The monks were thereby given time and space to create a sense of symbolic timelessness, 'a small portion from the world of meaningless change to make it a replica of eternity' (p. 29). The symbolic power invested in their way of life by the world around is evident from these words. The Rule was short and very clear on all details of daily life, yet flexible and universally adaptable to varying situations. It was a symbolic way of life that was to have immense influence from that day to this. David Parry, OSB (1980), writing a commentary on the Rule of St Benedict for the twentieth century, illustrates how the Benedictine spirit continues to provide thoughtful engagement with the world from the prayerful context and security of the communal house, and how Benedictine life continues to rely upon regular practices of communal prayer and the repetition of the Rule, read aloud as members eat.

> We propose, therefore, to establish a school of the Lord's service, and in setting it up we hope we shall lay down nothing that is harsh or hard to bear. But if for adequate reason, for the correction of faults or the preservation of charity some degree of restraint is laid down, do not then and there be overcome with terror, and run away from the way of salvation, for its beginning must needs be difficult. On the contrary, through the continual practice of monastic observance and the life of faith, our hearts are opened wide, and the way of God's commandments is run in a sweetness of love that is beyond words.

Let us then never withdraw from discipleship to him, but persevering in his teaching in the monastery till death, let us share the sufferings of Christ through patience, and so deserve also to share in his kingdom.

From the Prologue in Parry's edition, 1980, pp. 4–5

'[T]hrough the continual practice of monastic observance and the life of faith . . .' All activity was regulated with a given structure of time, to an extent difficult to conceive in today's world. As Parry comments: 'unlike us, they reckoned the day hours as corresponding to the period of light, and the night hours as corresponding to the period of darkness. Hence the length of each hour varied; in winter, when darkness was longer, the hours of the night were longer, and the hours during the day were correspondingly shorter.' This alternative community was in a position to make an entirely independent use of the 24 hours of the day (p. 53), and so time was regulated in order that it might have theological significance. The daily round of mealtimes and fasting, with the continual reading of the Rule and other theological matter, had a formative effect upon members, shaping them into an enduring community that offered a Christian alternative to the instability of the world outside.

As the community went about its daily routines and work, study of the psalms and Scriptures and other religious texts was also required, thus establishing the Benedictine order as one of the foremost repositories of theological study and knowledge throughout the Middle Ages. In chapter LXVI we hear the requirement that 'This rule we wish to be read frequently in the community, so that none of the brethren may plead ignorance of it' (p. 180). Parry's own edition divides the text up into amounts for daily consumption, indicating that within Benedictine communities of today the practice of hearing the rule continues. A chapter a day is still read, and the 'chapter' gives the name to the chapter house still to be found in monastic houses. The daily reading had a powerful constructive effect, creating and sustaining the order and identity of members into a stable communal life, with its deliberate order and regulated rhythms.

This theological construction of a community relied upon regular practices, and here the link between the meaning of 'regular' and its Latin derivations, meaning 'of a rule', become important. Regular practices of prayer and communal routines shaped the local faith community in distinctive ways, and illustrate another powerful model of corporate theological reflection. Pierre Bourdieu's work on how identity is formed through regular habits of life and performance, with his concept of *habitus*, offers an interesting contemporary parallel to this way of forming identity (see Bourdieu, 1977). Corporate identity, for the Benedictines, was a matter of allowing the self to be moulded by a regulated life of prayer, work and study into a community that symbolized immutability in a world of change and flux.

## The Beguines and the Vita Apostolica

The communities of Beguines of the twelfth century onwards developed, not around a formal rule of life, but as ordinary women (many made widows by the Crusades) who lived together in various and diverse communities in or near towns, and exhibited their devotion to Jesus Christ in prayer and service within society. They flourished in the twelfth century, initially around Liège in the Netherlands, and were formed as women sought to live together for mutual protection and to serve the poor and needy of nearby towns. Often intense experiences, visions and stigmatization would accompany their desire for the *Vita Apostolica*, so-called because those who espoused it sought to follow the example of the apostles, not so much by retreating from the world into religious life, but rather by pursuing the activities of preaching, teaching, converting, healing and serving in the world (see Southern, 1970, p. 252).

In beguinages, which might bring together thousands of members from different backgrounds in terms of social class and wealth, the women would not take vows, or follow a rule (although some did follow the rule of the third order of St Francis), and yet they enjoyed a religious and mystical way of life that did much to mould the popular piety of the age. Many of these communities were suppressed in later times, but in their heyday they were havens for widows and other women who did not choose the alternatives of marriage or nunnery.

If the communities of the Benedictine tradition established and sustained their corporate identity by following highly regulated lives, then the Beguine communities of the later Middle Ages held together with a very much looser organization and structure. They attempted to live religious lives, informed by their faith, but outside the structure and organization of the institutional Church. In doing so they often undermined and threatened the Church by the popular appeal of their witness.

From the point of view of our exploration of corporate theological reflection, it is difficult to find one consolidating metaphor, like 'the body of Christ', or set of regular practices, like eating and reading together, within the Beguine movement that could create and sustain corporate life. It is helpful to remember, however, how Cohen argued that the very notion of 'community' can function itself as a means of establishing corporate identity, and many Beguines gathered around the notion of the *Vita Apostolica* – even though it meant different things to different adherents in different places. Cohen writes that 'community is largely in the mind. As a mental construct, it condenses symbolically, and adeptly, its bearers' social theories of similarity and difference. It becomes an eloquent and collective emblem of their social lives' (1985, p. 114). For those who belonged to a beguinage, where there was a freedom to come and go in a way not found in the regulated life of a monastery, the idea of *Vita Apostolica* would have enabled a sense of cohesion even though each member would have understood it differently and lived the life with different emphases. With a way of life about which it is impossible to generalize, it is possible to see that there were sufficient factors about the spirituality that flourished in these communities at this time, and certain common themes that enable a shared understanding of a way of life, the *Vita Apostolica*, to create community.

This was a time of tremendous religious fervour, marked by such varied communities as the Waldensians, the Lollards, the Albigensians, the Spiritual Franciscans and flagellants, those of the Free Spirit. Some were orthodox, seeking the cleansing of the institutional Church. Others were heretical, for example the dualist Cathars (dualist because they believed in a strict division between good and evil in the world). Southern tells us that the Beguines had no quarrel with orthodoxy, indeed '. . . they had no distinctive theological ideas at all' (Southern, 1970, p. 322), seeking only to live together 'religiously'.

The adherents of the *Vita Apostolica* would, in the main, reject extreme wealth and the abuses they saw in the institutional Church. They would hunger for the life of the soul and the defeat of heresy, and be concerned to provide devotional literature in the vernacular, for the edification of the new urban populations of the day.

A strong devotion to the Eucharist was also an element in the spirituality of the Beguines. For many to receive the elements was to enjoy the real presence of Christ. Mary of Oignies, one of the founding Beguines, renounced her privileged background, and together with her husband with whom she lived a celibate life, nursed lepers and cared for the poor. Robert F. McNamara has written this of her:

Blessed Mary anticipated the particular devotion to the passion of Christ that the friars of St. Francis of Assisi were to spread a generation later. Among her mystical gifts was the 'gift of tears'. The mere mention of Jesus' passion was enough to make her weep. Part of her devotion to the Passion was her intense love of the Holy Eucharist as the sacramental renewal of Christ's death. Of her hunger for Holy Communion, Jacques de Vitry, her scholarly biographer, wrote: 'This is the only comfort she could not endure being without. To receive Christ's body was the same with her as to live.'

McNamara, 2005

Such passionate spirituality also often manifested itself in pious practices leading to stigmatization. Stigmatization first appeared in the thirteenth century, and it seems that Mary of Oignies may have received the stigmata contemporaneously with Francis of Assisi. Her renunciation of wealth, her dedication to chastity and service to the poor were highly influential during the early days of the Beguine movement, and the important support of Jacques de Vitry, her confessor and bishop, did much to foster the movement in its early days.

Other phenomena that heightened the piety of women of the age were extreme asceticism, trances and visions. The ecclesiastical structures attempted to rechannel this energy into more conventional paths, but perhaps inevitably the movement started to decline after the hostile Council of Vienne in 1312.

### Deitrich Bonhoeffer and 'Life Together'

In his short book, *Life Together* (1954) Dietrich Bonhoeffer laid out some guidelines for communal living in the mid-twentieth century. In doing so he provided a radical Christian alternative to the theological liberalism that, he believed, offered little to oppose the rise of Nazism in Germany in the 1930s and 1940s. The book represents a theological reappraisal and renewal in response to the rise of the Third Reich. In it Bonhoeffer presents a way of living in community where members are radically dependent upon the grace of God. Despite having the opportunity to flee Nazi Germany, Bonhoeffer stayed to protest, and ended up martyred as a result of his involvement in a plot to assassinate Hitler.

His theology reflects the stark choices that were forced upon Christians of the time who refused to capitulate to the Nazi movement. If humanity could be capable of such evil as Bonhoeffer saw around him during the Second World War, then theology needed to be based upon a radical alternative, the grace of God (p. 10). In developing his practical outline for what Christian fellowship might mean,

Bonhoeffer drew upon his Lutheran roots: a rich tradition of reflection upon the grace of God freely given to humanity, requiring the response of faith. Throughout this short work the contrast between the spiritual reality of the Christian fellowship and illusionary human community is made (p. 15).

> Innumerable times a whole Christian community has broken down because it had sprung from a wish dream. The serious Christian, set down for the first time in a Christian community, is likely to bring with him a very definite idea of what Christian life together should be and try to realize it. But God's grace speedily shatters such dreams. Just as surely God desires to lead us to a knowledge of genuine Christian fellowship, so surely must we be overwhelmed by a great general disillusionment with others, with Christians in general, and, if we are fortunate, with ourselves.
>
> By sheer grace God will not permit us to live even for a brief period in a dream world. He does not abandon us to those rapturous experiences and lofty moods that come over us like a dream. God is not a God of the emotions but the God of truth. Only that fellowship which faces such disillusionment, with all its unhappy and ugly aspects, begins to be what it should be in God's sight, begins to grasp in faith the promise that is given to it. The sooner this shock of disillusionment comes to an individual and to a community the better for both. A community which cannot bear and cannot survive such a crisis, which insists upon keeping its illusion when it should be shattered, permanently loses in that moment the promise of Christian community. Sooner or later it will collapse. Every human wish dream that is injected into the Christian community is a hindrance to genuine community and must be banished if genuine community is to survive. He who loves his dream of a community more than the Christian community itself becomes a destroyer of the latter, even though his personal intentions may be ever so honest and earnest and sacrificial.
>
> Bonhoeffer, 1954, pp. 15–16

The book deals with the foundation of evangelical Christian community. Bonhoeffer describes how the day with others might be shaped through prayer and reading, work and meals. He then considers solitude, silence, meditation, prayer. A part of the book is then given to the importance of ministry and he explores the ministries of holding one's tongue, of meekness, listening, helpfulness and bearing the burdens of others, as well as the more formal ministries of proclaiming

the word of God with authority. The final part deals with the centrality of confession and Communion; how sin results in the withdrawal
of a member from community, and how the confession of sin leads to
reconciliation in the common reception of the Holy Communion. The
fellowship of Communion is then 'the superlative fulfilment of Christian fellowship', enabling members to share in eternal community.

Bonhoeffer stresses the importance of the radical grace of God
that enables members to live in community through Jesus Christ and
in Jesus Christ (p. 10). This community is not a human creation, he
argues, but rather it is given by God, and on that basis members participate. As they do so, they belong to and in Christ, becoming Christ's
body. Bonhoeffer has recourse to the Pauline metaphor of 'the body
of Christ', using it as a theological symbol much as Paul did: 'This is
the proper metaphor for the Christian community. We *are* members
of a body, not only when we choose to be, but in our whole existence.
Every member serves the whole body, either to its health or to its
destruction. This is no mere theory; it is a spiritual reality' (p. 68).

In order to strengthen their mutual interdependence and the inclusion of the weaker members, Bonhoeffer also used the symbol of
the chain, arguing that it is essential for the community to secure
the smallest links in order not to break (p. 72). Everyone must be
employed so that even in hours of doubt, that person knows that they
are useful. When Bonhoeffer writes 'The elimination of the weak is the
death of the fellowship' (p. 72), perhaps he had in mind the Nazi pol-
icy of eliminating so many vulnerable peoples. For Bonhoeffer, Christian community, in small family-like units, offered a way of life that
ensured that each brother [sic] was accountable to the other, down to
the smallest concrete sin and action.

The life together that Bonhoeffer creates is counter-cultural in its
sole dependence upon the grace and gift of God. The life flourishes
or declines as God permits: members need only concern themselves
with living together in faith, bearing with one another in recognition
of the way God bears them. The congregation, then, relies upon a
theology of grace, and, according to Bonhoeffer, it perpetrates itself
in the light of that radical life-giving nature of the grace of God. Life
together is based upon a theological understanding of God's grace that
undermines any sense of this being a human construction and recalls
members away from reliance on self, and towards dependence upon
Christ. In many respects it could be argued that Bonhoeffer's understanding of life together coalesced the different ways we have looked
at corporate life in this section. He used metaphors like 'the body of
Christ' and 'the chain', as we have seen. He recognized the importance

of communal practices to foster cohesion, and he also recalled members to a radical apostolic life, seeking to recover the freshness of the initial responses that people made in the early Church, much in the same way that the Beguines expressed their dissatisfaction with the Church of their day. The 'Life Together' was understood symbolically by members, ensuring that there were distinctive characteristics that differentiated their life from that of those around them.

## The Method Realized

*Congregation: Stories and Structures: James Hopewell (d. 1984)*

In our exploration of these 'reflections from history' we have seen how faith communities have used metaphors, regular practices or a distinctive understanding of *Vita Apostolica*, to construct community, and we saw that there were elements of all these to be found in Bonhoeffer's vision of 'life together'. As we look at how the method is realized in contemporary times, these symbolic constructions can be seen to have continuing power to create community. We now explore how James Hopewell made evident some of the mechanisms contemporary Christians use to secure their communal identity.

Hopewell's book *Congregation: Stories and Structures* (1988) marks an important point in the contemporary development of this method of corporate theological reflection. Hopewell had an abiding love and interest in congregational life. In an appreciation of Hopewell on his death in 1984, James T. Laney wrote of how he was absorbed by 'that all too human body, with its unique ethos, stories, and struggles of hope and redemption; in Jim's words "an embodied community that dares to call its body Christ's" '(Laney 1984, p. 57).

Congregations were, for Hopewell, bodies that had their own unique identities. Each one different, it constructed its identity through the stories and narratives it told about itself.

Through spending time as a participant observer with a congregation he sought to uncover its symbolic life, expressed in its everyday activities and the values that emerged from understanding the stories that were told. He commented that such an approach had received little study to that point, remarking 'how scant has been the attention paid in the last quarter century to the congregation's culture, idiom, or identity – its storied dimensions' (1988, p. 50).

Hopewell's approach to the study of congregations was new, and to develop his understanding of narrative he used the literary theory of Northrop Frye's *Anatomy of Criticism* (1957). Unfortunately in many ways this choice of literary theorist meant that his work was dated even as he wrote, for literary theory had travelled a far distance in the 30 years since Northrop Frye wrote. However, the main innovation of Hopewell needs to be recognized, for in using literary theory at all, he opened up exciting hermeneutical possibilities in the whole field of congregational studies. He developed the idea that the identity of the congregation can be seen as a construction that was always narrative in form; and insisted that each congregation existed through the 'persistent imaginative construction of its members' (Hopewell, 1983, p. 82). For Hopewell, the identity of a congregation had its own plot, characterization and world-view. It was the researcher's job to uncover the story that was always implicit as part of the congregation's identity.

Following Frye, Hopewell argued that the plot of a narrative contained four elements (Hopewell, 1988, pp. 159–62) and he discerned them in the story of each congregation. A plot has 'linkages' through which it connects key features of past events into a significant sequence. It 'thickens' as previously unconnected elements are drawn into the emerging narrative. The plot 'unfolds', demonstrating cause and effect and suggesting reasons why things happen. The plot also 'twists' as unexpected circumstances carry it in new directions. Hopewell listened to stories told, identifying their plots and observing patterns of behaviour, and then worked with the congregation to characterize its narrative identity using Greek myths and archetypal fairy tales in which the congregation could see their ethos reflected.

Frye had argued that there are four narrative categories that correspond to four basic ways of interpreting the world. Hopewell translated Frye's genres of *comedy* (concerned with the development of harmony once the nature of reality is grasped), *romance* (tales of quests for great reward), *irony* (revealing the true nature of events and creating solidarity) and *tragedy* (submission to almighty power) into terms corresponding to recognizable Christian outlooks. He named these the *gnostic*, the *charismatic*, the *empiric* and the *canonic* world-views respectively. When applied to the stories told by a congregation, Frye's genres became ways of characterizing the narrative accounts into a communal world-view. Hopewell regarded the 'world-view' of a congregation as being the key to how it makes sense of communal life. Communal identity is reinforced as people tell the story of their community according to a particular established pattern.

Woven into the narrative construction of congregational identity, Hopewell also told the story of his own dying of cancer, illustrating how narrative could be used not only in the construction of corporate identity but also in the life of an individual. Hopewell wrote of his own ironic/tragic world-view as he went through the processes of dying.

> The tragic irony I tell about my mortal body reflects something of the approach I make to understanding the congregation. From neither bodily nor congregational habitation do I see miraculous escape, either by comic recognition that will give the special knowing at a higher stage of development or by a romantic quest that turns the parish outward into God's undomesticated presence in the larger context. Rather, the setting of my story and the congregation's portrays my own body and that of the local church essentially in human terms, but my factual portrait of the world is darkly shaded by the tragic inevitability of God's inexorable plan.
>
> Hopewell, 1988, p. 64

The way Hopewell worked with congregations to enable them to understand more fully their own corporate identity and life as story has contributed a great deal to the way this method of theological reflection has developed in contemporary times. His use of archetypal myths and fairy-stories shows an appeal to a popular, accessible canon of literature, which he correlated with the more obvious recourse to biblical sources and current theological symbols and practices. He wrote that the 'kerygma' of biblical stories and images challenged 'the self-characterizations that Christian households are wont to construct', giving a 'radical, critical, and finally redemptive meaning' (p. 114) to the congregation's mythic identity. He has been criticized, however, by Don Browning, for the limited range of literary genres that he employed, and it could be argued that he runs the risk of undermining the richness of his narrativity by restricting himself to the myths he knows. Browning points out that: 'This quasi-structuralism [of Northrop Frye] leads Hopewell to think that the fund of Greek myths more or less exhausts the mythic possibilities of the human imagination, and that the comedic, ironic, romantic and tragic perspectives more or less exhausts the fund of possible world views' (Browning 1991, p. 129). However, Hopewell's approach states clearly that one of the benefits of using narrative to tell the story of the congregation is that it is not authoritative and that the form is never final, and all in all he offers a liveliness of approach and an important contribution to the ways in which faith communities can be understood more deeply as a result of looking at how they use story and narrative to construct their corporate identity.

## Ecclesiogenesis: Giving Birth to Church

Our next contemporary example takes us to the base communities of Latin America, and Leonardo Boff's book *Ecclesiogenesis* (1997). This book explores how Church can be born from the 'bottom up' within traditional 'top down' ecclesial structures. This method relies upon the story-telling of members within base communities as they reflect theologically upon their faith and lives.

The central challenge of Boff's *Ecclesiogenesis* is directed at the structures of the Roman Catholic Church. He argues that new forms of community give birth and life to the Church. Basic church communities represent a new experience of Church by the working of the Holy Spirit. Boff explains how they grew originally out of the need, in the absence of priests in the 1950s, for lay-led worship and instruction, marking a growth in the influence of lay leaders (see Dawson, 1999, pp. 110ff.). But the base communities are not there merely to breathe new life into old hierarchies. It is the engagement with socio-political issues and injustice that gives these 'congregations' their central *raison d'être*.

Christian life in the basic communities is characterized by the absence of alienating structures, by direct relationships, by reciprocity, by a deep communion, by mutual assistance, by communality of gospel ideals, by equality among members (Boff, 1997, p. 4). Instead of a clerical institution, the church community becomes a group of people enthused by Christ and the Spirit. The People of God no longer merely receive from the hands of the cleric, but create and organize in response to the power of Christ in their midst, to bear prophetic witness, to sanctify (p. 27), to provide a community of services (p. 29).

Such a community is shaped by different theological assumptions to those of the institutional Church: it has to grow beyond the confines of clerical structures in order to be able to make decisions, and to relate with priests and bishops in different ways. A new style of cleric emerges: one who is 'now in the midst of the people as principles of animation and inspiration, of unity and universality' (p. 32). The people themselves then also emerge as genuine leaders, and the basic church communities then help 'the whole church in the process of declericalization, by restoring to the People of God, the faithful, the rights of which they have been deprived in the linear structure' (p. 32). A new praxis, a new way of thinking and doing, results.

This new praxis is intimately concerned with questions of justice, enabling the Church to become an oppressed people organizing for liberation. Acute social awareness prevails within the communities, with analysis of the working of the capitalist system, and engagement with political structures and systems. The freshness of this way of being Church perpetrates itself by doing theology differently, well-captured by Dawson in the following account, describing how a base community meets and follows a see-judge-act method of theological reflection. From this account emerges the centrality of communal story-telling, which is brought into creative correlation with biblical texts.

Our typical mid-week gathering, coordinated by a lay person or couple and possibly facilitated by a local priest or nun, is opened with the communal saying of a prayer, song or psalm. Following this formal commencement of proceedings, the next half-hour or so is given over to the recounting of the past week's events and concerns by each individual participating in the community gathering. Such concerns and events might include, for example, news of illness through lack of adequate sanitation facilities, proper housing or malnutrition, the sharing of hardships caused by redundancy or low pay, and information upon someone injured on account of dangerous working conditions . . . Following this review of the past week's happenings a scriptural passage might be read aloud by all present, with each person then sharing any comments felt relevant to both text and context of gathering. When the round is completed, the biblical text and shared comments are then drawn together in the form of a reflection, a further period of open discussion takes place, in which the scriptural passage is questioned in the light of present preoccupations and events, in the hope that it might shed light upon the situation at hand. In effect, the past week's life experiences provide the tool by which the biblical text is interrogated and made relevant to the life setting of the group. In such a way, the scriptural passage speaks in retrospect concerning recent events, whilst at the same time giving encouragement to those gathered concerning the week to come . . . Lasting for up to an hour or more, this time of reflection constitutes the moment of judging (evaluation) within the threefold methodology being utilised . . . The stages of seeing and judging thereby pass to a time of action; a time of action in which those empowered within the base ecclesial community immerse themselves within traditionally secular neighbourhood concerns such as local community centres, women's groups, cooperative ventures, political parties and unions, youth clubs, and ad hoc campaigns in the pursuit of a local health clinic, sanitation facilities, school and public transport provisions.

Dawson, 1999, pp. 117–18

The model of theological reflection employed here has had a profound influence upon other ecclesial groups and congregations throughout the world, enlivening institutions grown stale through tired theology ineptly applied. The attention to process and dynamic in the methods of theological reflection here ensure a lively and self-generating body, which constructs its own sense of community as it hears and responds to the issues of members. In the practice of community, the community itself is constructed. This is a real departure from the more institutional forms that traditionally established the church community and expected members to shape themselves to its form.

## *Don Browning and* A Fundamental Practical Theology

In the early 1980s James Hopewell participated in a research project that examined the life of a local church from different disciplinary perspectives, which was published as *Building Effective Ministry* (Dudley, 1983). One of his colleagues on that project was Don Browning, who, like Hopewell, went on to write more in the field of congregational studies. With the benefit of hindsight, Browning argued that *Building Effective Ministry* was interventionist (the researchers descended with their different theories, and studied the church as if it were an inanimate object), rather than his then preferred option, which took a more dialogical approach (engaging with the church in conversation). His influential book *A Fundamental Practical Theology* (1991) represents Browning's dialogical approach between researcher and congregation. He invited his readers to assume a similar perspective as they encounter the congregations he describes: 'Imagine being a friend to someone in one of these communities – someone who once, in the midst of a conversation, asked you with a sense of both playfulness and seriousness the following question: "Where do you think we should go from here?" ' (p. 18).

In *A Fundamental Practical Theology*, Browning studied three congregations to answer the question 'How are [congregations] both communities of memory and communities of practical reason?' (p. 3). In other words how do congregations exist in relation to their traditions of faith and in response to the concrete challenges of the day? How do they find a way of living out of the resources of the Christian story in a manner that unites them as one body in faithful action? He came with a particular way of understanding how communities might construct themselves as they worked through five dimensions of moral thinking. The first concerned the *visional* life of the congregation, as it addressed a particular issue with recourse to the relevant narratives and metaphors of its own tradition in its particular context (p. 105). Within those traditions, which formed the backdrop of the life of the church, more specific and rational consideration would be employed, which would emerge as the congregation explored the general principles of obligation it thought important. Browning calls this the *obligational* level of moral reasoning. The principle of neighbourly love, and the golden rule might be seen as examples of this level. The next level he called *tendency-need*, recognizing that human behaviour is driven by values that are selfish, social, intellectual or culturally induced. Moral reasoning often functions to manage these drives. The fourth level of moral reasoning is the *environmental-social*. This dimension shows how the individual or group is constrained by its social and environmental surroundings as it seeks to act in moral ways. The fifth dimension is the most concrete, the *rule-role* dimension. This category refers to the level of actual practices and behaviours (p. 106).

I make this kind of claim for my five dimensions of practical moral thinking. They are reconstructions of intuitive experience of what goes into practical moral thinking, whether conventional or critical. In the case of conventional practical thinking, the five dimensions are uncritically assumed and unthematized. In the case of critical practical thinking, they are conscious, thematized, and open to tests of various kinds. I call them dimensions of practical thinking because they generally interpenetrate so smoothly that we are unaware of them as differentiated aspects of experience. I occasionally use the metaphor of *levels* in contrast to *dimensions* to communicate that the visional and obligational dimensions are more comprehensive and influence our interpretations of the lower three levels. Nonetheless the so-called lower levels also influence the form and sometimes reshape the substance of the more comprehensive visional and obligational levels. Each of the five dimensions must submit to tests about its validity in ways similar to Habermas' consent of validity claims.

I invite the reader to try the five dimensions on for size and comfort. My claims for their usefulness are open-ended and modest. Do they help us describe the situations of our practical action? Do they help us think critically about the norms and strategies of our practical action? I believe that they will carry us a long way.

It is my present conviction that every instance of practical moral thinking that I have ever confronted sooner or later revealed these five dimensions. We will see all of these dimensions functioning in our three congregations. The dimensions will help us understand the situations of these congregations. They will help us analyze the practical thinking that the congregations do. They will guide our practical theological dialogue with these congregations.

Browning, 1991, pp. 108–9

Browning carried out ethnographic research in three different congregations. He examined how moral reasoning became a corporate activity and formed the faith community by the dialogues that happened in response to particular issues and problems that faced the congregation.

Browning saw the congregation itself as the place where theology is formed through processes of practical reasoning (or *phronēsis* in Greek). The congregation achieves its corporate, and its moral, identity when it engages in *phronēsis*. Theological reflection in this frame is a corporate activity undertaken in everyday life as ordinary people draw upon the traditions of faith, as these are encountered in scripture, worship and life together, in order to make concrete responses to the world in which they live. He called his theological method 'practical' because it begins when a congregation realizes that its habitual practices are no longer adequate to the situation in which it finds itself and new practices are required. 'When it hits a crisis in practice [the congregation] begins reflecting on these theory-laden practices. Eventually it must re-examine the sacred texts that constitute the sources of its norms. It institutes a conversation between its questions and the texts. As its practices change its questions change and new meanings are perceived in texts' (Browning, 1991, pp. 108–9).

It will be clear from the dialogical and conversational metaphors Browning uses that he envisages the congregation as engaged in a 'correlational' process of reflection leading to transformation (see Chapter 5). This conversation takes place by employing the dimensions outlined above, and will often be formed as the congregation seeks to practise an 'equal regard' in its life together. Browning considered this ethic of equal regard to be 'the inner rational structure of the Christian ethic' (p. 159), and one that will often be evident in the life of the community of faith as it struggles to find authentic ways of being the Church in its own situation.

One of the congregations he studied in the heart of Chicago was a black-led congregation called the Apostolic Church of God (ACG). The ACG revealed a deep concern for the problems of inner-city African Americans, a concern that it integrated with strong moral teaching. The result was a powerful congregational life. Coming from the university campus a few blocks away, Browning encountered something completely different to anything he had experienced before in his white, Liberal Protestant upbringing. He describes what he found:

> On this Sunday and over the following months, I heard a message that incorporated an extremely powerful and generous portrait of God as a source of affirmation and empowerment for the people of the Apostolic Church of God. This generous message of love, grace, recognition, and empowerment by the Holy Spirit was balanced with equally challenging demands to live a personal and social moral life at the highest level. Supported by electrifying joy and spontaneity, this demanding call for near moral perfection sounded amazingly light, bearable, unoppressive, and nonmoralistic to my white middle-class ears . . .
>
> p. 29

Browning came to research the congregations as a dialogue partner with particular precommitments, and at the ACG he encountered a way of constructing community that was different to anything he had experienced before. The teaching that united the congregation started with the premise that Christians were saved by faith and the gift of the Holy Spirit. This made the members 'saints', who did not drink alcohol, smoke, have premarital sex, use drugs or commit adultery. It was a moral code that was also realistically interpreted to be relevant to the context and the problems of the wider community. The teaching focused particularly on the family and on familial relationships. The pastor, Arthur Brazier, had the power to sanction husbands who were unfaithful, or did not show co-operation in attempting to save their marriage, or were lawbreakers, or alcoholic. The sanctions took the form of silencing, by the withdrawal of privileges until there was genuine repentance. Servanthood and accountability were consistent within the moral identity of the congregation, and had consequences in the practical programmes that strengthened the family in its conformity to this model.

Browning came to see that there was a dialogical interplay about morality going on within the congregation, one that he found deeply moving as he saw it alive in the pastoral and congregational care that was offered. The structures of congregational care were extensive, and Browning observed connections between the moral reasoning and the care programmes expressed in the preaching: 'the sermon was a complex dialogue between Brazier and the text, the questions of the congregation and the text, and Brazier's interpretation of the text and the congregation's questions . . . Pastoral and congregational care at the Apostolic Church proceeded in this context of dialogical worship, preaching and prayer' (p. 244).

Browning's vision of the congregation as a community of memory and practical moral reasoning has much to offer as a means of understanding corporate identity. It places the local Christian community in relation to the Church Universal and also acknowledges the dynamic particularity of each congregation's life. What gives a community its distinctive character is its practice and this practice emerges out of a dialogical relationship with its context – as can be clearly seen in the witness of the Apostolic Church. The encouragement he offers to respect the genius of local groups of committed believers in practising theological reflection represents a vital contribution to practical theology.

## Mary McClintock Fulkerson: Changing the Subject

Mary McClintock Fulkerson's work is included here because her research investigates what happens when a particular corporate construction excludes members by the power of its dominant discourses. She does not focus specifically upon congregations *per se*, but she does analyze different communities of faith and explores how women create space for themselves in contexts that traditionally have constrained them into restricted roles and subjectivity. She is attentive to the ways in which power works within those communities to construct an individual subjectivity that performs according to social expectations. Faith traditions that coalesce around a symbol or narrative can, she argues, create 'subject positions' (that is, roles that are accepted and played out in life) that inhibit and curtail women instead of liberating them. In *Changing the Subject* (1994), Fulkerson argues that feminist theo-logy should attend to the conditions and relations of power that produce the many different subject positions that locate women within capitalist patriarchy.

Fulkerson examines three communities of faith in particular: Pentecostal women preachers, affluent Presbyterian women in mainline churchwomen's groups, and women within the feminist academic community in the United States. She studies the different ways each uses the biblical texts. She writes: 'women's subject positions and their distinctive dependencies (problems of access) differ. The position occupied by the Pentecostal hillbilly woman differs from that of the middle-class Presbyterian churchwoman. The Pentecostal woman is related to a different scripture than that of the middle-class Presbyterian' (p. 143). She examines how each community of women uses the texts at their disposal to liberatory effect, often against the odds. She explores the process by which all texts and theological writing are rooted in traditions, and yet are used in the different social contexts in which they are interpreted and used – either to liberatory or oppressive ends (p. 10). Fulkerson writes: 'oppressive or liberating texts are not constants, then, but are socially activated, since I locate resistance neither in the biblical text, nor in women's contexts, nor in some combination of readers' and textual meaning' (p. 10).

The meaning, argues Fulkerson, is found in the social location in which women use those texts. In such social locations, women will often see their own subjectivity not just as something passive, as if they are victims to the oppressive structures in their lives (living with husbands, perhaps, who are forever telling them that they are no good). Instead Fulkerson shows how the faith of a Pentecostal woman, for example, can enable her to resist such powerful oppressive messages and help her find the strength to preach and lead others and exercise a high degree of autonomy. Such a woman, within her faith community, is able to change her subject. She is able to resist the way her faith community shapes her identity as a member and produce different meanings that create space to be different.

Fulkerson's analysis distinguishes between the dominant and subordinated in any group. She argues that the subordinated can develop strategies to create space within what is allotted to them by a powerful tradtion or institutional status quo. This 'space' enables those who are subordinated to develop a new sense of identity, to be creative, even to subvert the dominant structures and so 'change the subject'. In an important way, Fulkerson achieves a similar analysis of power as that of Paul when he argued that the rich and powerful Corinthians needed to attend much more to those who were subordinated within their church. Fulkerson is arguing, as Paul did, that the construction of community does not always serve each member equally, and it can be necessary to find ways to resist and 'change the subject' in order to create a different 'body of Christ' that reflects more authentically the needs and voices of all members.

## Emergent Church: A Dynamic Body of Christ

In the first few years of the twenty-first century there has been a groundswell of interest in local church communities and how they need to respond to a changing world. Many writers have characterized those changes by describing the impact of globalization, of the network society now 'wired up' in communication systems, and in changing patterns of spirituality and a sense of the diversity of culture. Pete Ward, in *Liquid Church*, has written that 'existing patterns of church fail to connect with the evident spiritual interest and hunger that we see in the UK and the US' (2002, p. 3). Similarly, in 2004 the Church of England published the report *Mission-Shaped Church* (Cray, 2004), which described various 'fresh expressions' of Church that respond more theologically and strategically to the needs of a changing society. Elaborating on this, the report states:

> The Internet is both an example of network society and a metaphor for understanding it. From one perspective the Internet has no centre. There is no one 'place' where choices are controlled. Everywhere is linked to everywhere else . . . But it would be untrue to say that the Internet has no centres of power. There are powerful financial networks that have significant control, and particular places (including London) that are physical hubs for the global network. Economic interests and the divide between the technological rich and the technological poor create their own forms of inclusion and exclusion.
>
> p. 5

Just as the workings of the Internet are diffuse, fluid and network society, so too are people's experiences of their social interactions and relationships on a daily basis. Two distinctive things happen to community in a changing world such as this. First, people are more likely to form community around networks rather than through location, and people are less likely to make lasting commitments (p. 7). The report addresses some of the ways in which the churches need to respond. It argues that, on the basis of the Trinity, which models diversity as well as unity, and the way in which creation reveals God's affirmation of diversity, mission to a diverse world requires a diverse Church (p. 20). Pointing at various examples in Britain of the ways in which fresh expressions of Church have emerged, the report says that the variety of fresh expressions is an encouraging sign of the creativity of the Spirit in our age. Fresh expressions should not be embraced simply because they are popular or new, but because they are a sign of the work of God and of the kingdom (p. 80).

Such thinking can be found in the 'EmergingChurch' movement, which offers online opportunities to create community, networks and friendships. The following analysis of a changing world is found at www.emergentvillage.com/Site/Explore/EmergentStory/index.htm:

- The world is changing politically, from Cold War era to a post-communist era, from a world of conventional and nuclear war to a world of terrorism and genocide, from a colonial world to a post-colonial one (or perhaps to a neo-colonial one).
- It is changing philosophically, from modern to postmodern, from a world of absolutes and certainty to a world of questions and searching, of challenge and anxiety, of opportunity and danger.
- It is changing socially and economically, as a growing global economy and the rise of the Internet and other global media make the world seem smaller and more connected, yet also more fragmented and tense.
- It is also changing spiritually as religions of the world cope with new challenges and opportunities . . . religious and ethnic strife . . . the loss of confidence in traditional authorities . . . the shift of Christianity's strength from the global north to the global south.

EmergingChurch seeks to foster growing networks based upon friendship that are able to generate new thinking on mission and leadership. On leadership, the website says:

This emergent friendship is among leaders – 'church leaders (staff and volunteer), organizational leaders, thought leaders, relational leaders, artistic leaders, spiritual leaders', and the intention to bring together thinking and practice in the service of mission is made explicit.

Emergent is practitioner-focused. We believe that the best theology arises in the context of mission, and the best mission is informed by good theology, so we seek to bring reflective practitioners together with missional scholars and thinkers for mutual enrichment. We seek to avoid both unreflective activism and intellectual cul-de-sacs that often divert reflective people from actually getting anywhere.

We have a special concern for leaders in local faith communities – pastors, youth workers, worship leaders, artistic leaders, lay leaders, etc. We believe that local faith communities are at the cutting edge of mission.

In this chapter on how faith communities reflect corporately and form themselves around a central motif, narrative or symbol, the notion of 'emergent' appears to have salient power as churches seek to respond to an increasingly networked society. The work of Brian McLaren (2004) and Kester Brewin (2004) both use the language of 'emergent' and they both develop ways in which community can be seen as dependent upon belonging and a willingness to enter into dialogue.

We have seen that in many of the examples through history and in contemporary times the Pauline metaphor of 'the body of Christ' has proved significant. Kester Brewin's book *The Complex Christ* uses it in a fascinating way that brings it together with the insights of James Fowler's *Stages of Faith* (1981). He argues that the faith of the Church itself should progress to move to Fowler's fifth (or 'conjunctive') stage. At this point the emergent church will possess the maturity to appreciate the complexity of existence and the need for growth and renewal to occur organically and locally. He writes:

This then is the complex Christ: it is Christ disestablishing the need for the temple, for people to gain access to God only by being in one place and through hierarchies of priests; it is Christ establishing his body as a decentralized network of believers, and thus giving birth to a complex, emergent church that could not be destroyed any more easily than the Internet could be. It is, to rephrase St Augustine, the body of Christ truly becoming the network whose nodes are everywhere and circumference nowhere.

This model of a complex, conjunctive church comes to us from the cities we live in, from the scriptures we read and the scientists we respect. Socially, economically, scientifically, politically and spiritually we are being given a clear message from Christ about the way to turn the Church into an organism fit for the challenges of this new century: we must die and re-emerge as the complex body of Christ.

This is nothing new. Though we have often blinded ourselves to it, Christ becoming complex is what we celebrate in the Eucharist. It is a meal to which we are invited, a gift that hangs heavy with potential for relationship in every plane. The bread and wine that begins centralized, in one place, is unleashed as it enters each *one* gathered and is taken out into the community. We symbolically split Christ up and each take Christ out with us. Thus decentralized, Christ becomes uncontrollable. The gifts of his body and blood have disappeared into mystery, become inseparable from our own flesh, and are spread out with us into the city in a manner that no power can reverse.

Brewin, 2004, p. 163

Here we see how suggestive the metaphor of 'the body of Christ' can be as a way of reflecting theologically upon the nature of faith community and Church. Brewin draws on social analysis, the insights of science and poetry, theological and scriptural resources to present a body of Christ that is dynamic and decentralized – and not more so than at the Eucharist, celebrated as meal and gift within local churches throughout the world, with transformative power. Whatever shapes of Church emerge from these relatively new developments in understanding the Church as inclusive communities of networks and friends, 'the body of Christ' shows its resilience as a theological motif, though now marked by a sense of kenosis, or emptying of power and brokenness in the place of Paul's call for unity.

## Evaluation

This chapter has attempted to show how different communities use theological reflection in different ways to construct their distinctive identity. We have seen how congregations in the past and present have formed and continued to shape themselves theologically, using a central image or metaphor, or by a set of practices that gives a sense of corporate identity. We have considered questions of power, raised from the beginning by Paul's intervention at Corinth, and the ways in which a faith community needs to ensure that no one is marginalized from the processes of theological reflection. We have seen how theology makes and shapes community and becomes the exploration in word and deed of embodied life.

The catalytic moment, when this method of theological reflection emerged as a explicit form, occurred with the development of congregational studies in the USA. We have looked at the work of Hopewell, Browning and Fulkerson, who have examined the life of local churches and communities with an increasing awareness of issues of culture and power. With their work we have seen how this method of theological reflection can encourage us to investigate how power relations and the way in which language and ethics are used shape the dynamics of community.

A main contribution of congregational studies has been to offer tools that enable church communities to reflect theologically – as a body. Facilitating this process requires, as Paul found at Corinth (and Browning found as he entered into research dialogues with different congregations), careful negotiation. These techniques help a congregation to reflect upon itself in a context where all involved need to be engaged in the processes of discerning the corporate vision of the church (see Cameron, *et al.*, 2005). It can be a complicated process to involve a significant part of the whole community, and questions need to be addressed about who is central and who is marginal in the processes of reflection.

The base communities inspired by liberation theology also encourage members to 'own' their theological reflection, by working with an analysis of power in their own locality and using stories and biblical resources to enable members to reflect theologically in order to transform their own situations. Basic ecclesial communities become powerful embodiments of principles of theological reflection emerging from the underside of history and return us to the radical witness of the first Christian disciples.

The responses of churches to the changes in society have resulted in theological reflection that is formative of community in new and different ways. We have seen from the reflection that is happening in books, reports and on websites that the metaphor of 'the body of Christ' has salience for 'emergent' churches. The notion of 'community' and corporate reflection takes on new forms as networking becomes a normative way of belonging and relating in contemporary times.

In the examples we have considered the motif of 'the body of Christ' has emerged again and again as a metaphor that has powerful resonance. It encourages us to view our corporate life as intimately connected to the divine life; which is expressed for Christians in the mutuality of the Trinity. It also enables us to see the faith community as something that lives, suffers, responds and acts. The form of this body is constituted in many different ways according to context. However, we have recognized that this diversity is a manifestation of the desire to incarnate the form of Christ in our varied experiences of 'life together'.

## Questions

- In what ways has the metaphor 'the body of Christ' changed in use and understanding throughout the texts considered in this chapter? What significance does it have in the context of debates about the changing shape of Church in a postmodern world?
- If you were to carry forward some research in a faith community, what issues would you think of addressing?
- What different understandings of 'community' emerge from the

material covered in this chapter? How would you characterize the differences?

## Annotated bibliography

Cameron, H. *et al.* (eds.) (2005), *Studying Local Churches: A Handbook*, London: SCM-Canterbury Press. A must for anyone interested in studying congregations in the UK context, this book offers an interdisciplinary approach with methodologies from anthropology, sociology, organizational studies and theology, to provide a new focus on studying the local church. There is a range of different research methods and approaches and comprehensive further reading.

Ammerman, N. T. *et al.* (eds.) (1998), *Studying Congregations: A New Handbook*. Nashville: The Abingdon Press. This provides a very useful text written by leading figures in and for the US context with a variety of different methods to enable a congregation to reflect theologically about its ecology, its culture and identity, its processes and dynamics, its resources and leadership.

Browning, D. (1991), *A Fundamental Practical Theology*, Minneapolis: Fortress Press. This book explores the complexities of participant observation research in faith communities, and offers ways to discern the moral values that shape corporate life.

Fulkerson, M. McC. (1994), *Changing the Subject: Women's Discourses and Feminist Theology*, Minneapolis: Augsburg Fortress Publishers. Fulkerson's text is an insightful analysis of different faith communities of women as they engage with and transgress the varying degrees of external limitation they experience.

Hopewell, J. F. (1988), *Congregation: Stories and Structures*, London: SCM Press. Hopewell's book continues to be a classic in the field and shows how narrative forms can offer the means to reflect theologically upon the culture and identity of the congregation.

# 5

# 'Speaking of God in Public': Correlation

## The Method in Outline

The correlative method is one that emphasizes the importance of theology's engagement with contemporary culture, be that philosophical, aesthetic, political or scientific. This approach to theological reflection regards the evolution of Christian thought and practice as necessarily taking place *in public*: the Christian tradition should be prepared to engage in an open exchange of ideas and debate with different cultural disciplines, values, images and world-views. Some see a dialogue between 'Christ' and 'culture' taking place in order to commend the gospel to a particular non-Christian philosophical system or world-view. However, other exponents of this method argue that the realms of human reason and enquiry are capable of manifesting God's truth, even if that remains to be brought to completion by a more complete revelation in Christ. This premise is taken further in some contemporary perspectives such as feminist theology, which argue that extra-theological sources and insights are often necessary as critical correctives to the failures and distortions of Christian history.

## Introduction

Historically, Christianity emerged from a pluralist cultural and religious context, and from its very beginnings was charged with the task of articulating norms of faithful discipleship alongside competing world-views. The correlational model thus represents a method of theological reflection that regards cultural pluralism as both challenge and opportunity. It is concerned to affirm cultural, philosophical and religious difference as a source for further dialogue and development.

In relation to the theological task of *adult induction and nurture*, correlation assumes that the individual subject of theological reflection is a person from a particular background who comes to Christianity never innocent of other philosophical influences. Like local theologies

(Chapter 7) therefore, the correlative method recognizes that 'talk about God' always takes place in a specific place and time. The task of adult formation and nurture involves working with the inherent potential of all human creatures to know something of the divine, by virtue of their (God-given) faculties.

In terms of facilitating theologically informed understandings of *corporate identity*, correlation stresses the community's locatedness in history and culture. The church community is called to participate in history and to some extent bring history to fruition through the gospel. Yet, given the possibilities of implicit revelation among those who do not explicitly profess Christianity, the boundaries between the Church and wider human community may be quite fluid, as in Karl Rahner's concept of 'anonymous Christianity'.

Correlation also assumes that theology is conducted, as our title suggests, in public as well as being an internal discourse of exclusively Christian identity. It acknowledges that the task of living within a pluralistic and fallen world will generate questions, anxieties and challenges to which the gospel must be seen to respond; and that the credibility of Christian truths must be argued in ways that fulfil prevailing standards of intellectual coherence. Part of the task of theological understanding is to commend the faith in the general marketplace of ideas, as the account of Paul preaching in Athens (see below) underlines.

In this chapter, therefore, we will present the 'dialogical' qualities of the correlational method as having two key dimensions: the apologetic and the dialectical.

1 The *apologetic* strand seeks to utilize prevailing thought-forms in order to indicate how Christianity fulfils and completes human questions. The effective proclamation of the gospel is dependent on it appearing relevant and accessible to its audience.
2 The *dialectical* strand stresses the possibility of theological understanding being glimpsed in 'secular' thought forms and argues that these make a vital contribution to a living theological tradition.

As our illustrations unfold, it will be clear that one or the other may have been given greater emphasis by certain writers; but essentially, both focus on locating Christian theology on the boundaries, or at the interface, between the insights of 'reason' and 'revelation' or 'nature' and 'grace'. They share a common assumption that the world beyond the Church, or Christian revelation, contains implicit or embryonic truths, although variations within this model differ to the extent to which such insights are admitted to exercise a correctional or revisionist effect on the revealed tradition.

Key questions within this method of theological reflection concern how accessible Christian theology can be to those outside the faith, and the extent to which insights from outwith the tradition may be admitted as theologically valid. Thomas Aquinas's project to consider the implications for Christendom of its encounter with the intellectual riches of the Arab world, and especially the latter's recovery of Greek philosophy, raised theological questions concerning the extent to which God had been revealed in the common language and wisdom of human discourse. In modern times, the German Jesuit theologian Karl Rahner embodied a correlational model in producing a theological apologetics that represented a return to Thomist theology informed by contemporary philosophy in general, and the work of Martin Heidegger in particular. Rahner's clear advocacy of a model of divine revelation in which God did indeed speak through 'intellect, nature and history' as well as the authoritative statements of the Church fuelled a sea-change within the Roman Catholic Church that came to fruition in the *aggiornamento* or 'openness' to the modern world of the Second Vatican Council. The work of Paul Tillich, David Tracy and, more recently, Rosemary Radford Ruether, has sought to engage in turn with modern psychotherapies, social theory and feminism. Theology is called to account for itself in relation to these new discourses and it is recognized that they might even exercise a corrective and renewing effect upon the Christian tradition.

## Reflections from History

### Paul preaches in Athens

While Paul was waiting for [Silas and Timothy] in Athens, he was deeply distressed to see that the city was full of idols. So he reasoned in the synagogue with the Jews and the devout persons, and also in the marketplace every day with those who happened to be there. Also some Epicurean and Stoic philosophers debated with him. Some said, 'What does this babbler want to say?' Others remarked, 'He seems to be a proclaimer of foreign divinities.' (This was because he was telling the good news about Jesus and the resurrection.) So they took him and brought him to the Areopagus and asked him, 'May we know what this new teaching is that you are presenting? It sounds rather strange to us, so we would like to know what it means.' Now all the Athenians and the foreigners living there would spend their time in nothing but telling or hearing something new.

Then Paul stood in front of the Areopagus and said, 'Athenians, I see how extremely religious you are in every way. For as I went through the city and looked carefully at the objects of your worship, I found among them an altar with the inscription, "To an unknown god." What therefore you worship as unknown, this I proclaim to you. The God who made the world and everything in it, he who is Lord of heaven and earth, does not live in shrines made by human hands, nor is he served by human hands, as though he needed any-thing, since he himself gives to all mortals life and breath and all things. From one ancestor he made all nations to inhabit the whole earth, and he allotted the times of their existence and the boundaries of the places where they would live, so that they would search for God and perhaps grope for him and find him – although indeed he is not far from each one of us. For "In him we live and move and have our being"; as even some of your own poets have said, "For we too are his offspring".

'Since we are God's offspring, we ought not to think that the deity is like gold, or silver, or stone, an image formed by the art and imagi-nation of mortals. While God has overlooked the times of human ignorance, now he commands all people everywhere to repent, because he has fixed a day on which he will have the world judged in righteousness by a man whom he has appointed, and of this he has given assurance to all by raising him from the dead.'

When they heard of the resurrection of the dead, some scoffed; but others said, 'We will hear you again about this.' At that point, Paul left them. But some of them joined him and became believers, including Dionysius the Areopagite and a woman named Damaris, and others with them.

Acts 17.16–33 (NRSV)

Having concentrated on preaching in synagogues and only then turning to sympathetic Gentiles, Paul's ministry takes a new turn upon his introduction to Athenian culture by beginning in the marketplace. As a condition of undertaking public preaching, Paul is summoned to a meeting of the city council, meeting on the Areopagus. There he argues that the 'unknown God' to whom that place is dedicated has not only been revealed through nature and human reason but also in the unique revelation of Jesus Christ.

The writer of Acts thus depicts Paul as debating not only with those of Jewish heritage but increasingly engaging with the intellectual roots of Graeco-Roman culture. A model of proclaiming the gospel (and of doing theology) emerges: initially, as a straightforwardly apologetic activity, using concepts familiar to a specific (and non-Christian) culture, and arguing that such human ideas are brought to fulfilment in the person and work of Jesus Christ. At another level, however, Paul must necessarily enter into the cosmopolitan, pluralist world of the Athenians on its own terms, and consider if their 'objects of worship' are entirely spurious or contain the seeds of authentic faith.

In this speech, therefore, Paul is portrayed as affirming the intellectual energy of the Athenians as indicative of a universal human search for truth. But Paul is in no doubt that, once explained, the good news of Christ crucified and risen will exercise a normative impact over indigenous world-views. Significantly, too, he is suggesting that human reason alone is insufficient to grasp the entirety of the nature of God. Nevertheless, the effectiveness of Paul's ministry – and his ability to win new, influential converts – depends on his willingness to harness the thought-forms of the prevailing culture and to depict it as an embryonic revelation of the God whose presence is already dimly apparent to human reasoning independent of revelation.

## Justin Instructs the Greeks on 'True Religion'

The formation of Christian theology from the second century to the Council of Nicaea (AD 451) may be understood as the codification of theological reflection based on three key practical endeavours: establishing patterns of Christian practice and formation; defining the normative boundaries of the Christian community against heterodoxy; and mounting a public account of itself to its surrounding cultural contexts. As well as the pedagogical, liturgical and pastoral tasks of forming new converts into a community of faith and of defending the boundaries of authentic belief and practice against numerous forms of 'heresy', Christians found themselves with an additional challenge of defending and proclaiming the faith within a pluralist intellectual context. As Christianity expanded beyond its original Jewish roots, it found itself engaging with the pagan cultures of the Graeco-Roman world. For Christianity to survive in the face of mounting political and philosophical opposition the new faith required ways of offering coherent and convincing accounts of itself. This was necessarily a dialogical task, involving rendering coherent the symbols and metaphors of Christianity to those of the dominant culture. In particular, that entailed a dialogue with Greek philosophy, which, together with the mystery cults, attracted most support from educated people. Christian writers of this era – and in particular the so-called 'Apologists' of the second century AD, such as Justin Martyr, Clement of Alexandria and Irenaeus – thus begin to construct 'a Christian culture in which philosophy plays an essential part in the education of the intelligent believer' (Stead, 1994, p. 133).

Many of these Apologists were Gentile converts. Their work had three main objectives: to instruct Greek converts to Christianity, to address Greek intellectual culture on its own terms, and to help mature Christians to deepen their faith. Their writings may therefore be seen as a form of practical theological formation in which Greek thought-forms are assimilated into emergent Christian theological formulations in practical pursuit of building up the faith community and presenting and defending the credibility of the gospel to an educated, pagan audience.

The writings of Justin (AD 100–165) represent some of the oldest extant texts of this kind. Justin was already well-versed in Stoic, Platonic and Pythagorean philosophy before his conversion to Christianity, and these remain an influential part of his continuing intellectual journey. What the poets, sages and philosophers glimpse partially, he argues, is brought to fulfilment in Christ. *Apology to the Gentiles*, addressed to the Emperor and Senators of Rome, portrays Christianity as sympathetic to the use of human reason in its search for truth, and invites dialogue with other philosophical traditions (Kee, *et al.* 1991, pp. 95–7). As well as fulfilling the prophecies of the Hebrew Scriptures and Jewish Law, Jesus may also be understood as the embodiment of the philosophical principle of eternal (divine) Reason – a concept articulated in Christian terms by the Johannine tradition of *Logos*, of Jesus as the incarnate, temporal manifestation of the transcendent God. Justin uses the term 'Christians before Christ' to suggest that those who have dedicated themselves to Greek philosophy (and the elevation of the principles of Reason) are already well on the way to understanding themselves as part of the community of those who follow Christ (as embodiment of divine *Logos*).

In *Hortatory Address to the Greeks*, attributed to Justin, he evokes the Greek philosophers in order to indicate the incoherence and inconsistency of their thinking in the light of Scripture, especially the testimony of the Hebrew prophets. He cites Plato, Socrates, Homer and others to demonstrate how limited and derivative is their teaching, a fact (he argues) they themselves acknowledge in references to the antiquity of Moses and the Law. Yet while the Greeks have shown themselves dedicated to the pursuit of 'true religion', he argues, it is impossible to learn it from sources proven unreliable. In contrast Scripture can be counted upon as the authentic revelation of God, surpassing the efforts of human wisdom.

> The time, then, ye men of Greece, is now come, that ye, having been persuaded by the secular histories that Moses and the rest of the prophets were far more ancient than any of those who have been esteemed sages among you, abandon the ancient delusion of your forefathers, and read the divine histories of the prophets, and ascertain from them the true religion; for they do not present to you artful discourses, nor speak speciously and plausibly . . . but use with simplicity the words and expressions which offer themselves, and declare to you whatever the Holy Ghost, who descended upon them, chose to teach through them to those who are desirous to learn the true religion . . .
>
> For neither will you commit any offence against your fathers, if you now show a desire to betake yourselves to that which is quite opposed to their error, since it is likely enough that they themselves are now lamenting in Hades, and repenting with a too late repentance; and if it were possible for them to show you thence what had befallen them after the termination of this life, ye would know from what fearful ills they desired to deliver you. But now, since it is not possible in this present life that ye either learn from them, or from those who here profess to teach that philosophy which is falsely so called, it follows as the one thing that remains for you to do, that, renouncing the error of your fathers, ye read the prophecies of the sacred writers . . . and learn from them what will give you life everlasting.
>
> Justin Martyr, 2001, Ch. XXXV

Justin's rhetoric is thus intended to convince his audience that the Christian gospel is superior in every way to the wisdom of the pagan world. The latter cannot be regarded as fully representing authentic religion; rather, as Justin argues, it offers but a partial prefiguration of Christianity.

## Thomas Aquinas on Reason and Revelation

The theological and philosophical system of the medieval theologian Thomas Aquinas (1225–74) was founded on the synthesis of Christian theology with Aristotelean philosophy. He was largely responsible for the rediscovery of ancient philosophy within the Western Church, but this was a revival largely mediated through his engagement with Arab philosophers, especially Averroes. He was also familiar with extant Jewish scholarship: the influence of Maimonides and Avicebron is evident within his great work *Summa Theologiae*, for example. So in the work of one of the greatest theologians of the Christian tradition we have a prominent example of a person who saw the development of Christian doctrine as necessarily proceeding in a dialogical fashion, via sustained engagement with the classics, with the philosophical systems of other faiths, and with what passed as 'scientific' enquiry of the time.

Aquinas is associated with the philosophical movement of 'scholasticism', which established itself in reaction to monasticism. Whereas the latter based its key sources of learning in study of Church fathers and ancient manuscripts – dependent, essentially, on interpretation of earlier authorities – scholasticism asserted that the exercise of reason was also a legitimate tool of intellectual enquiry. Although the scholastics read the ancients, their concerns were as much critical, synthetic and analytical as merely exegetical. A style of debate or interrogation of a text, known as the *disputatio*, was used to subject its meaning to logical scrutiny.

There is an important epistemology, or theory of knowledge, at the heart of scholasticism, which is also central to Aquinas's understanding of the nature of theology. It concerns the value of human rationality as a legitimate path to truth. This, in turn, is related to the doctrine of natural law, which argues that God can be genuinely discerned in the patterns of nature – including humanity's rational faculties – and that there is no fundamental contradiction between divine revelation and the natural order. To act in accordance with the dictates of reason, therefore, will not lead humanity astray, because God has set down in the laws of nature nothing that will contradict the laws of God (or as Aquinas put it, 'the reason of divine wisdom'). Even if nature (and reason) remained partial and flawed, Aquinas argued, it still represented one of the means by which humanity could apprehend the will of God. Indeed, natural law constitutes a body of moral principles that, by virtue of its universal character, is both available and compelling to all rational creatures and thus something to which humanity must conform themselves in order to realize its proper end or 'good'.

Now, although the truth of the Christian faith which we have discussed surpasses the capacity of the reason, nevertheless that truth that the human reason is naturally endowed to know cannot be opposed to the truth of the Christian faith. For that with which the human reason is naturally endowed is clearly most true; so much so, that it is impossible for us to think of such truths as false. Nor is it permissable to believe as false that which we hold by faith, since this is confirmed in a way that is so clearly divine. Since, therefore, only the false is opposed to the true, as is clearly evident from an examination of their definitions, it is impossible that the truth of faith should be opposed to those principles that the human reason knows naturally. Furthermore, that which is introduced into the soul of the student by the teacher is contained in the knowledge of the teacher – unless his teaching is fictitious, which it is improper to say of God. Now, the knowledge of the principles that are known to us naturally has been implanted in us by God, for God is the Author of our nature. These principles, therefore, are also contained by the divine Wisdom. Hence, whatever is opposed to them is opposed to the divine Wisdom, and therefore, cannot come from God. That which we hold by faith as divinely revealed, therefore, cannot be contrary to our natural knowledge.

*Summa Contra Gentiles* Bk 1, Ch. 7, in Pegis, 1955, p. 74

Thus, Thomas advances the conviction that the ordinary processes of human reasoning and knowledge are capable of grasping theological truths. The natural world and human experience are intrinsically valuable as theatres of divine revelation. It is not necessary to have been inducted into the propositions or theological 'grammar' of specific faith-traditions. God may be apprehended through the gift of revelation and the quest of rational enquiry. This extends to those beyond the Christian community, to embrace the classical, Jewish and Arab world. Aquinas was also adamant, however, that human reason – and thus, also, anything outwith the Christian revelation – was but a partial and approximate glimpse of the consummate, divinely revealed, truth:

Sensible things, from which the human reason takes the origin of its knowledge, retain within themselves some sort of trace of a likeness to God. This is so imperfect, however, that it is absolutely inadequate to manifest the substance of God. For effects bear within themselves, in their own way, the likeness of their causes, since an agent produces its like; yet an effect does not always reach to the full likeness of its cause. Now, the human reason is related to the knowledge of the truth of faith (a truth which can be most evident only to those who see the divine substance) in such a way that it can gather certain likenesses of it, which are yet not sufficient so that the truth of faith may be comprehended as being understood demonstratively or through itself. Yet it is useful for the human reason to exercise itself in such arguments, however weak they may be, provided only that there be present no presumption to comprehend or to demonstrate.

*Summa Contra Gentiles*, Bk 1, Ch. 8, in Pegis, 1955, pp. 75–6

Aquinas wrote his mammoth work, *Summa Theologiae*, as an exercise in demonstrating the compatibility of reason and revelation as routes to greater theological understanding. Thus, for example, his five proofs for the existence of God were an attempt to show that theological discourse could be conducted in language that was derived from logic rather than Scripture or tradition ('What God Is Not', in Aquinas, 1991, Bk 1, Ch. 1). Such a 'natural theology' takes as evidence the principles of scientific observation and argument, as Aquinas deduces divine presence from the very structures of nature itself – from the very order of things: 'Everything in nature, therefore, is directed to its goal by someone with understanding, and this we call *God*' (Aquinas, 1991, Bk 1, Ch. 1, p. 14).

This highly deductive (building on successive stages of logical argument) method is intended to demonstrate how theological conclusions can be arrived at from observation of natural phenomena and philosophical analysis, and that the discourse of faith is not incompatible with the discourse of experience. Nevertheless, although God has revealed Godself through natural law, which is accessible to human reason and constitutive of the moral good, there is for Aquinas always a limit to the power of human reason alone; for there are some aspects of divine mystery that will transcend and exceed human understanding – and thus the world of rational enquiry, human quest for truth, will never fully capture the true nature of God:

There is a twofold mode of truth in what we profess about God. Some truths about God exceed all the ability of the human reason. Such is the truth that God is triune. But there are some truths which the natural reason also is able to reach. Such are that God exists, that He is one, and the like. In fact, such truths about God have been proved demonstrably by philosophers, guided by the light of the natural reason.

*Summa Contra Gentiles*, Bk 1, Ch. 3, in Pegis, 1955, p. 63

## Schleiermacher and the 'Cultured Despisers'

Friedrich Schleiermacher (1768–1834) is regarded by many as the founder of modern liberal theology. Schleiermacher's theological legacy has been to establish the possibility of 'God-talk' as rooted in what David Tracy terms 'common human experience and language'. This is accessible as much through everyday experience as the specifics of doctrinal revelation. Such a 'sense and taste for the Infinite' (Schleiermacher 1960, p. 94) finds expression in cultural, artistic and scientific activity as much as it does in formal religion. Through his exposure to fashionable literary and cultural circles in Berlin from 1796, Schleiermacher began to put into practice his conviction that truth emerged dialectically, via intellectual interchange between friends and collaborators.

Schleiermacher was sympathetic to the humanist principles at the heart of the Western Enlightenment of the eighteenth century, yet he was also concerned to defend the credibility of Christianity against those who argued that the faith of miracles or divine intervention was no longer tenable in a scientific, rationalist world. Thus, in *On Religion: Speeches to its Cultured Despisers* ([1799] 1994), addressed to those who were intellectually sophisticated but sceptical towards religion, Schleiermacher argues that the deepest fulfilment of our humanity is to be found in the religious quest. Theologically, the goal of this quest is presented not as a supreme, transcendent Deity, mediated through the magisterial authority of the institutional Church, but rather the experiential ground of all being who is encountered within the individual's heart and mind. Thus Schleiermacher presents the outward forms of religious observance as less significant than the inward disposition of religious experience. Experiential religion is at the core of theological discourse; doctrinal codification is derivative and secondary. This approach bears the stamp of Pietism, a revival of personal religion in reaction to the rationalism of the Enlightenment. Inward experience and feeling is understood as the grounding of religious experience and knowledge. There are many similarities with the aesthetic movement known as Romanticism in which the immediacy of beauty and feeling become the paths to true knowledge.

This, for Schleiermacher, is the essence of religion. Everyone is possessed, potentially, of the capacity to experience such a 'God-consciousness', although he believed that the epitome of such awareness was Jesus of Nazareth himself. Thus, the general awareness of the transcendent God was given specific and ultimate expression in Jesus Christ.

It is said that the more clearly we conceive anything to be entirely conditioned by the interdependence of nature, the less can we arrive at the feeling of its absolute dependence on God; and, conversely, the more vivid this latter feeling is the more indefinitely must we leave its interrelatedness with nature an open question. But . . . we cannot admit such a contradiction between the two ideas. For otherwise (since everything would present itself to us as always in the system of nature), as our knowledge of the world grew perfect, the development of the pious self-consciousness in ordinary life would cease; which is quite contrary to our presupposition that piety is of the essence of human nature. And on the other hand, conversely, the love of religion would be opposed to all love of research and all widening of our knowledge of nature; which would entirely contradict the principle that the observation of creation leads to the consciousness of God. And besides, prior to the completion of both tendencies the most competent naturalist would have to be the least religious of men, and *vice versa*. Now, as the human soul is just as necessarily predisposed towards a knowledge of the world as towards a consciousness of God, it can only be a false wisdom which would put religion aside, and a misconceived religion for love of which the progress of knowledge is to be arrested.

Schleiermacher, 1830, quoted in Clements, 1987, p. 173

Schleiermacher was essentially concerned with the construction of a Christian apologetics, stressing the need to return to the essence of religious disposition that lay ultimately in the human heart and not in outward ecclesial structures, although corporate religious practice was an important element of the cultivation of one's religious sensibilities. Similarly, despite the primacy of feeling as the chief arbiter of authentic religion, the demands of human communication required that some kind of rationally accessible account be given of religious experience – hence the importance of theology as a means of mediating between the personal and the cultural. However, this means that Schleiermacher regarded all theological statements as conditioned by a particular cultural context. Concrete historical embodiments of religious experience were necessary, although they should always be differentiated from the transcendent, divine source of that feeling of utter dependency which characterizes the human encounter with the sacred.

## The Method Realized

*Karl Rahner and 'Aggiornamento'*

The German Jesuit priest and theologian Karl Rahner (1904–84) saw himself in many ways as the heir to the Thomist tradition, although he was frustrated at much of the defensiveness and sterility of scholasticism. It seemed to him to have become overly dependent on a relatively closed canon of authoritative texts rather than continuing the original vision of Aquinas in his engagement with significant philosophical movements of his day. Rahner's doctoral study concerned a section of Aquinas's *Summa Theologiae* on the nature of the intellect, and whether human enquiry into the nature of Being and ultimate reality was sufficient evidence for the mind's potential to grasp the nature of divine transcendence itself.

Under the influence of the French Jesuit Joseph Maréchal, Rahner immersed himself in contemporary philosophy – studying under Martin Heidegger at one stage – in order to bring such insights into creative dialogue with theology. Like Aquinas, Rahner suggested that there was an innate desire for God at the heart of human nature. Even if this was partially experienced as an ineffable reality beyond that of language and perception, it was nevertheless a stirring of consciousness towards the divine, although it awaited its ultimate apotheosis in the person and revelation of God in Christ.

> For everything human beings do (even their secular activity) in concrete freedom oriented to God, and open by God's grace upon immediacy to God, is free activity that is properly Christian (when rightly performed), and always and everywhere sanctified activity, activity with a sanctified meaning. This is verified even when this concreteness cannot be immediately deduced and procured from its ultimate religious purpose. Still, it can and must be a matter of a decision ultimately signed with a religious note – even though this decision cannot be immediately urged upon individual human beings and profane society by the official Church, but must be discovered by individual Christians themselves in an existential ethic.
>
> 'Courage to Let the World Be World'
> in Rahner, 1982, p. 195

At the heart of this theology lies a conviction that human reason has been designed with the capability of discerning the nature of transcendence in history. Rahner also places great emphasis on the power of divine grace as something universally given prior to any conscious or rational profession of faith, which effectively means that anyone is capable of theological reflection. Rahner is often associated with the exposition of something known as 'anonymous Christianity', which can be seen as an attempt to 'Christianize' the implicit faith-commitments of non-Christians. Given his understanding of the convergence of nature and grace, however, it is better appreciated as indicating the 'implicitness' of the apprehension of God than an attempt to colonize other faiths in a pluralist context, describing those who do not profess a doctrinal faith but nevertheless seek to incarnate divine virtues of compassion, charity and love in forms of practical action.

The fundamental problem of the relation between philosophy and theology is whether and how they can simultaneously be basic sciences (that is, shed light on being in general and existence in a reflexive, systematic way) in such a way that man need neither abandon, nor sacrifice the character of either discipline, that is, be faced with the choice of being either a philosopher or a theologian. In order to elucidate this problem we must first observe that Catholic theology draws an essential distinction between nature and grace, and consequently between natural knowledge of God and revelation; so that by its very nature it does not simply tolerate philosophy but actually needs it. That is to say, Catholic theology does not raise the structure of revelation and faith upon the ruins of the Christian intellect, sinner though man be. Furthermore, history shows that theology has always thought in philosophical terms, among others; and against Modernism and all religion of feeling, Catholic theology holds tenaciously to the historical fact that from the outset revelation and grace address the whole man, not least his intellect – a pertinent fact when one is considering the nature of religion.

The Christian believer as such lives in the conviction that intellect, nature and history are the creation, revelation, and property of the God who is the one truth, the source of all being and truth, and has produced historical, verbal revelation to perfect and exalt his creation. The fact, then, that a thing lies 'outside' a particular sphere of earthly reality (in this case outside historical revelation, the Church and theology) by no means removes it from God's domain so far as the Christian is concerned. So that it is neither necessary nor permissible for him to make a closed and final system of theology at the expense of philosophy.

'Philosophy and Theology'
in Rahner and Vorgrimmler, 1965, p. 355

Rahner had a considerable influence over one of the defining moments of twentieth-century Western theology, namely the documents and debates of Vatican II (1962–65), called by Pope John XXIII, and designed to be a thoroughgoing rearticulation of the self-understanding of the Church and the nature of faith in the light of contemporary social and cultural conditions. Following a century of resistance to modernity and secular culture on the part of the magisterium, the documents of Vatican II represent a very different emphasis on the part of Roman Catholic theology towards the nature of revelation and dialogue with the world. Vatican II continues much of the spirit of Rahner's work in relation to theology and secular culture, by establishing a new openness to contemporary thought and social movements on the part of Roman Catholic theology. It calls for a more dialogical, rather than dogmatic theological style, in which human problems and concerns are integrated into theological discourse, and the Church is regarded as a partner in a common human quest for meaning, truth and justice. Secular wisdom is to be respected for its ability to enlighten and expand the life of the Church.

In particular, the Pastoral Constitution on the Church in the Modern World (or *Gaudium et Spes* after the opening phrase of the document, 'The joys and hopes . . . of this age') is the fullest expression of the Council's predominant attitude towards social issues: a willingness to break with the caution and introspection of earlier traditions and embrace with enthusiasm a process of *aggiornamento*, or adaptation and openness towards the world. Essentially, the theology underpinning the document is one of a servant Church, affirming human strivings for the common good. As a result, much traditional ecclesiology is revised: the Church is no longer an exclusive, introspective community but one that exists for the perfection of the entire human community. Similarly, by virtue of the inherent dignity of all human persons, the document argues that the Church must recognize the integrity of human scientific, artistic and political activity as opportunities of divine disclosure, to the extent of fostering dialogue rather than condemnation.

### The Church and the Modern World

Just as it is in the world's interest to acknowledge the Church as a historical reality, and to recognize her good influence, so the Church herself knows how richly she has profited by the history and development of humanity.

Thanks to the experience of past ages, the progress of the sciences, and the treasures hidden in the various forms of human culture, the nature of man himself [sic] is more clearly revealed and new roads to truth are opened. These benefits profit the Church, too. For, from the beginning of her history, she has learned to express the message of Christ with the help of the ideas and terminology of various peoples, and has tried to clarify it with the wisdom of the philosophers, too . . .

To promote such an exchange, the Church requires special help, particularly in our day, when things are changing very rapidly and the ways of thinking are exceedingly various. She must rely on those who live in the world, are versed in different institutions and specialties [sic], and grasp their innermost significance in the eyes of both believers and unbelievers. With the help of the Holy Spirit, it is the task of the entire People of God, especially pastors and theologians, to hear, distinguish, and interpret the many voices of our age, and to judge them in the life of the divine Word. In this way, revealed truth can always be more deeply penetrated, better understood, and set forth to greater advantage.

Since the Church has a visible and social structure as a sign of her unity in Christ, she can and ought to be enriched by the development of human social life. The reason is not that the constitution given her by Christ is defective, but so that she may understand it more penetratingly, express it better, and adjust it more successfully to our times.

*Gaudium et Spes*, in Abbot, 1966, pp. 245–6

*Gaudium et Spes* demonstrates great openness to insights from the 'secular' world, and accepts that the Church might absorb the understandings of human psychology, the political and social sciences and scientific knowledge. Divine revelation is inseparable from the unfolding of history, by which all humanity is moving towards the fullness of truth. This reflects a theology of creation that regards the entire created order as capable of revealing the grace of God. While the Church makes a significant contribution to this process, it must also respect the value of autonomous wisdom, especially that of everyday, lived experience, as capable of facilitating the development and growth of human individuals and communities. Theological reflection thus becomes a matter of attending as much to the spirit of the world, and the revelation herein, as of interpreting classical texts and teachings. In theory, theological expertise is extended to the laity and those engaged in secular as well as ecclesial practice, principles which closely echo Rahner's project to reconcile the realms of nature and grace.

*Tillich's Method of Correlation*

Paul Tillich (1886–1965), a German Protestant theologian, also embodied the principle of Christian theology engaging with the contemporary *Zeitgeist,* or spirit of the times. After serving in the First World War he was convinced that the task of theology was to construct an 'apologetics' comprehensible to modern culture. Like Karl Barth, Tillich judged that the disillusionment of the war constituted a 'crisis' of Western culture (and Christianity, especially liberal theology), which required a response in the form of a re-evaluation of the tasks and nature of theological discourse. Tillich concluded that the existential and moral questions of each generation – the very symptoms of this crisis of confidence – constituted the real subject-matter to which Christian theology must address itself. The task of articulating a body of understanding by which people can live meaningfully in today's world is fundamental to the theological enterprise. This necessarily involves engaging with the dilemmas that preoccupy them and advancing responses that are both theologically authentic but culturally relevant. This Tillich termed a process of *correlation*:

> The answers implied in the event of revelation are meaningful only in so far as they are in correlation with questions concerning the whole of our existence . . . Only those who have experienced the shock of transitoriness, the anxiety in which they are aware of their finitude, the threat of non-being, can understand what the notion of God means. Only those who have experienced the tragic ambiguities of our historical existence and have totally questioned the meaning of existence can understand what the symbol of the Kingdom of God means . . .
>
> *Systematic Theology I*, 1953, quoted in Tinsley, 1973, p. 40

> . . . The method of correlation shows, at every point of Christian thought, the interdependence between the ultimate questions to which philosophy . . . is driven and the answers given in the Christian message. Philosophy cannot answer ultimate or existential questions *qua* philosophy. If the philosopher tries to answer them . . . he becomes a theologian. And, conversely, theology cannot answer those questions without accepting their presuppositions and implications. Question and answer determine each other; if they are separated, the traditional answers become unintelligible, and the actual questions remain unanswered. The method of correlation aims to overcome this situation.
>
> *The Protestant Principle*, p. xliii, quoted in Tinsley, 1973:39

In 1933 Tillich fled from the Nazi regime in Germany and settled in the United States. He joined the influential New York Psychology Group in the 1940s, which was concerned for dialogue between theo-logy and modern psychologies. Its membership included leading therapists and theologians such as Seward Hiltner, Eric Fromm, Carl Rogers and Rollo May. This opportunity pushed Tillich towards a very specific example of the correlative method, by enabling him to consider the nature of the connections between psychology and reli-gion and in particular how insights emerging from the psychothera-peutic movements – such as guilt, freedom, catharsis and repression – corresponded with traditional Christian concepts such as sin, grace and forgiveness. He regarded the former as contemporary expressions of enduring human dilemmas to which the gospel offers definitive answers. The theologian is bound to attend to such cultural specifics in order to understand how in each generation the generic existential issues are articulated. He concluded that there was an essential con-tinuity and convergence between the language of psychotherapy and the language of faith; and that the activities of counselling and therapy were akin to the functions of traditional pastoral care in creating and implementing 'the good news of acceptance'. For example, in the ser-mon 'You are Accepted', Tillich echoes psychological terminology by characterizing human malaise in terms of anxiety, rejection and estrangement, regarding them as psychologized versions of classical notions of sin. In response, Tillich moves to reiterate classic biblical doctrines of justification by faith through grace, although he presents this in the humanistic terminology of unconditional acceptance:

Grace strikes us when we are in great pain and restlessness. It strikes us when we walk through the dark valley of a meaningless and empty life. It strikes us when we feel our separation is deeper than usual, because we have violated another life, a life which we loved, or from which we were estranged. It strikes us when our disgust for our own being, our indifference, our weakness, our hostility, and our lack of direction and composure have become intolerable for us. It strikes us when year after year the longed for perfection of life does not appear, when the old compulsions reign within us as they have for decades, when despair destroys all joy and courage.

Sometimes at that moment a wave of life breaks into our darkness, and it is as though a voice were saying: 'You are accepted. *You are accepted*, accepted by that which is greater than you, and the name of which you do not know. Do not ask for the name now; perhaps you will find it later. Do not try to do anything now; perhaps you will do too much. Do not seek for anything; do not perform anything; do not intend anything. *Simply accept the fact that you are accepted.* If that happens to us, we experience grace.

'You Are Accepted', in Tillich, 1962, p. 63

Tillich did not believe, however, that the message of 'acceptance' in psychological terms could be a surrogate or substitute for theological truth. Rather, the work and theoretical perspectives of psychology represented partial prefigurations of a deeper theological truth. The 'power of acceptance' embodied in the therapeutic relationship went far beyond human or finite agency, and could only find its end and source in God, the 'Ground of our Being' that undergirds and animates everything. Certainly, the sermons in *The Shaking of the Foundations* reiterate the conviction that, no matter how meaningless or frustrating our human search for truth appears, or how exhausting our struggle to speak of God and faith in the modern world may feel, God will answer; and the Scriptures provide definitive assurance of God's promises and presence.

So a person's acceptance by others is to be seen as part of a universal order of love and grace sustained by the ultimate Ground and Power. God calls everything into being, and is therefore the source of humanity's struggle against non-being, and its affirmation into being by overcoming the powers of brokenness and alienation. And it follows, therefore, that correlation is both about recasting traditional religious language into a modern idiom and about placing psychological distress and existential angst within the primary (and normative) context of theological truth.

Tillich therefore affirmed the sufficiency of psychotherapy and the modern psychologies in general, arguing that their insights offered relevant insights into human experience for theologians, as part of a deeper existential and ontological framework that pointed towards God: a sort of 'prelude' to the Divine or ultimate. So he was not arguing, as humanistic and non-directive counsellors would, that humans have an innate capacity for self-actualization or healing, if only their therapist can create a sufficiently guilt-free zone of freedom. The question is whether the quality of the interpersonal relationship, or the technical procedures of analysis or regression or whatever, is sufficient for healing; or whether there is a transcendent or divine dimension that only works through grace. Tillich believes quite clearly in the transcendence of God, that God surpasses human knowledge and exceeds human efforts. There is a mystery and magnitude about God that leads Tillich to insist on the incompleteness of human reason, revelation and pastoral practice in the face of the radical otherness and supremacy of God (see, for example, 'The Escape from God' in Tillich, 1962).

Above all, he was concerned to explore the existential importance of psychological terms, and their significance as metaphors for the entirety of the human condition itself, rather than handy labels to describe a clinical disorder. However, it may be said that in so doing, Tillich actually abstracts such terms as anxiety, repression and guilt and severs their link into specific developmental patterns or contexts. Does he then so generalize these terms as to lose their origins in specific and acute psychological states, brought about not by simply being human, but by particular instances of abuse, psychological distress or mental illness?

Nevertheless, this approach was consistent with Tillich's overall professional goal to make Christianity understandable and relevant to religiously sceptical people living in a modern, secular, technological culture. Tillich was not the only person to believe that in the new psychologies and psychotherapies Christian theology and ministry had found not only a 'secular' language that brought to life older theological doctrines, but also an entire therapeutic discipline, with associated professional and clinical communities, which could offer paths of practical care that would embody and enact these principles. One of Tillich's important contributions was thus to stimulate those church-related practitioners to consider the theological implications of their work and to regard this as a continuing part of the development of theological discourse.

However, his correlational project was not limited to the psychotherapeutic sphere. For Tillich, the human quest to overcome existential anxiety and find meaning extended beyond the purely clinical and psychological and was also visibly demonstrated in much contemporary artistic, literary and philosophical endeavour.

> The analysis of the human situation employs materials made available by man's creative self-interpretation in all realms of culture. Philosophy contributes, but so do poetry, drama, the novel, therapeutic psychology, and sociology. The theologian organizes these materials in relation to the answer given by the Christian message.
>
> Tillich, 1968, p. 69

Tillich's understanding of cultural movements was that they represented a common human vocabulary that addressed in every era the perennial questions of anxiety, death, guilt, forgiveness and redemption. Artists, philosophers and social theorists frequently appropriated and reinterpreted classical theological themes, often unconsciously. Such activity represented a pressing invitation to the theologian to offer explicitly theological responses to the questions raised by culture; as a form of apologetic commendation of the Christian gospel, but also as an opportunity to engage in a common enquiry into the nature of the mysteries of the human condition.

In his commentary on Tillich's method of correlation, Seward Hiltner (1909–84), fellow member with Tillich of the New York Psychology Group in the 1940s, and latterly Professor of Pastoral Theology at Princeton and Chicago, introduced a significant area of critique that subsequently became an important area of development in correlational theology. Hiltner asks if Tillich's assumption that 'culture' provides the questions and 'theology' the answers is too simplistic. Hiltner speculates whether the correlation should be conceived as more of a 'two-way street'. In other words, cultural information, non-theological disciplines, art, literature and human sciences, may themselves contain new insights not already available within the Christian revelation, rendering the dynamic of interrogation and response mutual and dialectical.

Not everything is yet clear about Tillich's use of the key term 'correlation' to describe his theological method. Plainly he intends by it to establish theological relevance; theology does not talk in a corner by itself but speaks to the vital questions men ask. Thus he says to the theologian that culture and life cannot be neglected, and to the ordinary man that faith has a message for him. But to what extent is correlation a two-way method? . . .

We believe that a full two-way street is necessary in order to describe theological method. If we hold that theology is always assimilation of the faith, not just the abstract idea of the faith apart from its reception, then it becomes necessary to say that culture may find answers to questions raised by faith as well as to assert that faith has answers to questions raised by culture.

Hiltner, 1958, p. 223

## Revised Critical Correlation

Tillich's work and Hiltner's corrective criticisms have been developed more recently by the American Roman Catholic theologian David Tracy. Tracy has to a certain extent placed himself as the living successor to an earlier generation – Paul Tillich, but also Bernard Lonergan and Karl Rahner from the Roman Catholic traditions – within the context of twentieth-century North American liberal theology. Like his mentors and teachers, Tracy attempts to mediate between cultural concerns and theological truth-claims. The task of theology, he says, is to locate itself at the interface between human experience and culture, and Christian truth-claims. Tracy argues that the event of Jesus Christ, albeit mediated by historical tradition, tested and developed by the best literary, historical and critical enquiries, and correlated with our present situation, is the source of Christian revelation. He refers sometimes to the 'Christian fact' and this for him stands for the sum total of theological tradition.

> ... the word 'fact' serves to remind us that Christianity is not something we invent. Christianity exists and demands rediscovery and interpretation – the latter including retrieval, and critique and suspicion – but not invention. Second, the choice of the word 'fact' [over message/tradition] is also meant to remind us that the Christian fact includes the whole range of classic texts, symbols, events, persons, images, rituals, and practices from the New Testament forward ... Any interpreter of the Christian fact is likely to develop some selective principle as the central clue or focal meaning for the whole. For myself, that central clue is the event and person of Jesus Christ as the decisive disclosure of the Christian construal of God, self, and world. But any choice of either a central symbol ... must hold itself responsible to correctives from the full range of symbols, texts, images, events, and so forth. Only then is the full range of the Christian fact allowed to play its proper hermeneutical role.
>
> Tracy, 1981, p. 64

Crucially, however, Tracy argues that, in the process of hearing the claims of modern culture in all its urgency and complexity, Christian theology itself must be prepared to undergo *revision*. Unlike Tillich, Tracy wants to argue that the correlation between cultural problems and questions – including the data of the modern psychologies – and the Christian interpretation of life, may take a number of forms. There may be complete *identity* when a cultural expression and a Christian claim do say the same thing; but there may be occasions when the correlation is one of *analogy*, when there is similarity but not complete resemblance. However, there may also be points of *non-identity* between the values or answers of culture and Christian perspectives. In this case how do we decide between them? How do we proceed to discover what and where is truth in such a situation?

So what Tracy calls 'common human experience and language' (rather than 'culture') and Christian 'fact' (often represented for him as 'classic texts' which serve as paradigms of traditional truths) are mutually critical and corrective. Tracy's book *Blessed Rage for Order* sets out his model of 'revised critical correlation'.

> Fundamentally, the revisionist model holds that contemporary fundamental theology is best understood as philosophical reflection upon *both* the meanings disclosed in our common human experience *and* the meanings disclosed in the primary texts of the Christian tradition (1975, p. 237, our emphasis).

> In short, either the public character of the fundamental questions religion addresses (from the side of the 'situation') or the fully public character of the responses that any major religious tradition articulates (from the side of the tradition) demand a theological discipline which will investigate and correlate, through mutually critical correlations, questions and responses in *both* situation and tradition.
>
> Tracy, 1981, p. 64

What has to happen is a process of mutual interrogation, with further evidence or testimony given to support the insights and claims of both sides. Both sources of data thus pose questions *and* answers; both need to be investigated historically and hermeneutically, and in this way correlation exercises a mutually critical and revisionist influence. This opens theology to critique from the social sciences, from historical criticism, from feminist, post-colonial and other perspectives. So the philosophical and hermeneutical project of theology is to embark on 'the dramatic confrontation, the mutual illuminations and corrections, the possible basic reconciliation between the principal values, cognitive claims, and existential faiths of both a reinterpreted post-modern consciousness and a reinterpreted Christianity' (Tracy, 1975, p. 37).

Tracy represents the most accomplished example of Schleiermacher's tradition of addressing the 'cultured despisers' of religion. He considers that theological discourse must be accessible and accountable to a variety of vantage-points – and especially from the three 'publics' or constituencies of Church, academy and society. In this advocacy of a public theology Tracy brings together the two strands of the correlational model: (i) the apologetic, or an attempt to give a coherent account of Christianity in terms accessible to its cultural context; (ii) the dialectical, insisting on theology's openness to renewal from secular insights by virtue of their grounding in common human experience.

## Correlation Put to Work

In their book *Method in Ministry* (1980), James D. Whitehead and Evelyn E. Whitehead offer a practical theology of ministry in which theological reflection is understood to be the 'process of bringing to bear in the practical decisions of ministry the resources of Christian faith' (Whitehead and Whitehead, 1980, p. 6). Such a process of theological reflection is problem-centred, transformative – and correlational. 'The goal is a pastoral decision, a ministerial response to a contemporary decision' (p. 14). Theological competence is thus measured according to practical efficacy and the sources and norms for pastoral action are drawn from three 'sources of information: Christian tradition, personal and corporate experience and cultural information' (p. 1). All three sources are pluriform, overlapping and 'ambiguous'; and theological reflection entails a process of clarifying and interpreting their relevance for contemporary ministry. In what they characterize as their 'model' of correlation, Whitehead and Whitehead choose to represent it as a triangular conversation provoked by a ministerial concern, as follows:

**Theological Reflection in Ministry**

tradition
*pluriform in*
*Scripture and history*

MINISTERIAL CONCERN

cultural information
*data from the culture*
*(e.g. social sciences)*
*that influence the issue*

personal experience
*what the individual believer and the community bring to the reflection*

Like Hiltner and Tracy, the Whiteheads perceive the correlational dialogue as mutually transforming:

> On a complex pastoral question no ready-made answer is lying in wait in the tradition or in our experience. But in a truly assertive dialogue a solution – tentative, debatable, reversible – will be generated.

This is more than a confidence in educational technique; it is a theological conviction about how the Spirit generates a historical tradition.

p. 39

The three sources of practical-theological reflection are synthesized according to a three-fold 'method', similar to Joseph Cardijn's process of 'see-judge-act' in Roman Catholic practical theology (see Chapter 6):

THREE-STAGE METHOD OF THEOLOGICAL REFLECTION
IN MINISTRY

I ATTENDING
Seek out the information on a particular pastoral concern that is available in personal experience, Christian tradition, and cultural sources.

II ASSERTION
Engage the information from these three sources in a process of mutual clarification and challenge in order to expand and deepen religious insight.

III DECISION
Move from insight through decision to concrete pastoral action.

Whitehead and Whitehead, 1980, p. 22

In 'The Practical Play of Theology' (Whitehead, 1987) James Whitehead elaborates further on the correlative method, emphasizing that the dynamic of correlation is fuelled by both intellect and imagination, as critical engagement with experience, cultural information and tradition takes place at both rational and intuitive levels.

As we developed this model of reflection in ministry we were persuaded of the importance of imagination as an alternate source of religious information. We were convinced . . . that our deepest convictions and biases abide not in clear and available intellectual concepts, but in the images and fantasies often hidden somewhere within us.

p. 40

The centrality of imagination suggests that the model must be pursued heuristically, experimentally and provisionally: no truth in this respect is absolute, but must be tested in the 'play' of lived experience. Failure is thus a risk, but a necessary element of the maturing of faith-communities. What drives this process overall, however, is the desire to undertake practical (ministerial) action, in response to felt need, that is relevant to its particular situation and explicitly informed by the values of faith. As it emerges from the crucible of correlative interpretation, theology articulates the narratives and metaphors of faith in new imperatives for transformative action. In this respect, the Whiteheads' proposals continue Tillich's emphasis on the task of correlation as providing a route by which the practical or existential issues of human experience can be placed in creative dialogue with the resources of the Christian faith – in order to develop strategies for faithful living: 'The reality of theology, which theological reflection seeks to disclose, is the presence of God in people's experience, a presence that invites them to encounter God where they are and to participate in the divine life which is offered to them there' (Kinast, 2000, p. 3).

## Augmenting the Tradition: Rosemary Radford Ruether

The feminist theologian and historian Rosemary Radford Ruether stands in many respects within the revised Tillichian tradition described above, in that she is adamant that Christian theology must respond anew to the intellectual, political, cultural (and for her, ecological) challenges of each generation. Yet her feminist theological method is not only critical but also reconstructive. She argues that the Christian tradition stands in need of a radical corrective through the inclusion of extra-theological voices.

For Ruether, such a process is necessary because of the androcentric (male-centred or male-dominated) nature of much of Christian doctrine and the structures and practices of the Church. This represents a distortion of the essence of the Christian gospel, which for her is a message of equality, human dignity, reconciliation (between women and men, God and humanity, non-human nature and humanity) and justice. This constitutes a 'golden thread' within the historical tradition that is frequently obscured and degraded, but survives in marginal and oppositional traditions both in Church and wider society. The task, therefore, of rebuilding Christian theology in a more authentic (and, Ruether would argue, historically genuine) fashion requires a *critique* of the points at which tradition has misrepresented the spirit of the gospel; and then, a *reconstruction* of theology according to emancipatory principles.

The process of correlation may be seen as informing both stages of

Ruether's critical and reconstructive project. First, she seeks to expose the ways in which Christian tradition has fallen short of the criteria of justice and reconciliation. Ruether's *critical principle* of gender inclusion and equality forms the key criterion by which the received tradition is judged and which reveals how far the core revelation at its heart has become corrupted:

> The critical principle of feminist theology is the promotion of the full humanity of women. Whatever denies, diminishes, or distorts the full humanity of women is, therefore, appraised as not redemptive. Theologically speaking, whatever diminishes or denies the full humanity of women must be presumed not to reflect the divine or an authentic relation to the divine, or to reflect the authentic nature of things, or to be the message or work of an authentic redeemer or community of redemption.
>
> This negative principle also implies the positive principle: what does promote the full humanity of women is of the Holy, it does reflect true relation to the divine, it is the true nature of things, the authentic message of redemption and the mission of redemptive community. But the meaning of this positive principle – namely, the full humanity of women – is not fully known. It has not existed in history. What we have known is the negative principle of the denigration and marginalization of women's humanity. Still, the humanity of women, although diminished, has not been destroyed. It has constantly affirmed itself, often in only limited and subversive ways, and it has been touchstone [sic] against which we test and criticize all that diminishes us. In the process we experience our larger potential that allows us to begin to imagine a world without sexism.
>
> Ruether, 1993, p. 19

As the passage in the text box indicates, Ruether is not arguing for the total abandonment of the Christian tradition, but merely advancing a criterion by which it should be judged. This judgement also reveals what non-theological sources might be required to restore it to its own core values. These values Ruether understands as lodged most definitively in a doctrine of human nature as made in the image of God, male and female; the prophetic tradition of the Hebrew Bible and the ministry of Jesus of Nazareth, which proclaims an iconoclastic vision of social justice as true religion; and in communities of faith who strive for a world free of hierarchy, domination or alienation. So the purpose of correlating extra-theological sources is fundamentally a restorative one – the critical principle that guides such a process is both internal to Christianity (inclusion, prophecy, redemption, justice) and external insofar as non-Christian movements and values may often embody such principles more fully than theological tradition. They are acceptable resources for a renewed feminist theology because they remind us of the deeper 'golden thread' of an inclusive and liberating Christian message. They point out the inadequacies of the received tradition according to its very own standards buried within the past.

Chief among the extra-theological sources against which Ruether judges the adequacy of official tradition is the category of 'women's experience'. But Ruether is adamant that she is not departing significantly from orthodox theological method by using this as a key criterion (or *norm*) by which the adequacy of tradition is measured. For, she argues, all theology derives from human experience and understanding; feminist theology simply indicates how the perspectives of a minority (by and large, educated, white, Western men) have been allowed to stand as representative of *universal* experience. Ruether here deploys a hermeneutic (a strategy of critical interpretation) akin to Marxist exposure of 'ideology' (see Chapter 6): theologies that purport to portray universal and value-free truths may actually be exclusive of much human experience, serving to silence or even pathologize alternative perspectives.

> The uniqueness of feminist theology lies not in its use of the criterion of experience but rather in its use of *women's* experience, which has been almost entirely shut out of theological reflection in the past. The use of women's experience in feminist theology, therefore, explodes as a critical force, exposing classical theology, including its codified traditions, as based on *male* experience rather than on universal human experience. Feminist theology makes the sociology of theological knowledge visible, no longer hidden behind mystifications of objectified divine and universal authority.
>
> 1993, p. 13 (emphasis in original)

Ruether therefore argues for what she calls a 'usable tradition' (p. 21). This will be a new synthesis of mainstream and neglected sources – both Christian and non-Christian – that enable theology better to realize the values enshrined in her critical principles. These *sources* comprise the following. First, there are the Hebrew and Christian Scriptures, in which – like other liberation theologians – Ruether privileges the words of the Hebrew prophets, the teachings of Jesus and biblical visions of a transformed community. Note here how, whereas in the correlative methods of Justin, Aquinas or even Rahner, the partial insights of human reason are perfected by the more complete truths of revelation, Ruether suggests that the revelation of the biblical (here, prophetic) tradition is brought to a fuller, deeper apprehension via its interaction with a feminist critique.

> On another level, feminism goes beyond the letter of the prophetic message to apply the prophetic-liberating principle *to women*. Feminist theology makes explicit what was over-looked in male advocacy of the poor and oppressed: that liberation must start with the oppressed of the oppressed, namely *women* of the oppressed. This means the critique of hierarchy must become explicitly a critique of patriarchy. All the liberating prophetic visions must be deepened and transformed to include what was not included: women.
>
> p. 32 (emphasis in original)

Second, Ruether identifies 'fringe' or 'counter-cultural' traditions within Christianity that might renew the tradition. She nominates Gnostic, Montanist, Shaker and Quaker movements as containing emancipatory and egalitarian impulses, and often providing critical space for women to minister freely. She is aware that some of these traditions might be regarded as 'heretical' or marginal; but argues that this may have been due to their perceived threat to the patriarchal status quo rather than the irregularity of their teaching.

Third, Ruether advocates the inclusion of so-called 'pagan' sources, such as goddess thealogies and pre-Christian, earth-centred spiritualities within the usable resources of a transformed tradition. These testify to aspects of theological understanding suppressed by mainstream teaching and embody important principles of respect for the environment, embodied (rather than logocentric) spiritualities and the religious leadership of women. Finally, Ruether looks to modern 'post-Christian' (namely post-Enlightenment) sources, such as Marxism, romanticism and liberalism, that serve as a critical and corrective resource by offering visions of human dignity and emancipation akin to, and augmenting, the notion of *imago Dei*.

The feminist reconstruction of theological tradition is thus more than simply 'adding women in' but involves asking fundamental questions about theological method, sources and norms. Theology is recast under the scrutiny of feminist and emancipatory principles, and it is acceptable for the tradition to be revised and renewed as a result of new syntheses.

## Evaluation

In this concluding section we might wish to ask, what are the contemporary sources for critical correlation today? Whereas Thomas Aquinas regarded as a key task of Christian theology (as apologetics and public truth) a sustained engagement with Aristotelian thought, a twenty-first-century equivalent may well be the world of science and technology. This is the argument of writers such as Philip Hefner (2003) and Elaine Graham (2002b), who maintain that new technologies and techniques such as artificial intelligence, cloning, cybernetics and genetic modification represent vital challenges to Western culture's understandings of what it means to be human. It is important for the theologian and the Christian community to attend to these new developments, for the dilemmas they present are theological. As Hefner argues, what is understood to be authentically and normatively human relates directly to what might be proclaimed about the nature of God – and vice versa. Elaine Graham argues that representations of the impact of science and technology on what it means to be human are at their most vivid in forms of popular culture such as science fiction, and that these are refractions of deep-seated religious and theological impulses. Taking such understandings seriously is the point at which theology can engage in genuine dialogue with a largely secularized culture.

In both these perspectives there are clear echoes of Aquinas and Rahner, in that the preoccupations of contemporary culture may be considered to. be the precursor of deeper theological understanding; and in fact the resources of popular culture, imagination, art and creativity (such as science fiction) may serve as contemporary equivalents to Aquinas's and Rahner's choice of philosophy as a 'secular' conversation partner with theology.

Questions concerning the conversation partners of theology in the contemporary context lead us to consider other important issues. If this method rests on a dialogue between 'Christian tradition' and 'experience' then what do these categories actually contain? What kinds of experience are referred to, and how will it be articulated? What disciplines and methods will be adopted to bring such experience to light? Whose experience is deemed authoritative? And are there correctives to ensure that particular voices and perspectives are not neglected? How does engagement with 'Christian tradition' deal with the diversity of theological sources; and what counts as authentic tradition, and by what criteria? While these are important questions for those seeking a dialogue between contemporary culture and the

Christian faith, others have voiced a more fundamental concern that critical correlation risks becoming fatally wedded to the prevailing *Zeitgeist* and underestimates the counter-cultural dimensions of the gospel. Some critics, for example John Milbank (1990), argue that modern liberal theology's reliance on the social sciences fails to recognize how these disciplines have attempted to supplant the overarching vision of Christian theology, to the extent that liberal theology absorbs secular values without realizing it does so. And crucially the normative status of Christian theology remains unresolved within critical correlation. Does the gospel stand in judgement over all other insights into the human condition, which are at best proto-theological; or does the Christian tradition itself require correction and revision?

Finally, liberal revisionist theology appears to be progressive in its advocacy of dialogue with modernity and secular culture. However, even the critical correlative model operates within a particular cultural framework; and the emphasis of correlation since Schleiermacher and Tillich has tended to lie in addressing existential dilemmas rather than political concerns (the work of Ruether stands in contrast to this general trend). The danger is that a privatized, individualistic model of religious faith goes unchallenged, and that liberal theology simply baptizes culture without developing an independent critique. Contrast liberal correlative theology with liberationist traditions, in which the task is not to address existential, philosophical questions of belief and unbelief, but to challenge the dehumanizing structures of global capitalism. By exposing the ideological functions of religion, liberationists (including feminists) offer a critique of liberal theology's retreat into forms of personal, cognitive belief. Analysis of the 'cultural information' that forms one of the correlational sources must therefore be aware of its own ideological bias.

## Questions

- Can you think of any examples from science and religion or the performing and visual arts that adopt a 'correlative' method between theology and culture?
- Is this method of theological reflection in danger of simply baptizing the spirit of the age too uncritically, rather being than a properly theologically driven discourse?
- What kind of God is implied by this method of theological reflection?

## Annotated Bibliography

Clements, K. (1987), *Friedrich Schleiermacher: Pioneer of Modern Theology,* London: Collins. A useful introduction to Schleiermacher and his thought.

Ruether, R. R., (1993), *Sexism and God-Talk,* Boston: Beacon Press, 3rd edn. A staple of feminist theological literature, this book argues that all theologies, and not only feminist theologies, are codifications of human experience, and that the sufficiency of the Christian tradition must be put to the test by voices of liberation and justice from outwith its own sources.

Tillich, P. (1962), *The Shaking of the Foundations* (1948), Harmondsworth: Pelican. A collection of sermons that are perhaps the most accessible route into Tillich's views on the dialogue between religion and culture.

Tracy, D. (1975), *Blessed Rage for Order: The New Pluralism in Theology,* New York. Further exposition of Tracy's well-known claim that theological reflection must be accountable to the 'three publics' of Church, academy and society.

Whitehead J. D. and Whitehead, E. E. (1980), *Method in Ministry: Theological Reflection and Christian Ministry,* San Francisco, Harper & Row, 2nd edn, 1990. A good example of the critical correlative method put to work in practical case-studies.

# 6

# 'Theology-in-Action': Praxis

## The Method in Outline

This method of reflection characterizes theology as *'performative knowledge'*, that is, a way of knowing that is inseparable from doing. The fundamental assumption here is that theory and practice are inextricably joined. This conviction is often expressed in the use of the Marxist term *praxis* (denoting the centrality of value-committed action), and the insistence that proper theological understanding cannot be formed independently of practical engagement. *Theology-in-action,* therefore, places primacy on *orthopraxis* (right action) rather than *orthodoxy* (right belief). This is more than simply another form of applied theology in which systematic and historical theology provide norms for pastoral care or ethics. Rather, here, practice is both the origin and the end of theological reflection, and 'talk about God' cannot take place independent of a commitment to a struggle for human emancipation.

## Introduction

This method of theological reflection is most closely associated with the theologies of liberation that emerged in the two-thirds world from the end of the 1960s. These were partly inspired by Christian-Marxist debates on the nature of history and the role of religion in the process of social change. They were also inspired by the attempts of Christians actively involved in revolutionary struggles to articulate the fundamental relationship they perceived between their faith convictions and their political actions. The starting-point of this method of theological reflection has thus never been abstract speculation on timeless truths, but consideration of the obligations of communities of faith in the context of social, economic and political extremities. Theological reflection itself, therefore, is characterized as 'critical reflection on praxis' (Nickoloff, 1996, pp. 30–1). It is a process that enables the

Church to live out its commitment to the 'preferential option for the poor', a view reflected in José Miguez Bonino's assertion that 'truth lies at the level of history, not in the realm of ideas'(1979, p. 263).

This leads to particular understandings of the nature of the Christian calling, the shape of the Church in the world and the relationship between gospel and culture, or history. First, salvation is understood to include (although is not necessarily limited to) material, historical and political liberation. For Gutiérrez, the task is not to preach to the unbeliever but to proclaim to the dehumanized that they are God's children: 'Modern theology tries to answer the challenge of the "non-believer"; but in contrast liberation theology listens to the challenging questions of the "non-person" ' (Gutiérrez, 1983:57). The task of *Christian formation and nurture* is one of empowerment and liberation, and it means reinserting those on the underside of history back into *salvation* history, and transforming the poor from objects of others' abuse into subjects in control of their own destiny.

In terms of corporate reflection, the understanding of the Church is heavily influenced by a discernment of God as active in human history. Thus, the task of *forging Christian identity* and *building up the community of faith* involves taking a stand for human dignity and reconciliation in solidarity with those of all faiths and none who are similarly called to resist inequality, oppression and violence.

Gradually the processes involved in praxis-based theological reflection were schematized into the 'pastoral cycle' of action and reflection. This term evolved from the Roman Catholic usage of 'pastoral' to mean that which pertains to the life of the Church, its ministry, sacraments and social witness. In this frame '[p]astoral action necessarily includes action on behalf of justice' (Holland and Henriot, 1990), reinforcing an understanding that social change is as much an integral part of the Church's mission as personal conversion. The pastoral cycle embodies a synthesis of practice and theory, and offers what has become a much-used methodology for engagement with context that has been applied far beyond its original roots in twentieth-century Roman Catholic social activism.

While the theology of praxis may have crystallized in twentieth-century theologies of liberation under the influence of Christian Marxism, this method can trace a deeper continuity throughout history. This chapter will highlight a consistent reliance on biblically-grounded traditions of prophetic protest against social injustice and the vanity of empty rituals performed at the expense of observing covenant commandments of compassion, justice and righteousness. This prophetic impulse also manifests itself in Christian movements that have consistently insisted that authentic discipleship is to be found in the integrity of one's actions rather than in protestations of belief. Christian history contains many examples of radical movements such as the Society of Friends (or Quakers) for whom credal religion is secondary to one's duty to the realization of peace, justice and personal integrity. A sense that convictions must be lived rather than asserted can even be discerned in traditions of Christian existentialism (inspired by the work of Søren Kierkegaard) in which the encounter with a living God, and the ethical outworkings of such a revelation, are judged as the true measure of authentic faith.

We will also find that this method of theological reflection invites the recasting of theology itself as a transformative and practical discipline. Thus, the criterion of theological adequacy within the praxis method is to be found in the simple question, 'Will it liberate?' But although later developments in practical theology have widened our understanding of 'transforming practice' as embracing the sacramental or performative aspects of theology (as in Elaine Graham's postmodern theology of practice), it is important not to lose sight of the extent to which the praxis method remains rooted in the specific claims for social justice articulated in theologies of liberation from the two-thirds world.

## Reflections from History

### The Sheep and the Goats

When the Son of Man comes in his glory, and all the angels with him, then he will sit on the throne of his glory. All the nations will be gathered before him, and he will separate people one from another as a shepherd separates the sheep from the goats, and he will put the sheep at his right hand and the goats at the left. Then the king will say to those at his right hand, 'Come, you that are blessed by my Father, inherit the kingdom prepared for you from the foundation of the world; for I was hungry and you gave me food, I was thirsty and you gave me something to drink, I was a stranger and you welcomed me, I was naked and you gave me clothing, I was sick and you took care of me, I was in prison and you visited me.' Then the righteous will answer him, 'Lord, when was it that we saw you hungry and gave you food, or thirsty and gave you something to drink? And when was it that we saw you a stranger and welcomed you, or naked and gave you clothing? And when was it that we saw you sick or in prison and visited you?' And the king will answer them, 'Truly I tell you, just as you did it to the least of these who are members of my family, you did it to me.' Then he will say to those at his left hand, 'You that are accursed, depart from me into the eternal fire prepared for the devil and his angels; for I was hungry and you gave me no food, I was thirsty and you gave me nothing to drink, I was a stranger and you did not welcome me, naked and you did not give me clothing, sick and in prison and you did not visit me.' Then they also will answer, 'Lord, when was it that we saw you hungry or thirsty or a stranger or naked or sick or in prison, and did not take care of you?' Then he will answer them, 'Truly I tell you, just as you did not do it to one of the least of these, you did not do it to me.' And these will go away into eternal punishment, but the righteous into eternal life.

Matthew 25.31–46 (NRSV)

This parable reflects an eschatological world-view on the part of the early Church, anticipating that God would soon usher in a new order at the end of human history. The stark division between 'sheep and goats' may disturb a contemporary liberal conscience but it reflects the very clear expectation of a judgement to come – a judgement based on actions, charity, and the extent to which the earthly body of Christ is prepared to recognize and honour him in the face of the outcast, the poor, the sick and the marginalized. This is the test of one's fitness to participate in God's eternal kingdom.

One outstanding feature of this text is its strong identification of the person of Christ with the poor and the persecuted. Obedience to Christ is to be found in acts of mercy and compassion directed at all those in need, since they now embody the sufferings of the world to which Christ's passion was directed. This theme is later echoed by the letter of John, which exhorts the community to remember that it cannot claim to love God, whom it has not seen, if it neglects to love those in its very midst (1 John 4.7–21). Later, we will see how such an emphasis on true faith expressed in works of compassion becomes an argument to the effect that observance of the law without justice is false religion.

It is interesting to note how this method of theological reflection is one of the most biblical in inspiration. The dramatic parable of the sheep and the goats is entirely consistent with the description of Jesus' ministry presented in the Gospels. It is also congruent with other biblical traditions, such as God hearing the cries of the slaves in bondage in Egypt. It echoes with the same tone as that in which the Hebrew prophets spoke out against observing the forms of religion while acting without charity. It affirms the insight that God has very different priorities to those of the religiously orthodox:

> . . . and what does the Lord require of you
> but to do justice, and to love kindness,
> and to walk humbly with your God?
>                     Micah 6.8–9 (NRSV)

## Gregory and the Pastoral Rule

The writings of Pope Gregory I of Rome (*c.* AD 540–604), and especially his *The Book of Pastoral Rule*, completed in 590, are regarded as a milestone in pastoral care literature. It is essentially an extended reflection on the responsibilities of pastoral leadership, written to a bishop but revealing much about the directions in which Christian understandings of ministry were maturing at the time. In its seriousness of purpose and systematic attention to the many dimensions of the pastoral office, *The Book of Pastoral Rule* represents the first example of a handbook of practical ministry. Yet while it gives a full account of the qualities expected of those who exercised pastoral leadership, Gregory is at pains to connect practice with theory. The nature of pastoral ministry is for Gregory but an expression of divine care for creation: so it sets a significant precedent for theological reflection in rooting practice in biblical and philosophical musings on the nature of God.

Gregory began his career as a secular administrator and rose to the office of prefect of Rome. He only later made the decision to enter religious life, partly because he believed this would enable him to devote himself more fully to scholarship and contemplation. However, this was not to be his destiny, and for the rest of his life he combined the demands of ecclesiastical power with the realities of public life. Christianity was part of the cultural mainstream following the conversion of Constantine, and any bishop or pope needed to be concerned with public affairs as much as oversight of the Church. Peter Brown identifies this as the distinguishing feature of Gregory's career, and indeed his subsequent legacy: that he practised, and wrote, about 'the problem of power and its attendant cares and duties' (Brown, 2003, p. 139). Thus, Gregory's model of pastoral care is born of experience, and proceeds via an attempt to correlate the articulation of general principles with the exercise of *Realpolitik*. Gregory was also a pragmatist, advising his readers to exercise discretion and flexibility. Pastoral care requires discernment, responding to each person and situation yet Gregory insists that it must be informed by Scripture and tradition. The ability of a pastor to exercise the cure of souls is ultimately not a question of technique, but rests in their own humility and personal qualities.

According to Gregory, leaders should always practise what they preach and in their behaviour set an example for the way the community as a whole should be ordered. Power over the souls of others carried high responsibility, and Gregory's strategy was to draw as close an analogy as he could between the symbols of power within the Christian community and what he believed to be the nature of divine grace and power in the world. Hence Gregory's reputation as a reformer when he became pope: the integrity of the Church was, for him, a necessary part of its witness to the world.

Gregory's method of pastoral care was thus theologically informed. The pastor's concern for others should be an outworking and visible sign of God's grace. Human activity is a mimesis of divine action – in this case, Christ is the true and ultimate pastor. Just as there is a direct continuity between divine nature and human community, so there must be a match between the counsel of the pastors and leaders and their own integrity.

> The ruler should always be chief in action, that by his living he may point out the way of life to those that are put under him, and that the flock, which follows the voice and manners of the shepherd, may learn how to walk better through example than through words. For he who is required by the necessity of his position to speak the highest things is compelled by the same necessity to exhibit the highest things. For that voice more readily penetrates the hearer's heart, which the speaker's life commends, since what he commands by speaking he helps the doing of by shewing.
>
> Gregory the Great, 1976, Ch. 3: 'Characteristics of One Who May Exercise Pastoral Rule'

Gregory's emphasis on confession and penance locates *The Book of Pastoral Rule* as a founding text in the development of the Roman Catholic tradition of moral theology in which the administration of the sacraments is linked to the pastoral and moral welfare of the faithful. Via the practices of confession and absolution prior to the Mass, the penitent individual demonstrates their moral readiness to participate in communion. Penance is not a form of 'good works' to earn God's favour, but a sign, or enactment, of the reparation already achieved by Jesus. A person's conduct demonstrates their openness to God, rather than being a means of appeasement. Thus, Gregory once more identifies that *right action* and integrity work as a sign of a deeper relationship with God and one's fellow Christians.

In retrospect, many of Gregory's teachings seem outdated, and in his concerted attention to every detail of the disposition of the pastor he paves the way for a tradition of writings on pastoral theology that concentrate on the minutiae of 'hints and helps' at the expense of asking questions about the nature of the Church, of ministry, its values in relation to wider culture, and so on. Yet in his own insistence on the work of the pastor as being the tangible, temporal expression of divine reality, Gregory represents an early attempt to embody the indivisibility of theory and practice and to insist on theologically informed patterns of pastoral action and agency.

## The Witness of the Society of Friends

The seventeenth century in England was a time of political and religious turmoil. Tensions between royalist and parliamentary interests eventually erupted into civil war between 1642 and 45, which briefly re-ignited in 1648–49. While factors contributing to this era of ferment were complex, it was a period in which politics and religion were closely intertwined, particularly in giving expression to the nascent ambitions of an emergent middle class in supporting parliament against the power of the aristocracy. Various forms of Puritanism emphasized the immediacy of religious experience unmediated by ecclesial authority, and freedom of conscience unhindered by the alliance of Church and State. These groups stressed the primacy of religious self-expression but also found themselves calling for wider forms of political freedom. In their elevation of Scripture as the direct word of God, their use of the early Church as paradigm of primitive communism, and a doctrine of the Holy Spirit that stressed the openness of all persons to gifts of prophecy, preaching and ministry regardless of social station, many Puritan groups preached and practised theologically fuelled visions of what the historian Christopher Hill has called 'the world turned upside down'. They thus stand in a tradition of radical Christianity that denounces ecclesiastical power and magisterial authority in the name of a 'true Christianity' equated with justice, compassion and righteousness; or, in the words of the seventeenth-century radical Gerald Winstanley, 'action is the life of all' (quoted in Bradstock and Rowland, 2002, p. xxvi).

One such group was the Quakers, or Society of Friends, whose founder, George Fox, began his public ministry in 1644. Fox believed that there was what he called 'that of God in Everyone', something Quakers came to call 'the inner light' or 'inner Christ'. Knowledge of God was available to all people, independent of institutional mediation or authority, and all were ministers to one another. Conscience, prompted by the guiding of the Holy Spirit, was the ultimate arbiter. Despite a commitment to the authority of Scripture, Quakers argued that it must be moderated by experience.

Quakers cultivated a simple approach to personal behaviour and congregational practice, since anything but the immediacy of the prompting of the 'inner light' was seen as contingent. The essence of faith rested not in doctrine or institutional expediency but in the integrity of personal and collective witness to the Spirit within and to human dignity, peace and justice. Quaker testimonies thus eschewed credal orthodoxy in favour of radical discipleship in which the testimony of one's life is the essence of one's profession of faith.

> FRIEND,
> Thou that dost profess God and Christ, in words, see how thou followest him. To take off burdens, to visit them that are in prison, to show mercy, clothe thy own flesh, and deal thy bread to the hungry; these are God's commandments. To relieve the fatherless, to visit the widows in their afflictions, and to keep thyself unspotted of the world, this is pure religion before God. But if thou profess Christ, and followest covetousness and earthly mindedness, thou deniest him in life, deceivest thyself and others, and takest him for a cloak . . .
>
> George Fox, *Letter to Justice Bennett*, 1650,
> in Gwyn, 1990, p. 101

Traditionally, Quakers have met for public worship in silence, a practice they sometimes term 'expectant waiting'. When a member feels moved to speak, they will do so, believing it to be the promptings of the 'inner light'. This format emphasizes the equality of all members in relation to one another, eschewing the authority of preacher, priest or worship leader. Similarly, the custom of waiting in silence expresses something of the mystery of the divine, who is beyond words or creeds. In preference to the ambiguity of language Quakers choose personal communion free of coercion or dogma and the directness of charitable action and honesty.

Religious freedom is also paramount, since to prescribe a religious orthodoxy would be an abuse of the integrity of personal conscience. Fox and his followers thus endured years of persecution and imprisonment, not only for their religious dissent but also for their insistence on maintaining a distinctive way of life in other respects. Chief among these were a commitment to peace and non-violence, a refusal to swear oaths of loyalty (since only God could command such allegiance, which transcended that of any earthly power) and their practice of plain speaking and honesty in personal and business dealings. All life, all activity was sacred, because there were no privileged sources or mediators of religious truth beyond 'the spirit of Christ within' every woman and man. Hence the antipathy of Friends to social hierarchies and distinctions, and their insistence on equal respect being given to all, regardless of earthly rank or privilege. In this quotation from 1660, Margaret Fell petitioned King Charles II setting out the basis of the Quakers' peace testimony:

> We are a people that follow after those things that make for peace, love and unity; it is our desire that others' feet may walk in the same, and do deny and bear our testimony against all strife, and wars, and contentions that come from the lusts that war in the members, that war in the soul, which we wait for, and watch for in all people, and love and desire the good of all . . . Treason, treachery, and false dealings we do utterly deny; false dealing, surmising, or plotting against any creature upon the face of the earth, and speak the truth in plainness, and singleness of heart.
>
> Margaret Fell, 1660, in *Religious Society
> of Friends*, 1995, 19.46

This principle, that one's practice constitutes the strongest 'testimony' to faith, is echoed in contemporary Quaker guidance:

'Let your lives speak.' (Inscription on George Fox's Memorial Tablet)

The testimony of integrity calls us to wholeness; it is the whole of life open to Truth. When lives are centred in the Spirit, beliefs and actions are congruent, and words are dependable. As we achieve wholeness in ourselves, we are better able to heal the conflict and fragmentation in our community and in the world.

Integrity is a demanding discipline. We are challenged by cultural values and pressures to conform. Integrity requires that we be fully responsible for our actions. Living with integrity requires living a life of reflection, living in consistency with our beliefs and testimonies, and doing so regardless of personal consequences. Not least, it calls for a single standard of truth. From the beginning, Friends have held to this standard, and have often witnessed against the mainstream. When they suffered in consequence of their witness against secular order, their integration of belief and practice upheld them in adversity.

Cooper, 1991, p. 32

## Against Christendom: Søren Kierkegaard

The life and works of the Danish philosopher Søren Kierkegaard (1813–55) defy categorization and do not lend themselves easily to be included in any typological system. He was the first to recognize the singular and inimitable nature of his own thought. Yet in his emphasis on the need to return to 'simplicities' of faith free of the external trappings of formalism, and his – often tortured – search for an authentic form of Christianity unafraid to embrace the uncompromising example of Jesus Christ, Kierkegaard has something to say to theological reflection based on the primacy of praxis.

A chief preoccupation in his life and writings was the utter contrast, as he saw it, between the purity of New Testament Christianity and its subsequent development, particularly in the life of the Church and the pronouncements of those he called, with something approaching contempt, 'the professors'. Some of his impatience was directed at those for whom church-going or even a career in the Church (such as his old adversary, Bishop Mynster of the Lutheran Church of Denmark) had become a matter of conformity and social respectability. He was also appalled at the Hegelian tendencies of other philosophers who, as he believed, were diluting the distinctive (and even scandalous) nature of Christianity in favour of a universal human ethic of reason and progress.

Kierkegaard's radicalism was more than mere impatience with religious bureaucracy or the complacency of prosperous bourgeois Christians who failed to help the less fortunate. A deeper passion fired Kierkegaard, rooted in his very understanding of the nature of religious experience and of God. His understanding of the Christian faith was as a moment of encounter with the transcendent God, an encounter so terrifying and absolute that it caused all human certainties to melt into thin air. Religion was thus for him not essentially a matter of doctrine, or worship, or Church organization. It was an event in the life of each individual in which God was decisively revealed. This revelation was, for Kierkegaard, quintessentially exemplified in the paradox of the 'God-man' Jesus as one who transforms history through his incarnation.

Kierkegaard may in this respect be regarded as a precursor of modern existentialism, in which the authenticity of one's decisions and actions guarantee the quality of one's very life. In his view, the kind of progressive humanism of the Hegelians radically under-estimated the reality of sin, which Kierkegaard equated with despair and resignation to death. Since existence is characterized by human dependence on the divine, then authenticity comes through an acknowledgement of this. Despair, conversely, appears via a recognition of the precariousness and contingency of human experience. The only solution for Kierkegaard appeared to be to enter into the life of atonement and resurrection represented by Jesus, and to assent to the grace of God which can only be granted by the miracle of faith. This is effectively an experience of inwardness, in that each individual must apprehend the claim of God upon them as a leap of faith rather than something that can be persuaded via rational argument.

In *Fear and Trembling* Kierkegaard interpreted Abraham's willingness to sacrifice his son Isaac as an ultimate act of self-realization, since he is prepared to do so even with an awareness of the horrific nature of this act. Yet what is important is Abraham's willingness to transcend ethical conformity in pursuit of a deeper obedience to divine prompting. Thus, when one acts in 'fear and trembling' out of personal conviction rather than according to the dictates of external authority, one reaches a full comprehension of oneself and the moral life.

We can see this perspective as reflecting Kierkegaard's understanding of the essentials of religion as fundamentally rooted in the choices by which people's lives were shaped, and how it was at the very moment of acceptance of God's self-manifestation that one would achieve one's full humanity. Kierkegaard is thus an example of what we might call Christian existentialism, in that the way in which a person acts is regarded as the true arbiter of their convictions. Only by acting in pursuit of authentic self-determination can one truly experience the moral good.

Thus, for Kierkegaard, history and human existence themselves are shaped by authentic choices, both on the part of God to reveal God-self and on the part of humanity to undertake the 'leap of faith'. Yet that revelation, and the response, is focused around love rather than reason, around suffering and marginalized humanity (a factor with which Kierkegaard closely identified) rather than philosophical speculation. As Peerman and Marty assert, for Kierkegaard 'The Logos that became flesh is not the world reason but the creative Word that brings into being that which speaks' (1965, p. 141)

When Christianity was not a doctrine, when it was a few poor propositions, but these were expressed in life, then God was nearer to reality than when Christianity became a doctrine. And with each increase and embellishment, etc., of doctrine, God removes himself more. For doctrine and its spread mean an increase in the direction of appearance, and God is related inversely to appearance. When there were no priests, but the Christians were all brothers [sic], then God was nearer to reality than when there were priests, many priests, a powerful priesthood. For priests are an increase in the direction of appearance, and God is related inversely to the phenomenon . . .

And this is the history of Christendom: by strengthening the appearance it puts a distance between itself and God, or else (as in certain circumstances one speaks of removing someone in a refined manner) the history of Christendom consists of removing God more and more, in a refined manner, by building churches and splendid buildings, by elaborating monstrous edifices of doctrine, along with an endless horde of priests . . .

No, no, no: if you seriously wish to have God nearer, then to death and the devil with all that lying company of priests and professors, who publish *en masse* an excellent commentary on the text: Seek first the kingdom of God [Matt. 6.33], risk yourself in the very midst of reality, risk – and at the very same moment God is there, and believe and be assured that with a quite different certainty from when a doctor, rung up in the night, leaps from his bed, in the very second that a man really takes a risk for God's sake, he is there, he is immediately present, he who is infinite love.

[*In the margin*] The least possible place or phenomenon: a poor, solitary, needy, abandoned man – this the place for God, to such an extent is he negatively related to the phenomenon; and God must make this man, humanly speaking, even unhappier if he is to be present in him – to such an extent is he negatively related to the phenomenon. He must have the least possible phenomenon, and then he must deny it over and above everything.

Kierkegaard, *Journals* XI² A 51/52,
in Smith, 1965, pp. 211–12

Kierkegaard vehemently eschews any idea that Christianity is a comfortable panacea for human suffering, but rather sees it as the means by which individuals are confronted with the enormity of transcendence to which the only response can be awe and acceptance. Yet by virtue of its uncompromising nature, assent to such faith leads to a life of non-conformity, resistance to what Bonhoeffer was later to call 'cheap grace' or anything that substitutes authentic existence with mere lip service to the conventions of Christianity.

## The Method Realized

### Paulo Friere and Education for Freedom

The best-known manifestation of the praxis method, Latin American liberation theology, first emerged onto the theological scene in the late 1960s. Yet a number of theological, ecclesiastical and political currents had converged to produce the movement that spawned this method fully realized. First, there was the social, economic and political context of Latin America itself. Having gained political independence from its European colonizers during the nineteenth century, the countries of South and Central America continued to experience poverty and political fragility, which gave rise to several forms of social analysis, among which were derivatives of Marxist 'dependency theory'. This argued that the so-called 'developing countries' continued to experience a disadvantageous relationship with the industrial West, in terms of trade and other forms of neo-colonialism. In the face of poverty, malnutrition, lack of basic amenities, the displacement and migration of refugees, political instability (often due to the interventions of Western powers), Latin Americans drew inevitable parallels between their experience and Marx's original diagnosis of the inevitability of a polarization between rich and poor under capitalism.

Marxism thus held particular attractions for liberation theologians, with its scientific yet morally engaged analysis of poverty and extremes of wealth and power. First, they appropriated the historical materialism of Marxism, with its Hegelian model of history developing via conflict of opposing forces into a harmonious resolution, developed and adapted by Marx into a narrative of history that sees the contradictions of capitalism as eventually precipitating a crisis resolved in the emergence of communism. Yet they also used Marxism's critique of religious ideology, of regarding all knowledge as socially constructed and conditioned, of those who use religion to support an unjust status quo as cloaking the truth, and the poor as possessing a clarity and authenticity of vision that guarantees theological and moral deliverance.

These ideas were endorsed by many Christians concerned by the depth of social inequality they encountered on a daily basis. By the 1960s some elements of the progressive Roman Catholic Church in places like Brazil and Peru were developing programmes of social work, specializing in adult literacy, community organization and health care within the rapidly expanding cities. A method of action-reflection, pioneered in Europe by the Young Christian Workers under Joseph Cardijn, and following a three-fold pattern of 'see-judge-act', proved a highly effective means of sustaining lay Christians in their social engagement. The commitment expressed in Vatican II to active lay ministry seemed to approve pioneering efforts to find new ways of being Church. These were further endorsed by the Latin American bishops meeting in Medellin in 1968 and subsequently in Puebla in 1979. They made a commitment to 'God's preferential option for the poor' (Hennelley, 1990, pp. 253–8), which was to become the manifesto of those progressive elements within the Catholic Church who had come to see the liberation of the poor as integral to Christian mission.

The influence of the Brazilian educator and activist Paulo Freire (1921–97) has long been acknowledged on theologies of liberation. He was exposed to the influence of the Catholic Action movement in Brazil of the 1940s and 1950s. Catholic Action groups had motivated many educated lay people to engage in community work alongside the rapidly burgeoning urban poor of Brazil's big cities. This prompted him to abandon his first career as a lawyer and take up social work and adult education, becoming the director of the University of Recife's Cultural Extension Service, specializing in adult literacy programmes. His life-long work in adult education and the politics of literacy had begun and was to gain him an international reputation.

The core features of Freirean pedagogy include its emphasis on experiential learning; the collaborative and inductive method of facilitation on the part of the teacher; the situational nature of learning and the linkage between immediate and concrete experience and wider social forces; and the commitment to working for change (Heaney, 1995). In contrast to the 'banking' model, where the student is a passive receptacle of knowledge, Freire's method prioritized the concrete and immediate experience of the student and encouraged them to reflect critically on their experience, challenge the *status quo* and take control of their own destiny. It starts from the concrete problems of immediate concern, and is knowledge directed towards reversing the cycles of fatality and passivity and moving towards empowerment.

The influence of Freire's Marxist convictions may be felt here. Drawing upon Marx's early writings Freire recognized the significance of the 'alienation' of the poor in a society where they were separated not only from due reward for their labour but also divorced from their own resources of creative thinking. Grass-roots education, and particularly the process of *conscientização* ('conscientization'), was designed to restore to ordinary people the capacity for critical and constructive engagement with their own experience, enabling them to attain new levels of awareness and activism. Freire's thinking is Marxist in its affirmation of the transformative role of human agency in history and the possibilities of achieving liberation through the exercise of that self-determination. It is also deeply suspicious of ideological forms of knowledge – such as the banking model – believing that critical pedagogy releases the transformative power of self-realization. Freire's approach is 'praxis based' and in his educational interventions content and method are deeply interrelated.

> From my point of view, education for freedom implies constantly, permanently, the exercise of consciousness turning in on itself in order to discover itself in the relationships with the world, trying to explain the reasons which can make clear the concrete situation people have in the world. But it is not enough. It is important to point out that reflection alone is not enough for the process of liberation. We need praxis, or in other words, we need to transform the reality in which we find ourselves. But in order to transform reality, in order to develop my action upon reality, transforming it, it is necessarily and constantly, the unity between my action and my reflection.
>
> Freire, in Davis, 1980, p. 59

Thus Freire's pedagogy needs to be seen as both the means towards, and the anticipation of, the new social order of justice and equality. There is an explicit link between literacy, empowerment and humanization. We might therefore locate the distinctiveness of his pedagogy as resting in a process of literacy, linking to knowledge, leading to agency, facilitating community development, resulting in collective work for social change. *Praxis* for him entailed a constant dialectic of experience and action with reflection and learning. Methodologically, he was committed to the permanent process of harnessing critical knowledge – acquired through reflection on experience – towards empowerment and change. Through the activities of praxis we move from coercion to self-determination; from reaction to intentionality; and from passivity to creativity (Heaney, 1995). To transform the world is thus to humanize it: not simply in that the goal is greater justice, but that *praxis* is the very activity by which we transcend mere chance and contingency and realize our humanity as reflective and critically conscious beings.

*Gutiérrez and 'Critical Reflection on Praxis' as the Task of Theology*

Early liberation theologians from the two-thirds world from 1960s onwards adopted many of these themes. Gustavo Gutiérrez, in particular, crystallized strands from Freirean conscientization and Christian Marxism, understanding theology as 'critical reflection on Christian praxis in the light of the word of God' (Gutiérrez, 1988, p. xxix). In other words, theology is a form of 'talk about God' that begins in an analysis of the social context of the believer and finds its most authentic expression in the value-laden and purposeful practices of liberation and solidarity.

The notion of praxis is drawn, largely, from Marxist analysis. In a polarized society, in which the rich appropriated the fruits of the labours of the poor, religion was used to 'ideological' ends: that is, as a false representation of the world in which the status quo is rationalized as natural and inevitable when in fact it reflects the material interests of the ruling class. Taking Ludwig Feuerbach's protests against religion as a massive projection of human consciousness into an other-worldly realm where it assumes a pre-eminent status, Marx argued that material and historical existence, rather than consciousness, determined social relations. What counted as knowledge and truth was not a 'mirror of nature' but a function of economic polarization and injustice, as the outworking of the privileged interests of the powerful. The task of those seeking emancipation was thus not simply to engage with abstractions, but to facilitate the entry of the oppressed into self-consciousness, and thereby into struggle for change. As Marx put it, famously, 'Philosophers have only interpreted the world in various ways. The point is to change it.' (Marx in McLellan, ed., 1977, p. 158) Truth is, thus, a reflection of the triumph of human freedom over bondage, a process enacted in the agency of the oppressed in pursuit of their own emancipation, and realized in transformative action for social justice.

As theologies of liberation from the two-thirds world emerged, it was clear that their exponents regarded such a shift to the primacy of *praxis* as the defining mark of the 'new way of doing theology', and that this constituted more than simply a new variety of political theology traditionally understood. Rather, it represented a conviction that if faith were equated with liberating praxis, then the very nature of theology itself would be transformed:

> Many theologians . . . regard theology itself as a praxis. For them, theology is not the rational exploration of divine revelation to

increase its intelligibility; for them, the task of theology is not to provide abstract knowledge independent of the historical situation of the believing community. Instead, according to these theologians, theology is a rational exercise that follows upon the action of the poor and searches for an understanding of God's revelation that discloses its redemptive and liberative power. Theology as praxis is historically rooted; since history changes, praxis theology must move forward, through the interaction of the cognitive and agapic dimensions of faith, in an effort to formulate God's revealed word of rescue and hope addressed to people in the present.

Baum, 1999, pp. 182–3

In his earlier work, Gutiérrez was clearly influenced by Marxist social theory – particularly, understandings of dependency theory and ideas of praxis. Subsequently, he turned more to themes of the spirituality of liberation and to its historical antecedents, such as Bartolomé de las Casas (see Chapter 7). The spirituality of liberation, and its links with liturgy, has been a fertile area of debate. It demonstrates how the tasks of equipping faithful individuals and communities is regarded as one of fostering appropriate spiritualities and how the corporate praxis of liturgy and worship is understood as an enactment of the core values of the gospel, which are not to be separated from the secular praxis of the progressive Church.

In the following quotation, Gutiérrez explores the question of spirituality in relation to some already familiar themes: the notion of liberation entailing a humanization (as children of God) of the dehumanized; of faithful discipleship as an identification with the suffering Christ; and the centrality of God's preferential option for the poor at the heart of the Christian life.

Since the very first days of the theology of liberation, the question of spirituality (specifically: the following of Jesus) has been of deep concern. Moreover, the kind of reflection that the theology of liberation represents is conscious of the fact that it was, and continues to be, preceded by the spiritual experience of Christians who are committed to the process of liberation. That experience is at the heart of the movement set afoot by the poor of Latin America as they seek to assert their human dignity and their status as daughters and sons of God. This reaching out for life situates the place and time of an encounter with the Lord. And this encounter becomes in turn the starting point for a route to be taken in the following of Jesus Christ.

The importance assigned to this experience in the theology of liberation is in keeping with the purpose of that theology, which is to develop a reflection that is concerned with and based on practice in the light of faith. Consequently, in the area of spirituality too the varying conditions and ways of practice will lead to new perspectives and new themes. The breakthrough or irruption – as it has been called – of the poor in Latin America not only left its mark on the beginning of the theology of liberation but is daily becoming more urgent and massive, even where the effort is made to hide or repress it. This has simply reinforced the fact that the entrance of the poor onto center stage in Latin American society and the Latin American church has plowed new furrows for Christian life and reflection.

The furrows are watered at times with the blood of witnesses (martyrs) to that preferential love of God for the poor that is today leaving an indelible imprint on the life of the church in Latin America. This martyrdom is setting a seal on the following of Jesus and the subsequent theological reflections that are now coming into existence in Latin America. Ours is a land of premature and unjust death, but also of an ever stronger assertion of the right to life and the joy of Easter.

Gutiérrez, 1984, pp. 1–2

The spirituality of liberation is above all an insistence on the indivisibility of doctrine, worship and action. Action for social justice always needs to be rooted in the practices of faith, such as prayer and liturgy. Despite attempts to 'privatize' the Christian faith, Gutiérrez insists that spirituality must be a 'totality' informing every aspect of life. He defines this liberating spirituality as a way of living out the gospel such that life 'before the Lord' is equated with 'solidarity with all human beings' and vice versa (Nickoloff, 1996, p. 287). It implies a conversion, or radical transformation, towards a deep identification with the suffering of one's neighbour, and of a ready commitment to apprehending the face of Christ in that of the oppressed and exploited person. It also calls forth what Gutiérrez calls 'an experience of gratuitousness', an encounter with the presence of God in human affairs in which it becomes clear that 'at the root of our personal and community existence lies the gift of the self-communication of God, the grace of God's friendship' (1988, p. 116). To seek communion with God, who is at the heart of all life, therefore, is not to turn away from the world, but to engage more fully with its suffering in order to experience more fully the 'gratuitousness' of divine love and grace.

## The Pastoral Cycle

Many liberation theologians have refined the distinctive characteristics of theology as praxis into a distinctive *methodology*, which describes and systematizes the movement from practice to theory to practice. Drawing upon the threefold pattern of Young Christian Workers' 'see-judge-act' method, and also informed by Paul Ricoeur's hermeneutics via the work of Juan-Luis Segundo's *The Liberation of Theology*, first published in 1975, the so-called 'pastoral cycle' has been widely used in theological education and other contexts. Its influence extends far beyond the immediate impact of liberation theology.

The pastoral cycle assumes that each new reality or problem is calling people of faith to reinterpret the Word of God anew, but that theology, in the form of received tradition (doctrine, Bible, Church traditions) needs to be reinterpreted in the light of contemporary faith and tested against insights from other cultures and disciplines (see Chapter 7). This involves bringing the 'horizon' of social context (poverty, racism, oppression) into contact with that of theological world-views. Hence Segundo's use of the term 'hermeneutical circle', in that practical engagement fuels the process of interpretation in the service of *orthopraxis* (Segundo, 1982, p. 32). Thus, the hermeneutical circle or pastoral cycle actually embodies the method of theological reflection at the heart of theology as praxis: 'It is my feeling that the most progressive theology in Latin America is more interested in *being liberative* than in *talking about liberation*. In other words, liberation deals not so much with content as with the method used to theologise in the face of our real-life situation' (p. 9).

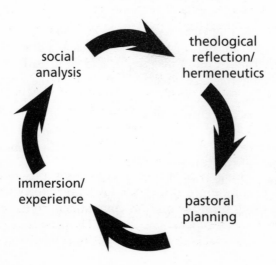

Segundo describes the process of theological reflection on praxis as containing four 'moments' or stages. It begins with 'immersion' in the very context of economic and political polarization in cultures such as Latin America to which theologies of liberation address themselves. 'Christians should not redefine social praxis by starting with the gospel message. They should do just the opposite. They should seek out the historical import of the gospel by starting with social praxis' (p. 85). Note, then, how implicitly this is not a method of 'applied theology' but a process of theological reflection that begins and ends in practical engagement:

> The novelty of liberation theology claims consists in its being a reflection in faith worked out from within a *practice* of liberation carried out by the oppressed in their movements. The first word is spoken by what is done, that is, by a conscious act aimed at changing social relationships. It is therefore an inductive theology. It does not start with words (those of the Bible or the magisterium) and end in words (new theological formulations), but stems from actions and struggles and works out a theoretical structure to throw light on and examine these actions.
>
> L. Boff, 1988, p. 23

This phase of pre-commitment, of conversion to the imperatives of a liberative theology, of a recognition of one's own complicity in the dynamics of oppression and structural sin, and a deeper solidarity with movements of resistance, therefore, leads to the second phase, or moment, aimed at gaining a deeper critical understanding of immediate experience. This element of the methodology focuses on the generation of deeper understandings of the experiences from which *praxis* is understood to emerge. It is an attempt to probe beneath the superficial or received accounts into a deeper understanding. It is thus a movement both from 'anecdotal' to 'critical' or 'analytical' experience; but it also begins to challenge the veracity and integrity of dominant, accepted forms of knowledge, be they political or ecclesiastical ideologies. It 'examines causes, probes consequences, delineates linkages, and identifies actors' (Holland and Henriot, 1990, p. 8).

Thus, the 'hermeneutics of suspicion' are activated; and as the critical and analytical processes of interpretation get underway, the guiding principles by which authentic knowledge is differentiated from ideology are taken from the *a priori* commitment to the preferential option for the poor (Segundo, 1982, p. 47). The perspectives and interests of those 'on the underside of history' are thus privileged as offering a fuller disclosure of the gospel and serve to unlock the 'transforming energy' of the biblical text (C. Boff, 1996, p. 16).

The third phase is that of 'hermeneutic mediation' (Boff and Boff, 1987, p. 32) – a return to the Christian tradition, renewed by a new hermeneutics of retrieval and reconstruction, generating narratives, values and visions that are tested against the contemporary situation. 'It attempts to see what the divine plan is with respect to the poor' (C. Boff, 1996, p. 11); but once more, a stance of active commitment is presumed, this time in the return to the resources of the faith tradition. In relation to biblical exegesis, rather than striving for an objective, 'rationalistic exegesis of intrinsic meaning' in order to distance the reader from the biblical texts and their socio-historical contexts, the hermeneutical method is consciously seeking to generate critical and reconstructive norms for committed *praxis* – 'denunciation and annunciation' (Vidales, 1979, p. 53).

The reader is also encouraged to see the bonds of affinity between the biblical texts and contexts and their own contemporary struggles. The Bible is thus to be read 'as a book of life, not as a book of curious stories' (C. Boff, 1996, p. 16); and the preferred books are Exodus, for its stories of liberation from captivity, Prophetic literature for its sustained denunciation of social injustice, the Gospels for their portrayal of Jesus as social iconoclast and suffering servant, the Acts of the Apostles for its depiction of an egalitarian community and the book of Revelation for its picture of the struggles of the Church against persecution and structural power (Boff and Boff, 1987, pp. 34–5; C. Boff, 1996, p. 17). Theology is not in the business of dispensing timeless certainties but to inform and inspire faithful *praxis*.

Fourth, therefore, comes the move back to faithful practice, informed by the values of theological reflection; what Boff and Boff term 'practical mediation' (p. 39) and Raul Vidales 'missionary proclamation' (p. 51). Practice is thus both 'foundation and aim' of a process of experience-analysis-action; and arguably, within such a method, even the activities of reading, reflection and interpretation are themselves forms of *praxis* because they serve to excavate the theological values by which faithful practice is to be guided. Similarly, while Clodovis Boff concedes that liberation theology is primarily a theology of *praxis* insofar as it leads to social action, it also embraces a broader spectrum of faithful discipleship. If theory and practice are indivisible, so too are spirituality and politics:

> [F]aith is not reducible to action, even liberative action. It is 'ever greater', and includes moments of contemplation, and profound

gratitude. The theology of liberation also leads to the temple. And from the temple it leads the believer, charged now with all of the divine and divinising energies of that Mystery of the world that is God, once more to the public square of history.

C. Boff, 1996, p. 20

## God as Love-in-Action

One of the first group of women ordained in the Episcopal Church in the United States in 1974, Isabel Carter Heyward has always believed in the radical (and God-filled) nature of actions as well as words. A writer known for her work on sexuality, she has grounded her ethical and political writings in a theology that seeks to reconceive the nature of the divine in ways that reflect the influence of liberationist and praxis models. Instead of a 'transcendent' God established over and against creation (human and non-human), she describes a God who comes into being among those who work to create right relationships. To speak of God – to act with God – is to identify with that which is encountered in the mending of brokenness, in intimacy and in the doing of justice, a God who is love-in-action:

> We touch this strength, our power, who we are in the world, when we are most fully in touch with one another and with the world. There is no doubt in my mind that, in so doing, we are participants in ongoing incarnation, bringing God to life in the world. For God is nothing other than the eternally creative source of our relational power, our common strength, a God whose movement is to empower, bringing us into our own together, a God whose name in history is love.
>
> Love, like truth and beauty, is concrete. Love is not fundamentally a sweet feeling; not at heart, a matter of sentiment, attachment or being drawn toward. Love is active, effective, a matter of making reciprocal and mutually beneficial relations with one's friends and enemies. Love creates righteousness, or justice, here on earth. To make love is to make justice. As advocates and activists for justice know, loving involves struggle, resistance, risk. People working today on behalf of women, blacks, lesbians and gay men, the aging, the poor in this country and elsewhere know that making justice is not a warm, fuzzy experience. I think also that sexual lovers and good friends know that the most compelling relationships demand hard work, patience, and a willingness to endure tensions and anxiety in creating mutually empowering bonds.
>
> For this reason loving involves commitment. We are not automatic

lovers of self, others, world, or God. Love does not just happen. We are not love machines, puppets on the strings of a deity called 'love'. Love is a choice – not simply, or necessarily, a rational choice, but rather a willingness to be present to others without pretense or guile. Love is a conversion to humanity – a willingness to participate with others in the healing of a broken world and broken lives. Love is the choice to experience life as a member of the human family, a partner in the dance of life, rather than as an alien in the world or as a deity above the world, aloof and apart from human flesh.

Heyward, 1984, p. 272

This is necessarily a sensual, embodied and passionate ethic, because Heyward understands the nature of God in this way. She has an incarnational, immanentalist understanding of the nature of the divine, as one who is brought into the world in and through human fellowship and passion. If God is love, she argues, then 'talk about God' is to realize God-in-action through acts of love, reconciliation and solidarity. Reminiscent of Paul Tillich's notion of God as ground of being, this is a concept also adopted by Mary Daly in her stress on Be-ing as divine, elemental source at the heart of women's energies. Heyward suggests that God is to be encountered in the acts of justice-driven people, and is thus more appropriately thought of in terms of verb rather than noun:

When a human being reaches out to comfort, to touch, to bridge the gap separating each of us from everyone else, God comes to life in that act of reaching, of touching, of bridging. The act is love and God is love. And when we love, we god. And I use the word god here intentionally as a verb. If we are as fully human as we are able to be, and Jesus suggested we *are* able to be, then we are godders, we god – human beings/created bodies bringing God to life again, and again. Serving God in the act of serving humanity. Loving God in the act of loving humanity and one another.

1984, p. 140

## Theology for an Age of Uncertainty

The principle of 'theology-in-practice' has been taken further in recent years by the British practical theologian Elaine Graham. In *Transforming Practice* (2002a), first published in 1996, she places the history of pastoral and practical theology under the scrutiny of postmodern thought, arguing that an 'age of uncertainty' has been engendered by the dissolution of many of the scientific, political and philosophical nostrums of Western modernity. Postmodernity may have exposed the illusion of knowledge as unmediated revelation of truth, but it is still possible to trace how sources and norms of knowledge rise up in concrete ways from human practice. As a result, the discipline of practical theology should be reconceived as 'the articulation and excavation of sources and norms of Christian practice', the discipline that 'enables the community of faith to practise what it preaches' (2002a, p. 11).

Graham's exposure of the limitations of modernity arise in part from her earlier work on gender theory and its impact on theology (Graham, 1995). Feminist thought, while owing its origins to the Western Enlightenment, has challenged many of the precepts of modernity, which were founded upon androcentric models of human nature, knowledge and ethics at the expense of more inclusive values. Thus, while the destabilization of fixed identities inherent in Enlightenment rationality has been liberative in many respects, postmodernity's scepticism towards modernity's narratives of progress, reason and human rights is also disturbing for all those, including Christians, concerned with the possibilities for moral action and human emancipation. What has become of the Enlightenment visions of human development and freedom? Is all hope swept away because of our recognition that the claims to truth upon which the modern world was founded were always partial and exclusive, denying the insights and experiences of marginalized groups? If the foundations of modernity have now been proven shaky, is it possible to rejuvenate our narratives of hope and obligation? In other words, 'Do Christian truth claims make any coherent sense amidst the multiple narratives of the public domain?' (Graham, 2002a, p. 2).

Graham's reconstructive project begins with a thorough critical assessment of the fragments of knowledge that inform faithful practice. The implicit value-commitments ('moral horizons') of all strands of knowledge that have informed pastoral theology must be excavated, including the so-called 'value-neutral' secular theories of care. Where do these discourses come from and whose values do they represent? By using this metaphor of excavation, Graham deliberately evokes the work of another practical theologian Don Browning. In his *Fundamental Practical Theology*, Browning envisages the congregation as the context of a renewed moral discourse within pastoral theology: 'I find it useful to think of fundamental practical theology as a critical reflection of the church's dialogue with Christian sources and other communities of experience and interpretation with the aim of guiding its action toward social and individual transformation' (1991, p. 36, see also Chapter 4).

This appeals to Graham's wish to draw upon a multiplicity of narratives that will be engaged in mutually critical dialogue. Yet in his model of practical moral reasoning, Browning seems to imply faithful people 'think' their way into their moral convictions; for Graham this perspective devalues the non-rational, performative, embodied *habitus* of faith communities as the crucial context within which value-commitments are actually realized. 'A critical task therefore remains to identify the possibilities of grounding Christian pastoral practice in alternative values other than those derived from rational ethical discourse' (Graham, 2002a, p. 112).

In *Transforming Practice* Graham is attempting to expose the particularity of the values of modernity, a loss of innocence rather than the absolute annihilation of value. Nevertheless, she is pursuing the possibility of coherent theological reflection and faithful action amidst such a fracturing of certainties. And that involves searching for ways of inhabiting consistently and authentically a tradition of binding values that recognize their own contingency but also seek to create some degree of coherence, discipline and transparency.

To achieve this Graham employs Pierre Bourdieu's idea that cultures have a 'logic of practice' (Bourdieu, 1992). He calls this shared practical sensibility the *habitus*. To be inducted into culture is to acquire a sense of how to behave, as expressed in the practical attitudes, preferences and actions of those around us. The *habitus* makes society possible. We enter a culture in which things are done – practised – in a certain way, and that is chiefly how we learn core values. Yet once more, the process is reflexive: we enter, we inhabit the culture, but we participate in it too and through our actions and agency contribute to the organic unfolding of *habitus*.

Bourdieu is presenting a model of tradition and continuity by which the values of the past are encoded in social life yet continually evolve because of human agency. Thus, Graham's 'turn to practice' does not represent a disregard for Christian tradition, but represents a way of understanding Christians as participating in and reshaping a living faith through their contemporary practices of worship, care and social concern. This tradition itself emerges directly out of Christian reflection upon God. Pastoral theology is theological because it always refers back to a transcendent reality, which forms the horizon over against which its praxis can be judged.

Furthermore, Graham's theology of practice is essentially of a discipline that enables people to live authentic lives by articulating a vision of the good and true in the concrete. Transformative practices are the embodiments and witnesses to 'Divine activity amidst human practice' (Graham, 2000, p. 113), as glimpses of the Word made flesh.

> My vision of pastoral theology portrays it as the systematic reflection upon the nature of the Church in the world, accessible only through the practical wisdom of those very communities. Therefore, as a discipline, pastoral theology is not legislative or prescriptive, but interpretative. It enables the community of faith to give a critical and public account of its purposeful presence in the world, and the values that give shape to its actions . . .
>
> Such a model of pastoral practice is thus a refutation of prescriptive pastoral care which seeks to enforce moral conformity to absolute norms on behalf of controlling and dominating interests. However, it does not abandon completely any notion of pastoral discipline or Christian perfection. In the face of uncertainty and Divine provisionality, Christian pastoral practices can still affirm some kind of (interim) truth and value by virtue of their location in the continuing life and work of the faith-community. The exact nature and purpose of ultimate reality may be cloaked in mystery; but at least a purposive and practising community meets to celebrate and realize the Divine possibility. It is within such a community that those who suffer may find support and healing, and through its celebrations and acts of compassion that healing and redemption may decisively be experienced and prefigured.
>
> Graham, 2002a, pp. 208–9

Yet the hub of Graham's work – and probably the matter on which readers remain convinced or unconvinced – is, essentially, whether one can speak of the infinite, undetermined world in the language of the contingent, finite world of practice. As Paul Lakeland puts it, 'What does it mean to say that God is real?' (1997, p. 49). Graham argues that those who express concern that exposure to postmodernity means we are descending into nihilism do not realize that theological discourse has always proceeded via dialogue with contemporary ideas and movements. Perhaps there are those who see the age of uncertainty as a chance to withdraw completely into the safety of an alternative Christian community; but for Graham, this merely denies the human vocation to bear faithful witness to God-in-the-world, to the world. The alternatives of nostalgia or fideism will not suffice. To be postmodern (which is not the same as being nihilist) is to realize the limits of human self-sufficiency and the provisionality of knowledge: that the very tradition by which Christian practice has been guided was founded on the exclusion of many voices, and that all temporal and cultural contexts are always already bounded by the limits of perception, language and self-interest. 'Only those who pretend to talk from everywhere or nowhere are to be feared as "playing God" and claiming the power of life and death by appealing to universal and totalizing vision and knowledge' (2002a, p. 157).

In writing *Transforming Practice* Graham was not alone among her contemporaries in inscribing a turn to *practice* in contemporary theology. Paul Lakeland's survey of postmodern theologies, published the year after *Transforming Practice*, notes that philosophical concerns about the significance of language were giving way to a commitment to faith in action, or 'faithful sociality' (Lakeland, 1997, p. 60). This echoes other theologians for whom postmodernity is about the resurgence of the sacred and the transcendent, but not as the assertion of the will to power, or the reinscription of absolutism (Ward, 1997). It is more about a movement towards transformation that cannot be contained in temporal discourse, of the importance of engaging with the immanent without illusions but also to know that the vitality and authenticity of that engagement depends on an openness to a divine providence beyond human self-centredness. This understanding relocates 'transcendence' away from other worlds or an immaterial, celestial space, and reconfigures it as 'ever beyond present actuality' (Jantzen, 1998, p. 271). It speaks not of projection but rather incompletion, as if the restlessness of human imagination and activity prompts further movement towards that which the present world cannot yet embody. For Graham, without practice, without narrative and culture, without incarnation, there can be no talk of God.

## Evaluation

This chapter has argued that the method of theology-in-action represents a paradigm shift in the epistemology of theology. It insists on a unity of action and reflection, emerging from concrete experiential knowledge, and adopts an inductive method that tests out the efficacy of Christian teaching in the arena of practical action. This demands a process of reflection on received tradition in the light of substantial problematics such as poverty, marginalization and social exclusion: a process of theological reflection on practice that emerges from 'grassroots' experience. Such reflection also seeks to integrate social analysis that addresses socio-political concerns with materialist readings of Scripture and Christian doctrine informed by the interpretative hermeneutic of the 'bias to the poor'.

This is thus a contextual theology emerging from the dilemmas of Christian and ecclesial identity in a context of extreme economic polarization and political oppression. What are the imperatives of the gospel in this situation? How to discern the signs of the times? These questions call forth a body of knowledge assisting the work of evangelization within the context of poverty and exploitation. If the Good News is to be preached, then this does not principally entail, as Gutiérrez puts it, bringing 'non-believers' to belief, but in assuring those reduced to 'non-human' status by poverty and powerlessness that they are indeed made in the image of God (see 'Introduction', this chapter, pp. 171–2). To proclaim God is not a propositional existential exercise but an event in which God's promise of justice, healing and reconciliation erupts into history, something that cannot be viewed dispassionately but demands a corresponding participation in the renewal of social reality. 'Ideas alone are never the message of the Gospel. Action is' (Rahner, 1968, p. 132). — *B*

Therefore, theological understanding is neither neutral nor universal in origin, but emerging from and reflecting its interests and authors. But due to the prior commitment to authentic knowledge as that which reveals the true purpose of history – understood here as the fulfilment of the biblical injunctions to identify with God's preferential option for the poor – then authentic theology is equated with that which furthers the purposes of divine deliverance from oppression. And in keeping with the Hegelian influence on Marx, God is understood as active and immanent within human history.

Thus, for Gustavo Gutiérrez, 'we cannot separate our discourse about God from the historical process of liberation' (1988, p. xviii) because the proclamation of the gospel is *primarily* embedded in transformative action. This means that theological reflection is necessarily a *second-order* discipline, responding to and systematizing the practices of faith, exercising a critical and instructive role in mapping the values by which Christian vocation is to be lived.

One chief criticism directed at theologies of liberation has been not so much their concern for the emancipation of the poor and oppressed or their commendation of social action for justice, as the sources used to inform such a project. While liberation theologians vary in their attachment to Marxism, critics accuse them of subordinating theological perspectives to dogmatic Marxist theory and to its vision of a secular humanist utopia. To quote *Centesimus Annus* (1991), Pope

John Paul II's encyclical on the 100th anniversary of *Rerum Novarum*, 'when people think they possess the secret of a perfect social organization which makes evil impossible, they also think they can use any means, including violence and deceit, in order to bring that organization into being. Politics then becomes a "secular religion" which operates under the illusion of creating paradise in this world' (John Paul II, 1991). In placing trust in Marxist analysis and account of history, say the critics, theologians are elevating humanism at the expense of God. Yet in their defence, liberation theologians argue that their understanding of the preferential option for the poor and the actions of God in history are *as much* biblical in inspiration as Hegelian and Marxist.

The kind of postmodern practical theology represented by Elaine Graham has also been criticized for commending practice as the guiding criterion of Christian theological identity as something entirely antinomian, spontaneous, merely led by the spirit of the age rather than rooted in proper Christian revelation. Yet such a commitment to practice, like that of the liberationists, is informed not by a disregard for Christian tradition, but in order to emphasize the way in which pastoral practice is both informed by, and constitutive of, an embodied and enacted narrative of faith. Transformative practice not only represents divine matters, but enables people to conform their lives to the divine.

## Questions

- Is the praxis method of theological reflection necessarily always a 'counter-cultural' voice within the churches?
- How would you assess the significance of the use of the Bible on the part of exponents of liberation theology?
- Does the political emphasis of theologies of liberation or the postmodern mood of Graham's theology of practice diminish or enhance a distinctively *theological* orientation to Christian praxis?

## Annotated Bibliography

Bradstock, A. and Rowland C. (eds) (2002), *Radical Christian Writings: A Reader*, Oxford: Blackwell. A chronological selection of primary sources from early Christianity to the twentieth century.

Freire, P. (1972), *Pedagogy of the Oppressed*, London: Penguin. An excellent introduction to the major themes in Freire's work, such as conscientization, literacy as humanization and effective pedagogy. Freire's influence extends far beyond liberation theology into education, community organizing and grass-roots politics.

Graham, E. ([1996] 2002a), *Transforming Practice: Practical Theology in an Age of Uncertainty*, Eugene, ON: Wipf and Stock, 2nd edn. As well as setting out her argument for a rejuvenated, postmodern practical theology, Graham offers a critique and overview of the history of pastoral care and practical theology since Schleiermacher.

Green, L. (1990), *Let's Do Theology*, London: Geoffrey Chapman. Laurie Green's illustration of how he enabled a group of people who knitted for a leprosy charity to reflect corporately and theologically upon what they were doing is a classic example of the pastoral cycle in operation in a communal context. As a result of the process Green embellished the method into what he terms the 'pastoral spiral'.

Gutiérrez, G. ([1973] 1988), *A Theology of Liberation*, New York: Orbis, 3rd edn. A foundational text for Latin American liberation theology. Gutiérrez's introductions to successive editions provide an interesting commentary to the evolution of the genre.

# 'Theology in the Vernacular': Local Theologies

## The Method in Outline

This method draws attention to the specific form the Christian gospel assumes in any given place or time. It demonstrates that theology is culturally, temporally and spatially located, and that the gospel cannot exist independent of particular, embodied expressions. If one motif unites all talk of 'local theologies' it is probably the attention to *culture* as a multi-dimensional lived reality that shapes the reception and transmission of the Christian faith. More recently, theologians have stressed the importance of theology taking on the characteristics of local and particular cultures in order to speak *in the vernacular*: utilizing the everyday language and symbols of ordinary people and paying attention to theological motifs in popular culture. The term 'vernacular' links this method to movements throughout Christian history that have sought to provide Biblical translations and liturgies in people's own native tongue, thereby breaking down the barriers of language or culture which might otherwise impede the reception of word and sacrament.

## Introduction

The issue of Christian distinctiveness in relation to its surrounding culture was a major preoccupation for the early Church. For some, such as Tertullian (d. AD 220), the absolute demands of the gospel were non-negotiable. 'What has Athens to do with Jerusalem?' he asked, attributing the highest authority to the unbroken integrity of apostolic witness. Conversely, Justin Martyr (c. AD 100–165) argued that converts to Christianity should not be expected to abandon prior cultural loyalties, if, as he argued, they could be proven consistent with the values of the gospel. Thus, for him, Stoicism and the teachings of

Plato and Aristotle – with their assent to the notion of a transcendent creator God and positive evaluation of the ability of reason to lead individuals to the truth – could be affirmed as containing 'the seed of the Word': a recognition of a common human experience in which the Gospel may be prefigured (see Chapter 5).

From the fifteenth century onwards, the expansion of Western colonial ambitions in Asia and the Americas brought an accompanying renewal of Christian missionary activity. In comparison to the pre-Constantinian era, however, the cross-cultural encounters between Christianity and local cultures were of a very different nature. Christianity was frequently assumed to be synonymous with Western culture. The colonial powers occupied the new lands with the explicit blessing of the Church, often with genocidal consequences. The indigenous (colonized) cultures were also regarded very differently: gone was the respect for the inherent integrity of pagan world-views, as articulated by Justin, Clement and Aquinas; in its place was an explicit 'civilizing' mission that saw the planting of the Christian gospel as a way of removing and suppressing the degenerate values of 'primitive' cultures.

Some notable exceptions to this perspective are significant, however, because they retain elements of a respect for the inbuilt integrity of local cultures as the seed-bed of proto-Christian values. They display the evolution of incarnational theology and the influence of Thomist understandings of natural law (in which human culture is affirmed as capable of representing aspects of God's will for creation). This cautious respect for local cultures developed into a more explicitly 'humanist' tradition that acknowledged the possibility of God's very presence in non-Christian traditions. While strong similarities are evident between this and the correlational method (Chapter 5), local theologies represent a more radical synthesis between traditions articulated in one context and the process of their transposition into different cultural, linguistic or geographical settings.

In the modern era, we shall see how two contributions – the documents of Vatican II (1962–65) and the cultural anthropology of Clifford Geertz – proved particularly influential. These fostered an appreciation of 'culture' as a human material and symbolic construct; and they also emphasized the need to understand the distinctiveness of each local context *from within* in order to offer theological responses that respected the integrity of that situation. As a result, terms such as 'contextualization', 'indigenization' and 'inculturation' have all been used to highlight the ways in which cultural diversity necessarily shapes the transmission and expression of the gospel. As Stephen Bevans has written, we may identify the primary focus of inculturation as one of reading 'culture', meaning 'the web of human relationships and meanings that make up human culture, and in which God is present, offering life, healing, and wholeness' (2002, p. 2).

It will therefore be plain that this method of theological reflection requires that particular attention be given to the local traditions, material and symbolic practices that make up the 'way of life' of a people. Such an anthropological model understands the process of theological reflection as being oriented towards a Christian community that stands in critical solidarity with the aspirations and insights expressed in the cultural context in which it is located. Its emphasis on the inherent goodness of human nature also extends to the work of communicating the gospel. Rather than implanting Christ into a particular culture, the work of theological reflection may be understood as more of a 'treasure hunt' seeking to bring to the surface signs of God's grace and activity present in the midst of culture. At a personal and corporate level, this model of theological reflection seeks to build faithful lives and communities by working within, and in partnership with, the cultural patterns and institutions already in existence. The task of *Christian formation and nurture* is to enable the believer to live more fully in their context, rather than attempting to remake them in the image of Western Christianity. Advocates of local theologies would argue that while the introduction of Christianity into a culture might challenge it in particular areas it would never completely change it; and that the Church must become deeply assimilated into culture in order to fulfil its incarnational calling.

## Reflections from History

### The Day of Pentecost

When the day of Pentecost had come, they were all together in one place. And suddenly from heaven there came a sound like the rush of a violent wind, and it filled the entire house where they were sitting. Divided tongues, as of fire, appeared among them, and a tongue rested on each of them. All of them were filled with the Holy Spirit and began to speak in other languages, as the Spirit gave them ability.

Now there were devout Jews from every nation under heaven living in Jerusalem. And at this sound the crowd gathered and was bewildered, because each one heard them speaking in the native language of each. Amazed and astonished, they asked, 'Are not all these who are speaking Galileans? And how is it that we hear, each of us, in our own native language? Parthians, Medes, Elamites, and residents of Mesopotamia, Judaea and Cappadocia, Pontus and Asia, Phrygia and Pamphylia, Egypt and the parts of Libya belonging to Cyrene, and visitors from Rome, both Jews and proselytes, Cretans and Arabs – in our own languages we hear them speaking about God's deeds of power.' All were amazed and perplexed, saying to one another, 'What does this mean?' But others sneered and said, 'They are filled with new wine.'

Acts 2.1–12 (NRSV)

The emergence of the first Christian communities occurred in a highly pluralist environment, and Christianity spread quickly, from its origins in Jerusalem, throughout the Roman world. One way of understanding what the day of Pentecost represents is as the preaching of the good news in all the languages of the known world. It is a clear indication of the global significance of the Christian gospel. The people represented as the potential recipients of the good news are drawn not only from the nation of Israel, but come from many regions of the Roman Empire. They include proselytes – or God-fearers, Gentiles sympathetic to Judaism – as well as Jews.

From its very beginnings, therefore, the Church was asking itself about the nature of the relationship between its exclusively Jewish origins and the Gentile cultures that came rapidly to assimilate it. On the one hand, this was a matter of moving from an exclusive to a more universal understanding of God's revelation in Christ; and this transition is apparent in the Church's memory of Peter's struggles to see beyond an exclusively Jewish expression of God's covenant with humanity towards an understanding of salvation as transcending creed, class or status (Acts 10. 9–16). Yet controversy continued to divide the Christians in centres such as Antioch and Jerusalem (see Acts 15) as to the extent to which the Good News was to be preached to the Gentiles or solely to the Jews, and if Gentiles should be expected to conform to Jewish religious customs. 'It would only provoke God's anger now, surely, if you imposed on the disciples the very burden that neither we nor our ancestors were strong enough to support? Remember, we believe that we are saved in the same way as they are: through the grace of the Lord Jesus' (Acts 15.10).

With the apprehension that the gospel was to be preached to all cultures and peoples – a realization of its universal and unconditional nature – came a second, related problem: how far should local variations of culture and custom be allowed to condition the way in which the Good News was to be proclaimed and received, not always with the greatest success (see Acts 14 for example). As with Paul's speech at Athens, therefore (see Chapter 5), the earliest disciples found themselves shaping their message according to the audiences among which they found themselves. But the question remained, of how far the unity of all Christians – in their corporate identity, moral conduct, theological language and practice – could be modified in the face of a diversity of cultural settings, and how far the distinctiveness of any given context should shape Christian doctrines and practices. These were to become perennial questions for theological understanding and Church polity.

## Origen Attempts a Synthesis with Greek Thought

As the discussion of the second-century Apologists in Chapter 5 on critical correlation revealed, early Christianity was engaging in a constant process of dialogue with surrounding cultures and philosophies. It is arguable that Christian theology was only consolidated with the assistance of concepts and rhetorical strategies borrowed from its Jewish and pagan interlocutors. Yet the degree to which early Christian writers were prepared to assimilate such thinking varied; and for some, such as Justin Martyr and Clement of Alexandria, the dialogical task was intended to turn the arguments of their non-Christian conversation partners against them. For others, however, there seems to have been a greater willingness to allow a fuller *synthesis*, whereby Christian doctrine becomes dependent on prevailing thought-forms for its maturation. One such example is Origen of Alexandria (AD 185–254).

Born into a Christian family, much of Origen's early education was in Greek philosophy – naturally enough, given that Alexandria was the centre of Hellenic civilization at the time. Christians were under extreme pressure, not only intellectually from their pagan detractors, but also from internal tensions occasioned by the emergence of Gnostic tendencies, as well as because of persecution under successive Roman emperors. Origen's *On First Principles* (around AD 212–15), written in Greek, represents one of the first systematic articulations of Christian doctrines of God, demonstrating in its arguments how deeply indebted he was to Greek philosophical traditions such as Platonism and Stoicism.

He begins the work with an extended meditation on the nature of God, imitating the structure of the Platonic thought of his day. This passage is believed by many commentators to reflect the influence of the Greek scholar Numenius, who posited a threefold quality to God. Following Numenius, Origen speaks of the hierarchical nature of the Trinity, in which the first person (God the Father) is a monadic unity, self-sufficient, and characterized by pure reason. Emanating from the Father is the second person, the Son, who is akin to Numenius's 'second God', whom he likens to a demiurge. The Spirit also derives from the Father, and the relationship of all three persons of the Trinity to material creation is similarly mediated, with God the Father as pre-eminent and the others relating only to strictly demarcated aspects of creation:

> The God and Father, who holds the universe together, is superior to every being that exists, for he imparts to each one from his own existence that which each one is; the Son, being less than the Father, is superior to rational creatures alone (for he is second to the Father); the Holy Spirit is still less, and dwells within the saints alone. So that in this way the power of the Father is greater than that of the Son and of the Holy Spirit, and that of the Son is more than that of the Holy Spirit, and in turn the power of the Holy Spirit exceeds that of every other holy being.
>
> Origen, 1985, Fragment 9

Platonism also influenced Origen's doctrine of humanity. He argued that God originally created a race of rational beings, which Origen called *logika*, who lived outside space and time with God until they fell away from the divine presence into temporal, embodied existence. Yet they retained free will and rationality, and were thus still capable of experiencing divine perfection and wisdom even in such a finite, imperfect realm. Origen's concept of God is as a great teacher, who will use the circumstances of each person to reveal Godself to them, drawing them closer to divine wisdom and grace by means of their inherent capacities for reason and moral discernment. Thus, knowledge of the good (and communion with God) is available to all created beings, despite their flaws; and traces of such divine wisdom can be found in human reason, culture and history. This means that reconciliation with God is anticipated for all humanity. Origen termed this 'the restoration of all things' (*apokatastasis*).

Origen offers a positive account of human experience, therefore, that, while displaying its Platonic roots, also acquires an eschatological flavour. He presents a benevolent God presiding over the evolution of human history and restoring the human form to its divine image and likeness. Platonic concepts of the hierarchy of creation are thus tempered with a more Stoic affirmation of the dignity and perfectibility of the human person, furnishing Origen and his successors with a potentially very inclusive understanding of divine grace and providence, which stresses the autonomy and freedom of the human person to seek out the good – equated with a gradual participation in the infinite and perfect mysteries of the divine origin of all things.

Origen was not afraid to break new ground, and to enlist Greek philosophy and metaphysics in the service of the further elucidation and development of Christian theology. His Neoplatonic theology was not acceptable to all his contemporaries. Yet his legacy is important in two ways: for demonstrating how Hellenic thought and culture helped shape doctrine, and for beginning to articulate a theory of culture in which human reason, self-discovery and history are themselves pathways to divine wisdom. At the heart of his convictions was a commitment to the incarnation and to the essential dignity of humanity as created in *imago Dei,* from which he deduced that God valued human culture and human reason for the furtherance of divine purposes. As a Neoplatonist, Origen's world-view was less about a world of material cultures than a spiritual world of souls inhabiting God, perceived as pure reason. Nevertheless, his benign view of human creativity and autonomy sowed the seeds for a form of Christian humanism that continued to place a high value on reason and culture, alongside revelation, as theological resources.

Methods of theological understanding containing synthetic or assimilationist tendencies, such as Origen's, often coexisted alongside understandings that stressed an altogether more counter-cultural message. An element of cultural distinctiveness, that the universal claims of the gospel require the faithful to transcend the values of the 'secular' world, was also an insistent voice within early Christian writings. The Letter to the Romans exhorts the faithful to be 'transformed' and not 'conformed' to the values of their surroundings (Rom. 12.1–2); and 1 Peter exhorts the Church to consider themselves visitors and pilgrims in a strange land, observant of its customs but subject to the higher law of God (1 Pet. 2.11–12). Other Christian writings, such as the Epistle to Diognetus – dating from the second century AD – continued in this vein, describing Christians as having, in effect, dual citizenship, fully committed to their surroundings and but never fully assimilated into prevailing, worldly norms. The demands of 'Christ' often overturn the expectations of 'culture', and the gospel can never be totally contained by any single human expression of it:

> For Christians are not differentiated from other people by country, language or customs; you see, they do not live in cities of their own, or speak some strange dialect, or have some peculiar lifestyle . . . They live in both Greek and foreign cities, wherever chance has put them. They follow local customs in clothing, food and other aspects of life. But at the same time, they demonstrate to us the wonderful and certainly unusual form of their own citizenship. They live in their own native lands, but as aliens; as citizens, they share all things with others; but like aliens, suffer all things. Every foreign country is to them as their native country, and every native land as a foreign country.
>
> Epistle of Mathetes to Diognetus, 2001, Chapter V

Nevertheless, the tradition of a receptivity to the integrity of different cultures, and the Gospel as transcending any one cultural expression to become something in which all humanity could participate, had some significant exemplars from the beginnings of Christian history. Indeed, from its very beginnings, Christianity was a multilingual, multicultural movement, conversing in Latin and Greek as well as Aramaic and Hebrew, factors that inevitably shaped its cultural diversity. Christianity spread rapidly from its original cultural setting, and before long it was competing with a variety of religious and philosophical world-views across the ancient Near East and North Africa. The understanding of early Christian writers of the inescapably culturally rooted nature of the gospel thus represents an important and enduring source for styles of theological reflection that seek to embody cultural particularity and diversity.

## Erasmus and the Dawn of Humanism

The rediscovery of Classical Greco-Roman culture and philosophy associated with the Italian Renaissance encouraged a reappraisal of Classical civilization. Its linguistic and intellectual fruits were put to work in the service of theology, for example in the retranslation and interpretation of Scripture. A leading scholar in this movement was Desiderius Erasmus of Rotterdam (1466–1536) who produced a definitive edition of the New Testament in Greek, eschewing much of the obscurantism of scholastic theology in favour of a less formal, more direct approach. Part of the motivation for Erasmus's interest in reading Scripture in its Latin and Greek versions may have been a wish on his part to return to the simplicities of 'primitive' textual sources, rather than relying on the complex, allegorical meanings favoured by scholasticism. His love of classical sources may also have been motivated by a desire to restore Scripture to its original cultural contexts, free of the embellishments of later translations and interpretations, consistent with his (often iconoclastic) contrast between the values of 'simple faith' and the corruptions of the institutional Church. It may also have explained his unwillingness to get involved in the politics of the Reformation, despite his ostensible affinities with much of its teaching.

As a theologian and biblical scholar, Erasmus was concerned to set out principles for ethical living, which he regarded as rooted in simple piety and knowledge of Scripture. He was also aware of the importance of making theology accessible and offering preaching and interpretation with a pastoral orientation. One such sermon, written in 1524, holds out the promise of forgiveness as a staple of God's miraculous work in creation. Characteristically, Erasmus cites sources from Old and New Testaments in support of his argument, showing how the goodness and mercy of God was known even before Christ.

Why do I bother to recite these examples of the Lord's mercy taken from the Old Testament? The entire scripture of the old covenant extols the mercy of God. Some men try to make two Gods out of one: one of the Old Testament, who was only just and not good, and one of the New Testament, who was only good and not just. These men are insane rather than heretical. For in the psalms it is often repeated, 'O give thanks unto the Lord, for He is gracious; and His mercy endureth forever.'

Manichaeus taught that He who spoke to us through the prophets and enacted the laws of Moses was not the true God, but one of the guilty demons. The same God is God of either law, the same truth, the same mercy through Jesus Christ our Lord, except that in the law of Moses there are only shadows; in the Gospel, truth. In the former there are promises, in the latter is their fulfillment. One shows great mercy toward the Jews, the other shows this mercy to all the world, destroying the sins of all mortals . . .

Why, then, do you despair, keeping yourself from salvation and the Lord from happiness? For He who grieves over the death of a sinner, and is happy at one's conversion, will not refuse to pardon those who repent. Then why do you tarry and fight against God's mercy? Christ is the wisdom of God. According to Solomon, 'And all the while Wisdom is publishing her message, crying aloud in the open streets; never a meeting of the roads, never a gateway, but her voice is raised, echoing above the din of it. What, she says, are you still gaping there, simpletons? Do the reckless still court their own ruin? Rash fools, will you never learn? Pay heed, then, to my protest; listen while I speak out my mind to you, give you open warning.'

'Concerning the Immense Mercy of God',
1524, in Dolan, 1964, pp. 256–8

Erasmus and other contemporaries, such as Thomas More, were also concerned to rehabilitate Stoic philosophy, with its emphasis on the innate human qualities of reason and self-determination. This was intended to cultivate the study of classical civilization as the basis for a reformed Christianity, free of the corruption of the institutional Church and capable of returning, via the renewal of linguistic and textual scholarship, to the unadulterated truths of Scripture. Yet underpinning this was an adoption of the Stoic theory of knowledge, which held that the natural light of reason guides all human beings toward a greater truth and moral sensibility. From this developed a particular kind of Christian humanism, which held the view that all religions express a common set of truths about God, a perspective endorsed by theologians such as Erasmus, More, Philip Melanchthon and Ulrich Zwingli, and which prefigured the Deism of the eighteenth century.

## Catholic Missions to the 'New World'

The humanist principles of the Renaissance are clearly articulated in the courageous protests of Bartholomé de las Casas, an outspoken critic of the Spanish conquest of South America – and, some would claim, proto-liberation theologian – against the Church's collusion in the enslavement of the native peoples. Audaciously, at a time when European settlers and theologians were debating whether the native peoples were to be considered fully human (and thus in possession of immortal souls, ripe for conversion rather than enslavement), las Casas defended their full equality and capacity to reason. At the heart of his doctrine of human nature was an essentially Stoic concept of humans as virtuous and rational creatures, capable of exercising free will. This underpinned a commitment to the essential unity of all humanity, informed by a rudimentary theory of cultural evolution. However 'primitive' or savage a people may appear to the outsider, they were capable of scaling the ladder of civilization by virtue of their innately rational faculties. As a result, the task of bringing the natives to faith did not need to involve coercion or conquest:

> The way of teaching people has to be a gentle, coaxing, gracious way. It wins the mind with reasons, it wins the will with graciousness. So, one way, one way only, of teaching a living faith, to everyone, everywhere, always, was set by divine Providence, a way that wins the mind with reasons, that wins the will with gentleness, with invitation.
>
> Las Casas, 1992, p. 68

Las Casas's theory of cultural evolution enabled him to judge the customs and beliefs of the indigenous peoples of the Americas within their own frame of reference, rather than imposing an absolute moral certainty drawn from European values. At a time when many settlers were content merely to plunder the reserves of wealth of ancient civilizations such as the Incas and Aztecs, las Casas made the case for regarding the intellectual achievements of such cultures as comparable with those of ancient Greece or Rome.

> For all the peoples of the world are men [sic], and the definition of all men, collectively and severally, is one: that they are rational beings. All possess understanding and volition, being formed in the image and likeness of God; all have the five exterior senses and the four interior senses, and are moved by the objects of these; all have natural capacity or faculties to understand and master the knowledge that they do not have; and this is true not only of those that are inclined toward good but those that by reason of their depraved customs are bad; all take pleasure in goodness and in happy and pleasant things and all abhor evil and reject what offends or grieves them . . .
>
> Thus all mankind is one, and all men are alike in what concerns their creation and all natural things, and no one is born enlightened. From this it follows that all of us must be guided and aided at first by those who were born before us. And the savage peoples of the earth may be compared to uncultivated soil that readily brings forth weeds and useless thorns, but has within itself such natural virtue that by labour and cultivation it may be made to yield sound and healthful fruits.
>
> Las Casas, in Keen, 1996, pp. 72–3

Las Casas, who became bishop of Chiapas in Mexico, returned to Spain in 1546 in order to continue the struggle on behalf of the indigenous peoples of the New World at the centre of power, the court of the Emperor, Charles V. His interventions had been instrumental in the publication of the New Laws of the Indies in 1542, which had aimed to bring an end to further enslavements of the native population. But when, under pressure from the Spanish settlers, Charles partially revoked these laws, Las Casas was bitterly disappointed and expressed his sorrow at being parted from his people, identifying their suffering at the hands of the conquistadors with that of the crucified Christ: 'I left behind me in the Indies Jesus Christ our God, scourged, tortured, crucified, not once but a million times' (quoted in Witvliet, 1985, p. 12). Rather than seeing the native people as a 'savage' race who must be subdued and Christianized, las Casas turns prevailing understandings on their heads, placing their situation at the centre of divine purposes, suggesting that their very predicament may itself be an epiphany of the human face of God.

The Roman Catholic *Sacred Congregation for the Propagation of the Faith*, founded in 1622, also attempted to counter the ethnocentrism of missionary activity. It laid down guidelines for the conduct of, and established elements of training for, missionaries. Its manuals also introduced, perhaps for the first time, a degree of reflection on the nature of the evangelization process itself; and while there were many who adopted a 'conservative' stance in which Western values and terminology were seen as non-negotiable, others advocated a closer identification with their host cultures and discretion in suppressing indigenous practices.

Another example of a Western missionary who practised a more sensitive strategy towards local culture was the Jesuit Matteo Ricci (1552–1610). On his arrival in China in 1582, he set himself the task of assimilating into local culture, by casting himself as scholar rather than priest and immersing himself in Chinese cartography, astronomy, languages and mathematics. He was particularly concerned to engage constructively with Confucianism, in order to mediate between Christian and Chinese world-views. Ricci was at pains to stress the convergence of Christianity and Confucianism on many important points, such as filial loyalty and piety. For him, there was no conflict between Christianity and Confucianism since the latter could not be considered a 'religion', but was simply a philosophical system. Nevertheless, Confucianism unlocked for him some key ethical and religious principles through which he could commend the Christian point of view; and Ricci permitted his followers to participate in Confucian rituals of venerating family ancestors, even though Church authorities tended to interpret such practices as 'ancestor worship' and therefore idolatrous. Indeed, despite the progressive sentiments of the Sacred Congregation for the Propagation of the Faith, in 1704 the Vatican gave orders that Chinese Catholics should not follow traditional Chinese rites that did not conform to Catholicism.

## The Method Realized

### Vatican II and the Evangelization of Cultures

The transition towards more fully realized notions of local theology within the second half of the twentieth century arose out of a number of convergent movements. The success of struggles for national independence and the moral outrage against colonialism provoked a growing realization amongst missionaries and progressive Christians alike that an unholy alliance had been forged between Western theology and Western imperialism. Along with this there developed within former colonial countries an energetic resistance to globalizing or universalizing tendencies of classical theology and a new celebration of the wisdom to be found within indigenous religious traditions.

There was also an increased theological interest in human dignity and autonomy. Writing from his prison cell shortly before his execution in 1945, the Protestant theologian Dietrich Bonhoeffer had declared that the world had 'come of age'. Archaic theological images were no longer adequate for modern times and the Church should not seek to shore up the ruins of theology but confidently proclaim that Christ was to be encountered in the midst of life. As Christ was to be found at the centre of human existence Christians were called to seek him there. Within the Catholic Church the Catholic Action groups (such as Young Christian Workers and Young Christian Students) had been articulating similar themes for many years. Priests who had served as chaplains to these lay groups began to develop theologies that reflected the significance of lay engagement within cultural life.

It is from within the Catholic Church that the first clear statements endorsing the trend towards local theologies emerges. In the documents of Vatican II (1962–65) a more responsive approach to evangelization begins to take shape. The Council recognized the autonomy of the Church in each culture to articulate the gospel without the mediation of Western thought forms. It also recommended the integration of 'younger' churches (that is, those from countries colonized by the West) into the global communion as equal partners with a developing local leadership. The local church, while part of the universal Church, was also seen as embodying sacramentally what it means to be the body of Christ in a certain place and time. The Church is thus imaged as a 'communion' of local churches.

Above all, the council was concerned with shaping Christian mission to meet the needs of its host cultures. The gospel was regarded as something that grew as much 'from below' as it was imposed 'from above'; and in keeping with its statements on religious freedom, the conciliar documents on mission emphasize the importance of non-coercive processes of evangelization:

> Man [sic] comes to a true and full humanity only through culture; that is through the cultivation of the goods and values of nature. Wherever human life is involved, therefore, nature and culture are quite intimately connected one with the other. The word 'culture' in its general sense indicates everything whereby man develops and perfects his many bodily and spiritual qualities; he strives by his knowledge and his labour, to bring the world itself under his control. He renders social life more human both in the family and the civic community, through improvement of customs and institutions.
>
> Throughout the course of time he expresses, communicates and conserves in his works, great spiritual experiences and desires, that they might be of advantage to the progress of many, even of the whole human family.
>
> Thence it follows that human culture has necessarily a historical and social aspect and the word 'culture' also often assumes a socio-logical and ethnological sense. According to this sense we speak of a plurality of cultures. Different styles of life and multiple scales of values arise from the diverse manner of using things, of labouring, of expressing oneself, of practicing [sic] religion, of forming customs, of establishing laws and juridic [sic] institutions, of cultivating the sciences, the arts and beauty. Thus the customs handed down to it form the patrimony proper to each human community. It is also in this way that there is formed the definite, historical milieu which enfolds the man of every nation and age and from which he draws the values which permit him to promote civilization.
>
> *On the Church in the Modern World,*
> paragraph 53, in Abbott, 1966

Vatican II focuses attention upon 'culture' as an artful human creation that is worthy of serious attention. The documents of the council seek to commend processes of evangelization that negotiate between a proper regard for the integrity of local cultures and the transformative effect of the gospel, as a later document, *Evangelii Nuntiandi* ('On Evangelization', 1975) makes clear:

> [The] Church, living in various circumstances in the course of time, has used the discoveries of different cultures so that in her preaching she might spread and explain the message of Christ to all nations, that she might examine it and more deeply understand it, that she might give it better expression in liturgical celebration and in the varied life of the community of the faithful.
>
> But at the same time, the Church, sent to all peoples of every time and place, is not bound exclusively and indissolubly to any race or nation, any particular way of life or any customary way of life recent or ancient. Faithful to her own tradition and at the same time conscious of her universal mission, she can enter into communion with the various civilizations, to their enrichment and the enrichment of the Church herself.
>
> ('On Evangelization', 1975 (online), available at:
> http://www.papalencyclicals.net/Paulo6/p6evan.html
> [accessed 03/01/05])

## Local and Catholic Theology in the Work of Robert Schreiter

The positive and confident approach to human culture that shines through the pages of Vatican II has been carried forward in the work of a number of progressive Catholic theologians who are concerned to deepen Christian understanding of the shape the Church should take in today's 'glocal' (global and local) societies. Among these the work of Robert Schreiter has been particularly significant. In his important text *Constructing Local Theologies* (1985) Schreiter draws upon the work of one of the most famous cultural anthropologists of the present day, Clifford Geertz. Geertz characterizes culture as a network of meanings, signs and symbols:

> The concept of culture I espouse . . . is essentially a semiotic one. Believing, with Max Weber, that man is an animal suspended in webs of significance he himself has spun, I take culture to be those webs, and the analysis of it to be therefore not an experimental science in search of law but an interpretive one in search of meaning.
>
> Geertz, 1973, p. 5

Geertz argues that cultures are bearers of complex and multidimensional messages – what he terms 'thick' meanings. These constitute 'an historically transmitted pattern of meanings embodied in symbols, a system of inherited conceptions expressed in symbolic forms by means of which people communicate, perpetuate, and develop their knowledge about and attitudes toward life' (p. 89). Following Geertz, Schreiter argues that culture must be interpreted 'semiotically'. That is, the signs and symbols people use to communicate among themselves and represent their identity offer the key to interpreting cultures. To understand any cultural context entails deciphering the profound clues embedded in everyday and commonplace practices. This work is undertaken in the service of articulating how the complex texture of a local culture shapes a people's sense of God and informs the manner in which Christ can be encountered as deeply incarnate in human life.

> How is a community to go about bringing to expression its own experience of Christ in its concrete situation? And how is this to be related to a tradition that is often expressed in language and concepts vastly different from anything in the current situation?
>
> Schreiter, 1985, p. xi
>
> Culture is the concrete context in which this happens. It represents a way of life for a given time and place, replete with values, symbols, and meanings, reaching out with hopes and dreams, often struggling for a better world. Without a sensitivity to the cultural context, a church and its theology either become a vehicle for outside domination or lapse into docetism, as though its Lord never became flesh.
>
> p. 21

In the work of Schreiter we can observe a sophisticated attention to anthropological and semiotic definitions of human cultures as a necessary aspect of Christian mission. In *Constructing Local Theologies* he employs the term *inculturation* to express this shift in missionary strategy and theological perspective. Schreiter explains the origin of the term to be an elision of the terms 'incarnation' as a theological principle and 'acculturation' a social-scientific term denoting the process by which the gospel came to birth: 'Inculturation is the dynamic relation between the Christian message and culture or cultures; an insertion of the Christian life into a culture; an ongoing process of reciprocal and critical insertion and assimilation between them'[5] (p. 17). In stressing the significance and integrity of the immediate and the specific, the model of inculturation engenders a strongly inductive theology. Just as cultural difference is valued, and the possibilities of what Eliade called 'hierophanies of the sacred' (Eliade, 1959) affirmed in many cultural contexts and expressions, so local theologies attend to drawing out the signs of divine disclosure from the values and symbols of a particular culture. A primary theological rationale for this is rooted in the doctrine of the incarnation: the local and specific and concrete is affirmed because it is the place of Divine revelation. Christians believe that it is supremely in the human that God is encountered most completely, because of the person of Christ. But theologians do not have to 'import' God; God is there already. So there is a clear belief that indigenous cultures are capable of apprehending the Divine in their midst. Local theology thus seeks to be a conduit by which some of those expressions might be realized: the values of a culture, its focal images, its social ills and problems, codes of conduct, habits and customs, cultural and political patterns and institutions.

Local theologies thus emerge from readings of culture as lived reality in order to 'discover its principal values, needs, interests, directions, and symbols' (Schreiter, 1985, p. 28). Yet for many, the prospect of the proliferation of many local theologies does raise the likelihood of loss of any sense of coherence or homogeneity of Christian theology. What is to prevent relativism and discontinuity between different local theologies? To what extent should some degree of 'family resemblance' be expected, either cross-culturally or historically throughout the generations? In response to these objections Schreiter has suggested that it is possible to talk of a 'catholicity' of local theologies, which fosters a comparative perspective against which particular expressions can gauge their authenticity. He advances five criteria for deciding the authenticity of local theological expressions, all of which need to be observed in order for a particular expression to be seen as adequately in step with Christian identity as consistently practised.

'The cohesiveness of Christian performance' ensures that local expressions of theological reflection reflect the breadth of historic tradition and do not 'skew' it too far in any particular direction. 'The worshipping context and Christian performance' argues for worship as a 'touchstone' of authentic identity. 'The praxis of the community and Christian performance' reflects many of the emphases of Chapter 6 by arguing that the integrity of faith is judged by its service in pursuit of justice. 'The judgement of other Churches and Christian performance' requires that a local community is prepared to be open to comparison with other churches. 'The challenge to other churches and Christian performance', conversely, argues that a local theology should be capable of moving beyond its own boundaries to contribute constructively to other local contexts (pp . 117–21).

In my view, the fact that any understanding of the faith has its roots in the particularity of a given situation should not cause us to neglect the comparison of what we are doing with efforts being made at the level of the universal church. Particularity does not mean isolation. It is true, of course, that each type of theological thinking cannot, and ought not, be applied mechanically to situations different from that in which it arose; whence the foolishness of attempts to do that with liberation theology, as if it resembled a pharmaceutical pre-scription. But it is no less true that any theology is discourse about a universal message. For this reason, and to the extent that it springs from an experience that is both deeply human and deeply Christian, every theology has a universal significance; or, to put it more accu-rately, every theology is a question and challenge for believers living other human situations.

Gutiérrez, 1988, p. xxxvi

This may still appear too slippery and relativistic for those who place great store by the universalism of theology and who regard the gospel as transcending the particularity of human cultures. Yet it is an attempt to introduce a concept of 'catholicity' into the process of vali-dating and authenticating local theologies that runs consistent with Vatican II's principle of the universal Church as 'communion' of local churches.

## Vincent Donovan and Theology among the Masai

Schreiter's work offers a sophisticated theological rationale for a deep engagement with local cultures. However, much of his writing con-cerns the theoretical principles that underlie the construction of local theology. In contrast, Vincent Donovan's *Christianity Rediscovered* ([1978] 1982) is an actual case study in constructing local theology from a cross-cultural perspective. It records Donovan's work as a missionary among the Masai people of Tanzania and traces the dawn-ing realization on his part that many of his presuppositions needed to be revised in the light of the encounter between his culture and that of his hosts.

Donovan talks of going to people with a 'naked gospel', or a 'stripped-down skeletal core' freed of its Western, colonial trappings. He is reluctant to 'distil' the substance of Christianity as if it were a 'final and fundamental' essence. It cannot be articulated independent of each culture in which it finds root. At the heart of the gospel is the 'God-human named Jesus Christ' who is implicit in all human cultures, a basic message of God as transcendent Creator, characterized by love, forgiveness, compassion and justice (Donovan, 1989, p. 143). This 'minimalist' gospel carries Donovan into a risky dialogue with the Masai people, in order to enable them to rework these core assumptions into the symbols and value-systems of their culture. 'Evangelization is a process of bringing the gospel to people where they are, not where you would like them to be' (Donovan, 1982, Preface to 2nd edn, p. 2). Thus, the process of evangelization is one of commending the gospel to a culture in order that people can engage in dialogue with the bearer of the message in order to reach a new understanding; yet the emphasis is not on the proclamation – and the bearer of the message – so much as its reception within a situation, and the community's mature expression of the gospel in its own way. Donovan refers to this as the 'refounding' of the Church. The process of a rediscovery of Christianity in a particular time and place leads the host community into unexpected and unpredictable places, including new expressions of the gospel:

> When the gospel reaches a people where they are, their response to that gospel is the church in a new place, the song they will sing is that new song, that unwritten melody that haunts all of us. What we have to be involved in is not the revival of the church or the reform of the church. It has to be nothing less than what Paul and the Fathers of the Council of Jerusalem were involved in for their time – the refounding of the Catholic church for our age.
>
> Donovan, 1982, Preface to 2nd edn, p. vii

Donovan quotes a Masai creed that emerged from such a synthesis. It is interesting to note how the creed combines elements of 'catholicity' and 'particularity'. On the one hand, the pattern of the creed's affirmation is structured along traditional lines; yet on the other, it contains new perspectives drawn from its African context.

### An African Creed

We believe in the one High God, who out of love created the beautiful world and everything good in it. He created man and wanted man to be happy in the world. God loves the world and every nation and tribe on the earth. We have known this High God in darkness, and now we know him in the light. God promised in the book of his word, the bible, that he would save the world and all the nations and tribes. We believe that God made good his promise by sending his son, Jesus

Christ, a man in the flesh, a Jew by tribe, born poor in a little village, who left his home and was always on safari doing good, curing people by the power of God, teaching about God and man, showing the meaning of religion is love. He was rejected by his people, tortured and nailed hands and feet to a cross, and died. He lay buried in the grave, but the hyenas did not touch him, and on the third day, he rose from the grave. He ascended to the skies. He is the Lord.

We believe that all our sins are forgiven through him. All who have faith in him must be sorry for their sins, be baptized in the Holy Spirit of God, live the rules of love and share the bread together in love, to announce the good news to others until Jesus comes again. We are waiting for him. He is alive. He lives. This we believe. Amen.

Donovan, 1982, p. 200

## Chung Hyun Kyung: 'Very Third World, Very Asian and Very Women'

Vincent Donovan's vivid work inspired many Christians with a vision of the powerful regeneration of Christianity that can take place through a deep engagement with local culture. However, Donovan does not engage with many of the issues concerning pluralism and globalization that must be considered when talking about local theologies in the contemporary context. A more recent encounter between 'classical' Western Christian theological discourse and 'local' theologies is well illustrated in the work of the Asian feminist theologian Chung Hyun Kyung, from South Korea. A number of distinguishing features characteristic of Asian religions and societies inform Chung's approach to theology: gender issues, religious and cultural pluralism and the post-colonial context. Chung's analysis of the afflictions inhibiting the realization of women's full humanity, together with her diagnosis of how theology offers resources for healing and justice, represents one of the most fully articulated examples of 'local theology' of recent years. It is a theology that Chung herself characterizes as 'very Third World, very Asian and very women' (Chung, 1990, p. 23). Her theology weaves itself around a number of themes.

First, like other Asian theologians of the past thirty years, Chung addresses the need to forge appropriate resources for the construction of an authentically Asian Christianity. As Kwok Pui-lan argues, Asian Christians 'are seen more as "missiological objects" of Christian mission, rather than . . . "theological subjects", expected to participate in the dialogue' (Kwok Pui-lan, 1994, p. 64). Further, if indigenous cultures and theologies have been held captive by Western presuppositions, concerns and methods, then part of the process of freeing Asian theological minds and hearts has to be a serious engagement with the historical, religio-cultural, economic and philosophical heritages of Asia. Christianity, whether in Western, colonial form or in its local indigenous expressions, is after all a minority faith. Thus, the development of a genuinely Asian Christian theology will be one that takes place out of the encounter between different cultures, including the encounter between the many religious traditions of Asia.

Chung's theology has a third component: she attends to the historical subordination of women in Asian societies and the Christian tradition, and raises the corresponding need to 'recontextualize' theology in order to give credence to women's experience. In adding this third element, Chung raises the question not only of the way in which one dominant (colonial) culture can silence another (indigenous) expression; but also how issues of power and difference within a culture can be adequately considered and addressed. Thus, under the influence of theologies of liberation, the articulation of what might be classified as a 'local theology' for Korea incorporates the question of gender bias, an issue that is also, despite diversity in its manifestations, a cross-cultural phenomenon.

Much of Chung's theology is focused around a renewed theological anthropology: one that affirms the dignity of Asian women as fully human, and made in the image of God. Yet in order to address the dehumanizing influences of neo-colonialism, poverty, sexism – along with their theological rationales – Chung finds new perspectives and resources drawn directly from Asian contexts and women's experiences. Concepts introduced from Korean folk traditions serve to refashion Western doctrines of God, Mary and Jesus. What results is a paradigm shift in the method and content of her theology:

> To choose the despised women of Asia as the primary context for my theology means to do theology that is accountable to their experience. Theological languages, paradigms, and questions that come from the life experiences of Western male intellectuals, who are the brains of the cultural hegemony which reduced poor Asian women to the status of non-persons, cannot serve as a source of Asian women's theology. The resources for Asian women's liberation theology must come from the life experiences of Asian women themselves. Only when we Asian women start to consider our everyday concrete life experiences as the most important source for

building the religious meaning structures for ourselves shall we be free from all imposed religious authority.

Chung, 1990, p. 5

Further characteristics of Chung's Asian women's theology are suggested by this quotation. First, women's experiences generate both the context and text for doing theology, providing the questions and challenges to which the Good News presents itself. Correspondingly, Chung adopts a liberationist, praxis-based criterion for theological authenticity: the test of theology is its capacity to restore full humanity to the dehumanized, which in Asia means women, as the poorest of the poor. Third, a variety of sources and images inform this contextual theology of liberation, as Chung draws upon concepts from Asia and beyond Western classical Christianity. Here Chung, like other Minjung theologians in Korea, employs the concept of *Han*, meaning oppression, violation and grief. In shamanistic traditions, the shaman performs rituals of *Han-pu-ri* by which the evil of Han is exorcised and dispersed; and Chung appropriates this tradition as one of the vital tasks of a liberating theology.

Chung's theology has proved controversial because of the way in which she has consciously worked to synthesize a number of religious and cultural perspectives alongside Christian tradition into her theology. Her address to the World Council of Churches General Assembly in Canberra in 1991 attracted much negative attention for its invocation of the spirits of victims of genocide and war in the style of Korean shamanistic ritual and the integration of traditional Australasian first nations' music and dance – a use of the performative and aesthetic that further indicated its distance from the conventions of the Western lecture theatre (Ruether, 1998; Chung, 1994). Chung defended herself against charges of 'syncretism' (the mixing together of different religious systems with the end result that the original identities are destroyed) by professing accountability not to Western criteria but the demands of Christian solidarity with the peoples (especially the women) of her own region. This she terms a 'survival-liberation centered syncretism':

In their struggle for survival and liberation in this unjust, women-hating world, poor Asian women have approached many different religious sources for sustenance and empowerment. What matters for them is not doctrinal orthodoxy. Male leaders of the institutional church always seem preoccupied with the doctrinal purity of their religions. What matters to Asian women is survival and the liberation of themselves and their communities. What matters for them is not Jesus, Sakyamumi, Mohammed, Confucius, Kwan In, or Ina, but rather the life force which empowers them to claim their humanity. Asian women selectively have chosen life-giving elements of their culture and religions and have woven new patterns of religious meaning.

Syncretism has been such a 'dangerous' word for Western theologians. They believe 'syncretism' destroys Christian identity and will eventually lead people to confusion. Syncretism, for them, is the lazy and irresponsible way of combining different religious principles without any principles. They talk as if Christian identity is an unchangeable property which they own. Any radical break of Asian theologians from orthodoxy in an effort to dive deep into our Eastern traditions and be transformed by them has been considered suspicious by Western church leaders. Traditional Western theologians seem to say to us that they have the *copyright* on Christianity: 'All rights reserved – no part of our teaching may be reproduced in any form without our permission.'

Chung, 1990, p. 113

## Local Theology in the Vernacular: the Work of Robert Beckford

Another example of how theology is finding new sources and expressions under the impetus of inter-cultural encounter is to be found in the work of the Black British theologian Robert Beckford. His theology is concerned with finding sources and norms appropriate to articulating the experiences of second- and third-generation Black British Christians in the face of their exclusion from official Church structures and the overwhelmingly White, Eurocentric nature of theology. 'We Black Christians who are concerned with a Black liberation theology cannot depend on White academic theologians to do theology on our behalf, or even to consider our interests' (Beckford, 1998, p. 5).

Beckford draws from a liberationist paradigm in arguing that the test of authenticity for such a theology will be its ability to empower and affirm the spiritual and political identity of Black Christians in Britain. To this end, Beckford advocates using what in *Jesus is Dread*, his first major work, he terms 'Black expressive cultures': the sources and resources of Black culture, especially that of the North Atlantic diaspora. His work since then has been characterized by interrogation of many Black artistic and cultural forms for just such an inspirational direction: in the political message of Bob Marley, in dub culture and in visual arts inspired by the Black Muslim artist Faisal Abduallah. These function as representative art forms, speaking on behalf of Black experiences in West Indies, Europe and North America, offering the articulation of an identity invisible within dominant Western culture.

As with Chung's theology, Beckford's work once again raises the question of Christian distinctiveness amidst cultural diversity. Although Beckford identifies himself as a Christian – a Pentecostalist – many of the resources he uses for his Black theology are not of a 'Christian' tradition. Yet Beckford justifies these choices on the grounds of their shared African roots, as an alternative source to European predominance in theology. He prefers that they speak of a Black culture rather than worrying about the exclusively Christian nature of their outlook. Here, the liberationist hermeneutical criterion – favouring the degree to which these voices empower Black people, and render them visible – informs his preference. He maintains that orthopraxis – the political and practical efficacy of an expression of faith – must be privileged over orthodoxy (see previous chapter). But Beckford, along with other liberation theologians, would argue that the preoccupation with 'right belief' and intellectual correctness over political action, is yet another Eurocentric assumption, and one that he is free to reject.

As with theories of inculturation, therefore, Beckford emphasizes the centrality of culture as the totality of lived material and symbolic experience in furnishing a disenfranchised people with the necessary resources to reclaim a gospel relevant to their condition, and root it once more in their experience. As with Chung's work, Beckford's sources are eclectic, especially in the way he draws on sources from popular culture in his theology.

His use of the lyrics of the Rastafarian singer/songwriter and political activist Bob Marley (1945–81) is a case in point. While ostensibly part of the world of mainstream entertainment, Marley's work was also a critical conduit for the emergent political ambitions of a generation of diasporate West Indians, and served as a prominent focus for concerns about Black self-determination in the face of apartheid, racism, poverty and social exclusion. Beckford uses Marley's lyrics as latter-day sacred texts in order to bring into speech these aspirations; yet part of their political and moral power is their form of expression, in the performance of reggae music. More recently, Beckford's work on 'dub' music emphasizes its democratic nature via the availability of cheap technology, further underlining its significance as a medium that privileges the voices and performances of ordinary young people (Beckford, 2005).

Beckford's emphasis on 'Black expressive cultures' draws together a number of key elements. It speaks of the specificity of a 'contextual' theology born of the experience of a marginalized group, young Black Britons, who have been disenfranchised by dominant, White culture. It offers an example of 'local' theology that reminds us of its powerful geopolitical dimensions, representing the source of an irruption into the mainstream of voices hitherto marginalized and undervalued as legitimate insights into the *nature* of God. Yet he also highlights the significance of the performative and aesthetic, and not only the 'semiotic', as well as voices from so-called 'popular' culture and not simply 'high culture', for his sources of inspiration and critique.

Beckford's work joins that of other theologians concerned with the relation between theology and the arts in emphasizing the significance of the vernacular, the popular and the everyday as the vehicle through which people's theological aspirations achieve expression. Detweiler and Taylor, for example, ascribe a special status to what they term 'common grace' (2003, p. 16) in which the products of the human creative imagination engage with ultimate questions of meaning and open up new theological possibilities. They insist that 'secular' culture, and in particular mainstream entertainment, can be a site of such disclosures as much as formal religious discourses or institutions.

> We want to 'look closer' to examine where God might be lurking in the songs, shows, and films kids continually return to for solace and meaning. We celebrate the rise of pop culture, as among the most profound, provocative, exciting expressions of legitimate spiritual yearning in at least one hundred years. We turn to pop culture in our efforts to understand God and to recognize the twenty-first-century face of Jesus.
>
> Detweiler and Taylor, 2003, p. 9

This is local theology as, essentially, 'theology in the vernacular', in the sense that it is deliberately couched in the language of the everyday and the popular, in order to be able to reflect the cultural and religious realities of those who identify least with organized religion or elitist approaches to theology.

## The Space of the Local in Postmodernity

We have seen how within the general trajectory of the 'inculturation' movement, local theologies might emerge out of an engagement between Christianity and a particular culture. Yet the precise meaning of 'local' has also in recent years been contested and expanded. In an era of globalization, for example, how are we to distinguish the 'local' from the 'global'? There is a danger that 'global' becomes a synonym for 'Western', and that the process of globalization is assumed to be one in which the dominance of transnational consumer capitalism obliterates local particularity in the name of global homogenization. It may be, however, that local cultures negotiate more creatively with global forces, and that the result is forms of *hybrid* or *glocal* cultures. In which case 'local' is more a question of a continuing negotiation between the universal and particular.

The expression *glocalism* usefully focuses attention upon how the wider social nexus impacts in material ways upon the lives of communities and is now also appearing more frequently in the work of contextual theologians (see, for example, Schreiter, 1997). As well as drawing attention to the political constraints that shape local life it signals a reawakening to the importance of space and place in contemporary theology (Gorringe, 2002; Inge, 2003; Sheldrake, 2000). We now see more clearly that the physical environment of a culture, its local ecology, takes shape as a result of the influence of outside forces as well as the creative building work of local people. This corresponds with perspectives emerging from disciplines such as economics, sociology and geography, which argue that, whereas modernity tended to privilege time over place and space, a move to postmodernity protests against the objectification and reification of space, recognizing it as a fundamental experiential category by which we make sense of the world. Rather than 'local' indicating the semiotic aspects of human cultural activity by which we make sense of the world, or even the suppressed perspectives of subjugated peoples, this emergent perspective emphasizes the physical, material, embodied reality of a particular geographical area, or perhaps of the built environment.

As Inge in particular has argued, a devaluation of the particularity of local space and place in the Christian tradition often went hand-in-hand with certain models of mission and evangelism that assumed truths articulated in one cultural setting were universally representative (Inge, 2002). It may also be present in the philosophy of 'mega-churches' that pay little attention to the communities or locale in which they are planted. Thus, in part, the reawakening of interest in the geographically local reflects another dimension of the re-evaluation of universalism in favour of a greater appreciation of the contextual nature of knowledge. It stresses the importance of specific physical location for the ways in which one might enter into 'talk about God'.

In many respects such attention to the theological nature of the built environment is clearly a continuation of the positive evaluation of culture expressed throughout this chapter, although culture now appears in material form rather than as 'a web of meaning'. It takes as its starting-point the potential of any product of human fabrication – technologies, cities, performing and visual arts – to be redolent of deeper values and aspirations, as embodiments of implicit statements about ultimate reality. Tim Gorringe speaks of the built environment as humanity's 'third skin' (2002, p. 82) and any attempt to undertake a theological reading of material culture will necessarily acknowledge its rootedness in the everyday texture of human lives, and the opportunities it offers to reflect theologically on issues of land, home, the integrity of creation, technologies, globalization and power. The notion of the local is helpful, therefore, in illuminating the influence of *culture* in its broadest sense on theological understanding and practice; furthermore, as something expanding into all sorts of new directions. It may be better understood as a composite category, embracing the term in its geopolitical, spatial, anthropological *and* theological manifestations.

> Human beings, says Clifford Geertz in a famous image, are animals suspended in webs of significance they themselves have spun. 'Culture' is the name for those webs. It is what we make of the world, materially, intellectually and spiritually. These dimensions cannot be separated: the Word is necessarily flesh. In constructing the world materially we interpret it, set values on it. To talk of values is to talk of a culture's self-understanding, its account of its priorities. The everyday world, the built environment, rituals, symbols, ideals and practices all rest on these values . . . Culture, we can say, is concerned with the spiritual, ethical and intellectual significance of the material world. It is, therefore, of fundamental theological concern.
>
> Gorringe, 2004, p. 3

## Evaluation

As we have seen, talk of 'local theologies' disguises a variety of approaches and understandings of what is happening when 'Christ' and 'culture' interact. The articulation of 'local theologies' always involves a degree of tension between the immediacy of experience and cultural context and the claims of tradition that transcend any particular, specific geographical or temporal setting. Yet much of the argument of this chapter has been that no timeless essence of the gospel exists outwith its embodied expression in a particular time or place. Theology always addresses specific human dilemmas; and its continuing incarnation in the midst of different circumstances will of itself contribute to the continuing unfolding of revelation. Similarly, inculturation need not necessarily entail accommodation or assimilation as the gospel merely adapts to its host culture. Rather, something like a correlational or dialogical process needs to take place, in which 'Christ' and 'culture' engage in *mutual* critique: 'The gospel must be culturally contextualized, yet it must "gospelize" the cultural context itself. The incarnation is the ultimate event of contextualization. This means that the gospel remains a stumbling block and no contextualization can domesticate it' (Koyama, 1993, p. 703).

Yet there is a potential tension within this method of theological reflection. It concerns the relative authority of the particular over the universal. Certainly the doctrines of creation and incarnation might be seen as crystallizations of Christian traditions that affirm the goodness and God-givenness of the created order and that seek to endow human history and material culture with a providential provenance. If God, in Christ, renders human experience sacred as the arena of divine action and salvation, then the Church, as people of God in a particular time and space, is also called to complete God's work of creation and redemption within a material and temporal context.

Christianity contains other strains as well that speak of a loyalty to a God who transcends tribalism, or the limits of time and place. For example, the Hebrew Bible attributes special, even sacred, value to the local and the specific, in which the land, the temple, Mount Sinai, are all suffused with a sense of awe and wonder as places of divine self-disclosure. By contrast, however, the New Testament is altogether less territorial and more universal, replacing ideas of the land as holy, and the exclusive covenant of one people with God as founded in a particular territorial community, with the vision of a holy *God* whose love is universal, and a holy *people* who are dispersed throughout the temporal world, united only by their anticipation of the world to come.

This tension between local and universal is even evident in the story of Pentecost, with which this chapter opened. Alongside the valuing of the particular – 'all together in one place', 'in our own languages we hear them' – this story speaks of the universality of those who witness the coming of the Spirit – 'from every nation under heaven'. If, as many commentators have noted, the story of Pentecost is a reversal of the story of the Tower of Babel (Genesis 11), where humanity is scattered and fragmented into different cultural and linguistic communities, then the coming of the Spirit in Acts 2 might be regarded as the realization of unity in diversity. It is still an affirmation of the movement of the Holy Spirit not through one authorized or prescribed official culture, but in its manifestation in the *vernacular* medium of all known languages, and emerging in Gentile piety as well as Jewish law. These are themes in the method of 'local theology' that are perennial.

## Questions

- Can the tension between global and local, or universal and particular, ever be resolved within Christian theology?
- What critical principles might be needed in order to distinguish between cultural values that are consistent with Christianity, and which are incompatible?
- What understanding of the nature of God is at the root of this method of theological reflection; and how does it differ from the correlative method?

## Annotated Bibliography

Arbuckle, G.A. (1990), *Earthing the Gospel*, London: Geoffrey Chapman. Arbuckle's approach stands within Schreiter's model of local theologies and inculturation. This book provides a framework for practical development of many of the themes within this chapter.

Chung, Hyun Kyung (1990), *Struggle to Be the Sun Again: Introducing Asian Women's Theology*, New York: Orbis. A clear, vivid and challenging example of a local theology. It provides a valuable case study of the interaction of gender, culture and religious pluralism in theological reflection.

Gorringe, T. (2004), *Furthering Humanity: A Theology of Culture*, London: Ashgate. A recent contribution to the debate on the category of 'culture' in theology. Considers issues of inculturation, the role of popular culture and globalization, as well as classic perspectives from the history of theology.

Kingsolver, B. (1999), *The Poisonwood Bible*, London: Faber and Faber. A powerful fictional account of Western missions to the former Belgian Congo during the 1960s, told through the eyes of the family of an American Baptist missionary. The precise lack of connection between 'local' and 'universal' expressions of the gospel leads to tragedy.

Schreiter, R. (1985), *Constructing Local Theologies*, London: SCM Press. The essential introduction to the concept of inculturation and its significance for mission.

# References

Abbott, W. A., ed. (1966), *The Documents of Vatican II*, London: Geoffrey Chapman.

Albrecht, G. (1995), *The Character of Our Communities: Toward an Ethic of Liberation for the Church*, Nashville: Abingdon.

Aquinas, Thomas (1991), *Summa Theologiae: A Concise Translation*, ed. and tr. T. McDermott. Allen, Texas: Christian Classics, Bk 1 (God).

Aquinas, Thomas (1997), *Summa Contra Gentiles, Volume I: God*, ed. A. C. Pegis, Notre Dame, IN: University of Notre Dame Press.

Aquinas, Thomas (1999), *Selected Writings*, ed. R. McInerny, Harmondsworth: Penguin.

Anderson, H. and Foley, E. (1998), *Mighty Stories, Dangerous Ritual: Weaving Together the Human and the Divine*, San Francisco: Jossey-Bass.

Arbuckle, G. A. (1990), *Earthing the Gospel*, London: Geoffrey Chapman.

Armstrong, E. P. (1992), '"Understanding by Feeling" in Marjory Kempe's Book', in Sandra McEntire (ed.) *Marjory Kempe: A Book of Essays*, London and New York: Garland Publishing.

Auerbach, E. (1953), *Mimesis: The Representation of Reality in Western Literature*, Princeton: Princeton University Press.

Augustijn, C. (1991), *Erasmus: His Life, Works, and Influence*, trans. J. C. Grayson, Toronto: University of Toronto Press.

Augustine, (1961), *The Confessions*, trans. R. S. Pine-Coffin, Harmondsworth: Penguin.

Ballard, P. and Pritchard, J. (1996), *Practical Theology in Action: Christian Thinking in the Service of Church and Society*, London: SPCK.

Barth, K. (1928), *The Word of God and the Word of Man*, tr. D. Horton, Boston: Pilgrim Press.

Baum, G., ed. (1999), *The Twentieth Century: A Theological Overview*, Maryknoll, NY: Orbis.

Beckford, R. (1998), *Jesus is Dread*, London: Darton, Longman & Todd.

Beckford, R. (2005), *Jesus Dub: Faith, Culture and Social Change*, London: Routledge.

Bevans, S. ([1996] 2002), *Models of Contextual Theology*, Maryknoll, NY: Orbis, revised and expanded edition.

Boff, C. (1996), 'Methodology of the Theology of Liberation' in Jon Sobrino and Ignacío Ellacuría, eds. *Systematic Theology: Perspectives from Liberation Theology*: Maryknoll, NY: Orbis, 1996, 1–21.

Boff, L. (1988), 'What are Third World Theologies?' *Concilium* 199, 3–14.

Boff, L. (1997), *Ecclesiogenesis: The Base Communities Reinvent the Church*, Maryknoll, NY: Orbis.

Boff, L. and Boff, C. (1987), *Introducing Liberation Theology*, Tunbridge Wells: Burns & Oates.

Bolle, S. D. (1987), *Christian Dialogue as Apologetic: The Case of Justin Martyr*, Manchester: Manchester University Press.

Bolton, G. (2001), *Reflective Practice: Writing and Professional Development*, London: Paul Chapman Publishing Ltd.

Bonaventure, St (1991), 'The Major Life of St Francis', in M. Habig (ed.), *St Francis of Assisi. Writings and Early Biographies: English Omnibus of Sources for the Life of St Francis*, Quincy, IL: Franciscan Press, pp. 615–787.

Bonhoeffer, D. (1954), *Life Together*, London: SCM Press.

Bonino, J. M. (1979), 'Historical Praxis and Christian Identity', in Rosino Gibellini, ed., *Frontiers of Theology in Latin America*, Maryknoll, NY: Orbis.

Bons-Storm, R. (1996), *The Incredible Woman: Listening to Women's Silences in Pastoral Care and Counselling*, Nashville: Abingdon Press.

Bourdieu, P. (1977), *Outline of a Theory of Practice*, trans. R. Nice, Cambridge: Cambridge University Press.

Bourdieu, P. (1992), *The Logic of Practice*, Cambridge: Polity Press.

Bourdieu, P. (1998), *Practical Reason: Or the Theory of Action*, Cambridge: Polity Press.

Bradstock, A. and Rowland, C., eds. (2002), *Radical Christian Writings: A Reader*, Oxford: Blackwell.

Brewin, K. (2004), *The Complex Christ: Signs of Emergence in the Urban Church*, London: SPCK.

Brown, P. (1988), *Augustine of Hippo: A Biography*, London: Faber and Faber.

Brown, P. (2003), *The Rise of Western Christendom: Triumph and Diversity A.D. 200–1000*, 2nd edn, Oxford: Blackwell.

Browning, D. S. (1991), *A Fundamental Practical Theology: Descriptive and Strategic Proposals*, Minneapolis: Fortress Press.

Bunyan, J. ([1678] 1907), *Grace Abounding and the Pilgrims Progress*, Cambridge: Cambridge University Press.

Burck, J. R. and Hunter, R. J. (1990), 'Pastoral Theology, Protestant', in R. J. Hunter, ed., *Dictionary of Pastoral Care and Counseling*, Nashville: Abingdon, 867–72.

Busch, E. (1976), *Karl Barth: His Life from Letters and Autobiographical Texts*, London: SCM Press.


Cameron, H. *et al.* eds. (2005), *Studying Local Churches: A Handbook*, London: SCM Press.

Celano, T. (1991), 'The Second Life of St Francis', in M. Habig, ed., *St Francis of Assisi. Writings and Early Biographies: English Omnibus of Sources for the Life of St Francis*, Quincy, IL: Franciscan Press, 359–443.

Charry, E. T. (1997), *By the Renewing of Your Minds: The Pastoral Function of Christian Doctrine*, New York: Oxford University Press.

Chopp, R. (1995), *Saving Work: Feminist Practices of Theological Education*, Louisville, KY: Westminster/John Knox Press.

Christ, C. P. and Plaskow, J. (1989), *Weaving the Visions: New Patterns in Feminist Spirituality*, San Francisco: Harper & Row.

Chung, Hyun-Kyung (1990), *Struggle to Be the Sun Again: Introducing Asian Women's Theology*, Maryknoll, NY: Orbis.

Chung, Hyun-Kyung (1994), 'Come, Holy Spirit – Break Down the Walls with Wisdom and Compassion', in Ursula King, ed., *Feminist Theology from the Third World: A Reader*. London: SPCK, 392–4.

Clements, K. W. (1987), *Friedrich Schleiermacher: Pioneer of Modern Theology*, London: Collins.

Cohen, A. (1985), *The Symbolic Construction of Community*, London and New York: Routledge.

Cooper, W. (1991), *Testimony of Integrity of the Society of Friends*, Pendle: Pendle Hill Pamphlets.

Cray, G. *et al.* (2004), *Mission-Shaped Church: Church Planting and Fresh Expressions of Church in a Changing Context*, A Report of the working group of the Church of England's Mission and Public Affairs Council, London: Church House Publishing.

Crites, S. ([1971] 1989), 'The Narrative Quality of Experience', in S. Hauerwas and L. Gregory Jones, eds., *Why Narrative?*

*Readings in Narrative Theology*, Grand Rapids, MI: William B. Eerdmans.

Davies, B. (1993), *The Thought of Thomas Aquinas*, Oxford: Oxford University Press.

Davis, R. (1980), 'Education for Awareness: a talk with Paulo Freire', in R. Mackie, ed., *Literacy and Revolution: The Pedagogy of Paulo Freire*, London: Pluto.

Dawson, A. (1999), 'The Origins and Character of the Base Ecclesial Community: A Brazilian Perspective', in C. Rowland, ed., *The Cambridge Companion to Liberation Theology*, Cambridge: Cambridge University Press, 109–28.

Detweiler, C. and Taylor, B. (2003), *A Matrix of Meanings: Finding God in Pop Culture*, Grand Rapids, MI: Baker Academic.

Dolan, J. P., ed. (1964), *The Essential Erasmus*, London: New English Library.

Donovan, V. J. (1989), *The Church in the Midst of Creation*, London: SCM Press.

Donovan, V. J. ([1978] 1982), *Christianity Rediscovered: An Epistle from the Masai*, 2nd edn, London: SCM Press.

Dudley, C., ed. (1983), *Building Effective Ministry: Theory and Practice in the Local Church*, San Francisco: Harper & Row.

Dulles, A. (1974), *Models of the Church*, London: SCM Press.

Dulles, A. ([1983] 1992), *Models of Revelation*, Maryknoll, NY: Orbis, 2nd edn.

Dunn, J. (1998), *The Theology of Paul the Apostle*, Grand Rapids, MI: William B. Eerdmans.

Elford, R. J. (1999), *The Pastoral Nature of Theology*, London: Cassell.

Eliade, M. (1959), *The Sacred and the Profane: The Nature of Religion*, London: Harcourt.

Eliot, T. S. (1933), *The Use of Poetry and the Use of Criticism*, London: Faber and Faber.

Epistle of Mathetes to Diognetus ([124 CE] 2001), (online), available at: www.earlychristianwritings.com/text/diognetus-roberts.html [accessed 03/01/05].

Estep, W. (1996), *The Anabaptist Story*, Grand Rapids, MI: William B. Eerdmans.

Farley, E. (1983), *Theologia: The Fragmentation and Unity of Theological Education*, Philadelphia: Fortress Press.

Ford, David F. (1981), *Barth and God's Story: Biblical Narrative and the Theological Method of Karl Barth in the Church*, Frankfurt: Peter Lang.

Ford, D. F., ed. (1998), *The Modern Theologians*, 2nd edn, Oxford: Blackwell.

Foskett, J. and Lyall, D. (1988), *Helping the Helpers: Supervision and Pastoral Care* London: SPCK.

Fowler, J. (1981), *Stages of Faith: The Psychology of Human Development and the Quest for Meaning*, New York: HarperCollins.

Frei, H. (1974), *The Eclipse of Biblical Narrative: A Study in Eighteenth and Nineteenth Century Hermeneutics*, New Haven: Yale University Press.

Frei, H. (1993), *Theology and Narrative: Selected Essays*, eds. G. Hunsinger and W. C. Placher, New York: Oxford University Press.

Freire, P. (1972), *Pedagogy of the Oppressed*, New York: Seabury Press.

Frye, N. (1957), *Anatomy of Criticism*, Princeton: Princeton University Press.

Fulkerson, M. McC. (1994), *Changing the Subject: Women's Discourses and Feminist Theology*, Minneapolis: Augsburg Fortress Publishers.

Geertz, C. (1973), *On The Interpretation of Cultures: Selected Essays*, New York: Basic Books.

Gerkin, C. (1979), *Crisis Experience in Modern Life: Theory and Theology for Pastoral Care*, Nashville: Abingdon Press.

Gerkin, C. (1984), *The Living Human Document: Revisioning Pastoral Counselling in a Hermeneutical Mode,* Nashville: Abingdon Press.

Gerkin, C. (1986), *Widening the Horizons: Pastoral Responses to a Fragmented Society*, Philadelphia: Westminster Press.

Gerkin, C. (1991), *Prophetic Pastoral Care: A Christian Vision of Life Together*, Nashville: Abingdon Press.

Gerrish, B. A. (1984), *A Prince of the Church: Schleiermacher and the Beginnings of Modern Theology*, London: SCM Press.

Goldberg, M. (1982), *Theology and Narrative: A Critical Introduction*, Nashville: Abingdon.

Gorringe, T. J. (2002), *A Theology of the Built Environment*, Cambridge: Cambridge University Press.

Gorringe, T. J. (2004), *Furthering Humanity: A Theology of Culture*, Aldershot: Ashgate.

Graham, E. L. (1995), *Making the Difference: Gender, Personhood and Theology*, London: Mowbray.

Graham, E. L. (2000), 'Practical Theology as Transforming Practice', in S. Pattison and J. W. Woodward, eds., *The Blackwell Companion to Practical Theology and Pastoral Studies*, Oxford: Blackwell, 104–117.

Graham, E. L., ([1996] 2002a), *Transforming Practice: Pastoral Theology in an Age of Uncertainty*, Eugene, OR: Wipf & Stock, 2nd edn.

Graham, E. L. (2002b), *Representations of the Post/Human: Monsters, Aliens and Others in Popular Culture*, Manchester: Manchester University Press.

Green, L. (1996), *Let's Do Theology*, London: Mowbray, 2nd edn.

Gregory the Great (1976), *The Book of Pastoral Rule*, Grand Rapids, MI: William B. Eerdmans.

Gutiérrez, G. (1983), *The Power of the Poor in History*, Maryknoll, NY: Orbis.

Gutiérrez, G. (1984), *We Drink from Our Own Wells: The Spiritual Journey of a People*, London: SCM Press.

Gutiérrez, G. ([1973] 1988), *A Theology of Liberation*, revised edn, London: SCM Press.

Gwyn, D., ed. (1990) *The Works of George Fox, Vol. I*, State College, PA: George Fox Fund, Inc.


Hauerwas, S. (1978), 'Jesus: The Story of the Kingdom', *Theological Digest*, 26:4, Winter 303–24.

Hauerwas, S. (1981), *A Community of Character*, Notre Dame, IN: University of Notre Dame Press.

Hauerwas, S. ([1983] 2001) 'The Servant Community: Christian Social Ethics', in S. Hauerwas, *The Hauerwas Reader*, Durham: Duke University Press.

Hauerwas, S. and Willimon, W. (1989), *Resident Aliens: Life in the Christian Colony*, Nashville: Abingdon.

Hawkins, P. and Shohet, R. (2002), *Supervision in the Helping Professions: An Individual, Group and Organizational Approach*, Buckingham: Open University Press.

Heaney, T. (1995), 'Issues in Freirean Pedagogy' (online), available at: http://www.nl.edu.ace/Resources/Documents/FreireIssues.html [accessed 16/02/02]

Hefner, P. (2003), *Technology and Human Becoming*, Minneapolis: Fortress Press.

Hennelley, A. T. (1990), *Liberation Theology: A Documentary History*, Maryknoll, NY: Orbis.

Heyward, I. Carter (1982), *The Redemption of God: A Theology of Mutual Relation*, Lanham, MD: University Press of America.

Heyward, I. Carter (1984), *Our Passion for Justice: Images of Power, Sexuality and Liberation*, New York: The Pilgrim Press.

Hill, C. (1988), *A Turbulent, Seditious and Factious People: John Bunyan and his Church*, Oxford: Oxford University Press.

Hiltner, S. (1958), *Preface to Pastoral Theology*, Nashville: Abingdon.

Holland, J. and Henriot, P. (1990), *Social Analysis: Linking Faith and Justice*, 2nd edn, Maryknoll, NY: Orbis.

Hopewell, J. (1983), 'The Jovial Church: Narrative in Local Church Life', in C. S. Dudley, ed. (1983), *Building Effective Ministry: Theory and Practice in the Local Church*, San Francisco: Harper & Row, 68–83.

Hopewell, J. (1988) *Congregation: Stories and Structures*, B. Wheeler, ed., London: SCM Press.

Hughes, G. (1985), *God of Surprises*, London: Darton, Longman & Todd.

Inge, J. (2003), *A Christian Theology of Place,* London: Ashgate.

Ivens, M. (1998), *Understanding the Spiritual Exercises: Text and Commentary: A Handbook for Retreat Directors*, Leominster: Gracewing.

James, William ([1901–2] 2002), *The Varieties of Religious Experience: Centenary Edition*, London: Routledge.

Jantzen, G. (1998), *Becoming Divine: Towards a Feminist Philosophy of Religion*, Manchester: Manchester University Press.

John Paul II (1991), *Centesimus Annus: The Hundredth Year* (online), available at: http://www.osjspm.org/cst/ca.htm [accessed 21/03/02].

Justin Martyr (2001), *Hortatory Address to the Greeks*, trans. Roberts-Donalds (online) available at: www.earlychristianwritings.com/text/justinmartyr_hortatory.html [accessed 05/01/03].

Kaufman, G. D. (1993), *In Face of Mystery: A Constructive Theology*, Cambridge, MA: Harvard University Press.

Kaufman, G. D. (1995), *An Essay on Theological Method*, Cambridge, MA: Harvard University Press, 3rd edn.

Kee, H. C. *et al.* (1991), *Christianity: A Social and Cultural History*, New York: Macmillan.

Keen, B., ed., (1996), *Latin American Civilization: History and Society, 1492 to the Present,* Boulder, CO: 6th edn Westview Press.

Kelsey, D. H. (1979), *The Uses of Scripture in Recent Theology*, Minneapolis: Fortress Press.

Kempe, M. (1985), *The Book of Margery Kempe,* Harmondsworth: Penguin.

Kempe, M. (2003), *The Book of Margery Kempe: An Abridged Translation*, tr. Liz Herbert McAvoy, Woodbridge: D. S. Brewer.

Killen, P. O. and de Beer, J. (1994), *The Art of Theological Reflection*, Maryknoll, NY: Orbis.

Kinast, R. (2000), *What Are They Saying About Theological Reflection?*, New York: Paulist Press.

Kolb, D. (1984), *Experiential Learning: Experience as the Source of Learning and Development*, New Jersey: Prentice Hall Inc.

Koyama, K. (1993), 'Christ's Homelessness', *The Christian Century*, July 14–20, 702–3.

Kwok Pui-lan (1994), 'The Future of Feminist Theology: An Asian Perspective', in U. King, ed., *Feminist Theology from the Third World: A Reader*, London: SPCK, 63–75.

Kraemer, R. S., ed. (2004), *Women's Religions in the Greco-Roman World*, Oxford: Oxford University Press.

Lakeland, P. (1997), *Postmodernity: Christian Identity in a Fragmented Age*, Minneapolis: Fortress Press.

Laney, J. T. (1984), 'James Franklin Hopewell: An Appreciation', *Theological Education*, Autumn, 57–9.

Lartey, E. Y. ([1996] 2000), 'Practical Theology as a Theological Form', in S. Pattison and J. W. Woodward, eds., *The Blackwell Reader in Pastoral and Practical Theology*, Oxford: Blackwell, 128–34.

Las Casas, Bartolomé de (1992), *The Only Way*, ed. Helen Rand Parish, tr. F. Sullivan, New York: Paulist Press.

Lindbeck, G. (1984), *The Nature of Doctrine: Religion and Theology in a Post Liberal Age*, Philadelphia: The Westminster Press.

Lindbeck, G. (2002), *The Church in a Postliberal Age*, London: SCM Press.

Loughlin, G. (1996), *Telling God's Story*, Cambridge: Cambridge University Press.

Mackie, R., ed. (1980), *Literacy and Revolution: The Pedagogy of Paulo Freire*, London: Pluto.

Mahoney, D. (1992), 'Margery Kempe's Tears and the Power over Language', in S. McEntire, ed., *Marjory Kempe: A Book of Essays*, London and New York: Garland Publishing.

McAvoy, E. H., ed. (2003), *The Book of Margery Kempe: An Abridged Translation*, Woodbridge: D. S. Brewer.

McLaren, B. (2004), *A Generous Orthodoxy*, New York: Zondervan.

McFague, S. (1987), *Models of God: Theology for an Ecological Nuclear Age*, London: SCM Press.

MacGillivray, C. (1994), 'Introduction: The Political Is – (and the) Poetical', in H. Cixous, *Manna to the Mandelstams to the Mandelas*, tr. C. MacGillivray, Minneapolis: University of Minnesota Press, vii–ix.

Macintyre, A. (1981), *After Virtue: A Study in Moral Theory*, Notre Dame, IN: University of Notre Dame Press.

McLellan, D., ed. (1977), *Karl Marx: Selected Writings*, Oxford: Oxford University Press.

McNamara, R. (2005), 'Mary of Oignies' (online), available at: www.stthomasirondequoit.com/SaintsAlive/id686.htm  [accessed 25/02/05].

Meeks, W. (1983), *The First Urban Christians: The Social World of the Apostle Paul*, New Haven: Yale University Press.

Milbank, J. (1990), *Theology and Social Theory: Beyond Secular Reason*, Oxford: Blackwell.

Miles, M. (2004), *The Word Made Flesh: A History of Christian Thought*, Oxford: Blackwell.

Milner, M. ([1934] 1986), *A Life of one's Own*, London: Virago Press.

Milner, M. ([1937] 1986), *An Experiment in Leisure*, London: Virago Press.

Milner, M. (1987), *Eternity's Sunrise: A Way of Keeping a Diary*, London: Virago Press.

Mudge, L. and Poling, J. N. (1987), 'Editors' Introduction', in L. Mudge and J. Poling, eds, *Formation and Reflection: The Promise of Practical Theology*, Minneapolis: Fortress Press, xiii–xxxvi.

Murray, S. (2000), *Biblical Interpretation in the Anabaptist Tradition*, London: Pandora.


Nickoloff, J. B., ed. (1996), *Gustavo Gutiérrez: Essential Writings*, London: SCM Press.

Niebuhr, H. R. (1951), *Christ and Culture*, San Francisco: Harper & Row.

Niebuhr, H. R. ([1929] 1957), *The Social Sources of Denominationalism*, Cleveland: World Publishing Co.


Oden, T. C. (1984), *Care of Souls in the Classic Tradition*, Minneapolis: Fortress Press.

O'Malley, J. (1993), *The First Jesuits*, Cambridge, MA: Harvard University Press.

Origen (1985), *On First Principles*, trans. G. Butterworth, New York: Harper & Row.

Parry, D. (1980) *Households of God: The Rule of St Benedict, with Explanations for Monks and Lay-people Today*, London: Darton, Longman & Todd.

Pattison, S. ([1989] 2000), 'Some Straw for the Bricks: A Basic Introduction to Theological Reflection', in S. Pattison and J. W. Woodward, eds. *The Blackwell Reader in Pastoral and Practical Theology*, Oxford: Blackwell, 135–45.

Pattison, S., Thompson, J. and Green, J. (2003), 'Theological Reflection for the Real World: Time to Think Again', *British Journal of Theological Education*, Vol. 13, No. 2, 119–31.

Peerman, D. G. and Marty, M. E., eds. (1965), *A Handbook of Christian Theologians*, New York: Collins.

Perkins, J. (1995), *The Suffering Self: Pain and Narrative Representation in the Early Christian Era*, London: Routledge.

Perpetua ([d. 203] 1989), *The Passion of the Holy Martyrs Perpetua and Felicitas: Ante-Nicene Fathers The Writings of the Father Down to AD 325: Latin Christianity: Its Founder Tertullian*, A. C. Coxe, ed., Grand Rapids: William B. Eerdmans.

Pickett, R. (1997), *The Cross in Corinth: The Social Significance of the Death of Jesus*, Sheffield: Sheffield Academic Press.

Placher, W. (1993), 'Introduction to Hans Frei', in Humsinger and W. Placher, eds., *Theology and Narrative: Selected Essays*, New York: Oxford University Press.

Rack, H. ([1989] 2002), *Reasonable Enthusiast: John Wesley and the Rise of Methodism*, Peterborough: Epworth Press.

Radice, B., trans. (1974), *The Letters of Abelard and Heloise*, Harmondsworth: Penguin.

Rahner, K. (1968), *Theology of Pastoral Action*, New York: Herder & Herder.

Rahner, K. (1982), *The Practice of Faith: A Handbook of Contemporary Spirituality*, K. Lehmann and A. Raffelt, eds., London: SCM Press.

Rahner, K. and Vorgrimmler, H. (1965), *Concise Theological Dictionary*, Freiburg: Herder.

Religious Society of Friends (1995), *Quaker Faith and Practice*, Warwick: Warwick Printing Co.

Ricoeur, P. (1994), *Oneself As Another*, K. Blamey, trans., London and Chicago: University of Chicago Press.

Ricoeur, P. (1998), *Critique and Convictions*, K. Blamey, trans., New York: Columbia University Press.

Roemer, M. (1999), *Postmodernism and the Invalidation of Traditional Narrative*, Maryland: Rowman & Littlefield.

Ruether, R. R. (1998), *Women and Redemption*, London: SCM Press.

Ruether, R. R. ([1983] 1993), *Sexism and God-Talk: Toward a Feminist Theology*, Boston: Beacon, 3rd edn.

Salisbury, J. (1997), *Perpetua's Passion*, London: Routledge.

Schleiermacher, F. ([1799] 1994), *On Religion: Speeches to its Cultured Despisers*, J. Oman, trans., Louisville, KY: Westminster/John Knox Press.

Schleiermacher, F. ([1830] 1960), *Brief Outline on the Study of Theology*, ed. with intro. by T. N. Tice, Richmond, VA: John Knox Press.

Schön, D. (1983), *The Reflective Practitioner: How Professionals Think in Action*, New York: Basic Books.

Schön, D. (1987), *Educating the Reflective Practitioner: Toward a New Design for Teaching and Learning in the Professions*, New York: Basic Books.

Schreiter, R. (1985), *Constructing Local Theologies*, Maryknoll, NY: Orbis.

Schreiter R. (1997) *The New Catholicity: Theology between the global and the local*, Maryknoll, NY: Orbis.

Schweizer, E. (1984), *Good News According to Luke*, Louisville, KY: Westminster/John Knox Press.

Segundo, J. L. ([1976] 1982), *The Liberation of Theology*, third impression, Maryknoll, NY: Orbis.

Sharrock, R., ed. (1976), *The Pilgrim's Progress: A Casebook*, London: Macmillan.

Sheldrake, P. (2000), *Spaces for the Sacred: Place, Memory, Identity*, London: SCM Press.

Smith, R. G., ed. (1965), *Kierkegaard: The Last Years. Journals 1853–55*, London: Fontana.

Snyder, A. (2004), *Following in the Footsteps of Christ*, London: Darton, Longman & Todd.

Southern, R. (1970), *Western Society and the Church in the Middle Ages*, London: Penguin.

Stead, C. (1994), *Philosophy in Christian History*, Cambridge: Cambridge University Press.

Stokes, A. (1985), *Ministry After Freud*, New York: The Pilgrim Press.

Theissen, G. (1982), *The Social Setting of Pauline Christianity*, Edinburgh: T & T Clark.

Tidball, D. J. (1995), 'Practical and Pastoral Theology', in D. J. Atkinson and D. H. Field, eds., *New Dictionary of Christian Ethics and Pastoral Theology*, London: IVP, 42–8.

Tillich, P. ([1949] 1962), *The Shaking of the Foundations*, Harmondsworth: Penguin.

Tillich, P. ([1951, 1957, 1963] 1968), *Systematic Theology*, combined volume, Welwyn: James Nisbet.

Tinsley, E. J., ed. (1973), *Paul Tillich: Modern Theology 3*. London: Epworth.

Tracy, D. (1975), *Blessed Rage for Order: The New Pluralism in Theology*, New York: Seabury.

Tracy, D. (1990), 'On Reading the Scriptures Theologically', in B. Marshall, ed., *Essays in Conversation with George Lindbeck*, Notre Dame, IN: Notre Dame University Press, 35–68.

Tracy, D. (1981), *The Analogical Imagination: Christian Theology and the Culture of Pluralism*, London: SCM Press.

Troeltsch, E. ([1911] 1931), *The Social Teaching of the Christian Churches*, London: Allen & Unwin.

Valdes, M. J., ed. (1991), *A Ricoeur Reader: Reflection and Imagination*, Hemel Hempstead: Harvester Wheatsheaf.

Van Braght, Thielman J. ([1660] 1938), *Martyrs' Mirror*, Scottdale: Herald Press.

Vidales, R. (1979), 'Methodological Issues in Liberation Theology', in R. Gibellini, ed., *Frontiers of Theology in Latin America*, Maryknoll, NY: Orbis, 34–57.

Walton, H. (1993), 'Breaking Open the Bible', in E. L. Graham and M. Halsey, eds., *Life Cycles: Women and Pastoral Care*, London: SPCK, 192–9.

Walton, H. ([1999] 2000), 'Passion and Pain: Conceiving Theology out of Infertility', in D. Willows and J. Swinton, eds, *Spiritual Dimensions of Pastoral Care: Practical Theology in a Multidisciplinary Context*. London: Jessica Kingsley, 196–201.

Walton, H. (2002), 'Speaking in Signs: Narrative and Trauma in Practical Theology', *Scottish Journal of Healthcare Chaplaincy*, 5(2), 2–6.

Walton, H. (2003a), 'Women Writing the Divine', in P. Anderson and B. Clack, eds., *Feminist Philosophy of Religion: Critical Readings*, London: Routledge, 123–35.

Walton, H. (2003b), 'Advent: Theological Reflections on IVF', *Theology and Sexuality*, 9(2), March 2003, 201–9.

Walton, H. (2005, forthcoming), 'Literature and Theology: Sex in the Relationship', in D. Bird and Y. Sherwood, eds., *Bodies in Question*, Aldershot: Ashgate.

Walton, R. (2003), 'The Bible and Tradition in Theological Reflection', *British Journal of Theological Education*, 13.2, 133–151.

Ward, F. (2005), *Lifelong Learning: Theological Education and Supervision*, London: SCM Press.

Ward, G., ed. (1997), *The Postmodern God*, Oxford: Blackwell.

Ward, P. (2002), *Liquid Church*, Carlisle: Paternoster.

Warren, H. A. Murray, J. L. and Best, M. M. (2002), 'The Discipline and Habit of Theological Reflection', *Journal of Religion and Health*, 41(4), Winter, 323–31.

Weber, M. (1949), *The Methodology of the Social Sciences*, New York: Free Press.

Wesley, J. ([1986] 2003), *The Journal of John Wesley: A New Selection from Wesley's Own Account of his Life and Travels*, abridged by C. Idle, Oxford: Lion Publishing.

Whitehead, J. D. (1987), 'The Practical Play of Theology', in L. Mudge and J. N. Poling, eds., *Formation and Reflection: The Promise of Practical Theology*, Philadelphia: Fortress.

Whitehead, J. D. and E. E. ([1980] 1990), *Method in Ministry: Theological Reflection and Christian Ministry*, San Francisco: Harper & Row, 2nd edn.

Williams, R. (1986), 'On Ricoeur', *Modern Theology*, 2(3), 197–211.

Wire, A. (1990), *The Corinthian Women Prophets: A Reconstruction through Paul's Rhetoric*, Minneapolis: Augsburg Fortress Press.

Witvliet, T. (1985), *A Place in the Sun: Liberation Theology in the Third World*, London: SCM Press.

Wogaman, J. P. (1988), *Christian Perspectives on Politics*, London: SCM Press.

Yoder, J. H. (1972), *The Politics of Jesus*, Grand Rapids, MI: William B. Eerdmans.

## WEBSITES

http://www.anewkindofchristian.com
http://www.emergentvillage.com/Site/Explore/EmergentStory/index.htm
http://www.earlychristianwritings.com

# Index